GUINNESS W★RLD RECORDS 2015

GAMER'S EDITION

British Library Cataloguing-in-Publication Data: a catalogue record for this book is available from the British Library.

ISBN-13: 978-1-908843-66-1

ISBN-10: 1-908843-66-7

Check the official **GWR Gamer's Edition** website at: **www.guinnessworldrecords.com/gamers** for record-breaking gaming news as it happens, plus exclusive interviews and competitions.

© 2014 Guinness World Records Limited, a Jim Pattison Group company

OFFICIALLY AMAZING

GAMER'S EDITION 2015

SENIOR MANAGING EDITOR
Stephen Fall

LAYOUT EDITORS
Eddie de Oliveira,
Lucian Randall

ASSISTANT EDITOR
Adam Millward

EDITORIAL CONSULTANTS
Rob Cave, Stace Harman,
Eddie de Oliveira

INDEX
Marie Lorimer

PROOFREADING
Matthew White

PICTURE EDITOR
Michael Whitty

DEPUTY PICTURE EDITOR
Fran Morales

PICTURE RESEARCHER
Wilf Matos

TALENT RESEARCHER
Jenny Langridge

ORIGINAL PHOTOGRAPHY
Richard Bradbury,
Paul Michael Hughes

PRINTING
Courier Corporation, USA

VP PUBLISHING
Jenny Heller

EDITOR-IN-CHIEF
Craig Glenday

DIRECTOR OF PROCUREMENT
Patricia Magill

PUBLISHING MANAGER
Jane Boatfield

PUBLISHING EXECUTIVE
Ebyan Egal

DESIGN
Paul Wylie-Deacon, Richard Page and Matt Bell at 55design.co.uk

CONTRIBUTORS
Louise Blain, Matt Bradford, Rob Cave, David Crookes, Andrew Davidson, Matthew Edwards, Rachael Finn, Ellie Gibson, Stace Harman, Tyler Hicks, Phil Iwaniuk, Joel Meadows, John Robertson, Dan Whitehead, Ben Wilson, Alex Wiltshire

GUINNESS WORLD RECORDS

THE JIM PATTISON GROUP

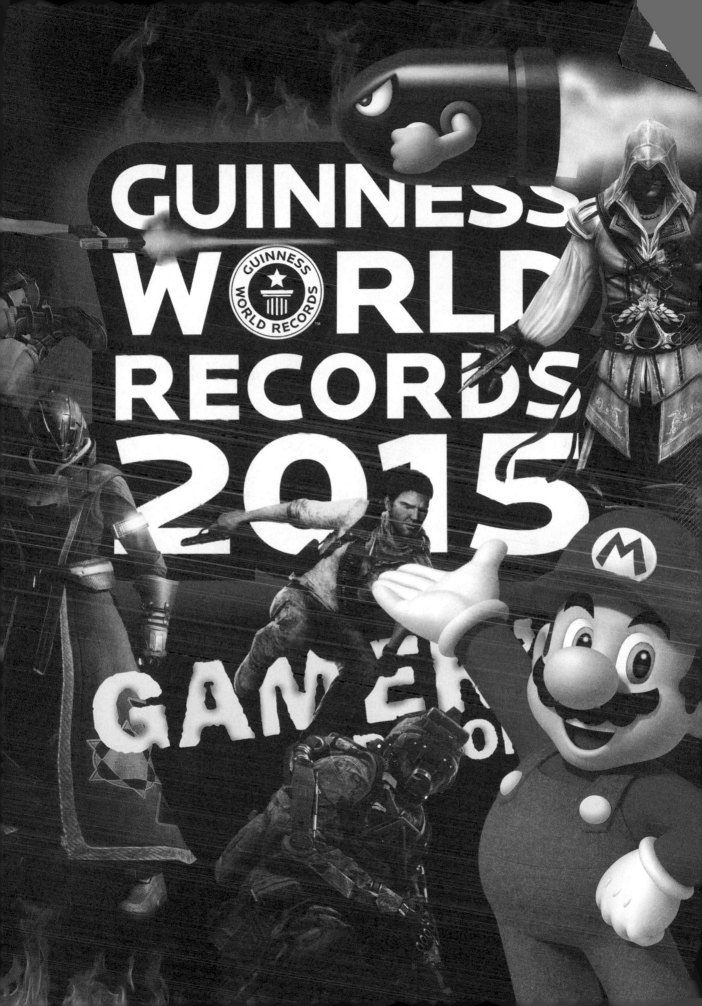

GUINNESS WORLD RECORDS 2015

GUINNESS WORLD RECORDS

GAMER'S

CONTENT

This year's book is based around the top 50 games of all time, as voted for by our readers…

INSIDE THE BOOK…

The "Countdown" pages break up the games according to their position in the readers' poll, and introduce each section.

Look out for game tips and hints in the form of our handy "For the Win" boxes.

Once again, we've included special features on a wide variety of topics, including a look at the GT Academy (pp.40–41), the toys-to-life phenomenon (pp.144–45) and prominent women in the gaming industry (pp.158–59). Some of the most significant firsts in gaming history appear on pp.22–23, while we celebrate the speediest gamers of them all on pp.24–25. Games in the *Alien* franchise – including *Isolation* – are profiled on pp.94–95, and across pp.186–194 we look at the major developments in gaming hardware.

GENRE ICONS

Listed below are the icons
for each gaming genre
represented in the book.
You'll find them in
the top left corner
of each game-
based page.

ACTION-ADVENTURE

ARCADE

FIGHTING

MMOs

PLATFORMERS

PUZZLES

RACING

RHYTHM

RPGs

SHOOTERS

SPORTS

STRATEGY & SIMULATION

INTRODUCTION

Welcome to *Guinness World Records Gamer's Edition 2015* – the ultimate videogame guide. Our eighth annual edition is packed with new and updated records from all your favourite games, plus news and feature reports from across all aspects of gaming.

LONGEST *MINECRAFT* MARATHON

"It's a big honour being part of this giant Guinness World Records family," said Austria's Martin Fornleitner after securing his first ever world record. Martin, who posed for a *Minecraft* photo shoot for this year's book (see pp.170–73), played for 24 hr 10 min on 19–20 August 2011.

COUNTDOWN

Instead of organizing games by genre, as we sometimes do, this edition counts down the 50 games that were voted the most popular in our online readers' poll. This gives us the chance to include games we've not covered in detail previously (such as *Crash Bandicoot* and *World of Tanks*), and also means that we could revisit old favourites in more depth (see our double spreads on *Call of Duty*, *Grand Theft Auto*, *Minecraft*, and so on). We've also included related games that we know you'll enjoy – or those we felt were simply too good to ignore – so look out for the extra records marked with the ▶▶ symbol.

If you're keen to improve your gaming, you can make the most of our "For the Win" top tips. You'll also find quirky and fascinating games trivia in boxes dotted about these pages, along with insightful quotes from leading figures within the industry. Not only that, but this book features more exclusive interviews than ever before. We've spoken to game designers, voice actors, indie developers, scriptwriters and programmers to get their insider view of the gaming industry.

LARGEST COLLECTION OF *TOMB RAIDER* MEMORABILIA

Rodrigo Martin Santos (Spain) owns a record number of *Tomb Raider* items (see p.19). "The first," he tells us, "was a figure of Lara Croft raiding Area 51 that my parents gave me for Christmas. I started buying items of Lara Croft because I liked them, not just to collect." Eventually, he admits, "there comes a day when you have so many that you have become a collector".

HIGHEST MARGIN OF VICTORY (VS COMPUTER) ON *2014 FIFA WORLD CUP BRAZIL*

Patrick Hadler (Germany) won by 321 goals on 28 May 2014. The most difficult part, he tells us, was "holding your concentration over the whole 90 minutes as you have to keep on scoring with such intense rapidity. You must get the ball back as quickly as possible after each restart and one mistake can cost you the record score."

FEATURES

This book is bursting with features on everything from sports videogames to speed-runs. In our 2014 edition, we took a look at the evolution of consoles; this time we trace the way handhelds have progressed from Mattel's Auto Race in 1976 to the mobile gaming revolution of the present day. There's also a look at the *Alien* franchise, MMO landmarks, gaming firsts through the decades, the best of party games, and even the outlandish clothing worn by certain game characters.

And if you're wondering about the games you'll be playing next, turn to pp.184–85 for our summary of upcoming titles. Written by an assortment of experts from every corner of the gaming world, these features give you a fully rounded picture of gaming today.

Gamer's Edition 2015 is a visual feast, too. Our picture team have worked hard to bring you the best images of your favourite games and some of our high-achieving record holders.

And we hope you like the fresh new style of the page layouts, brought to us by our friends at 55 Design.

Finally, if you think you might be able to set a record that could appear in our next book, turn to p.8 to find out how to get started.

LONGEST *WORLD OF WARCRAFT* MARATHON

"Kinumi Cati", aka Hecaterina Kinumi Iglesias Pérez (Spain), has set records on both *WoW* and *Final Fantasy* (see pp.88–89 and p.137). "I started watching anime when I was a little kid," she said. "First I watched it in Galician, but then I discovered that Japanese versions were different – so I started watching anime in Japanese with English subtitles. Since then I've never watched anime in any other language except Japanese. I also started reading manga, and most games I like are Japanese."

Kinumi Cati in costume as Yuna from *Final Fantasy* (above) and Tyrande Whisperwind from *World of Warcraft* (right).

BE A RECORD-BREAKER

If you're a speed-runner, a high-scorer, a marathon-gamer, a pioneering developer or you have the biggest collection of any kind of gaming memorabilia, GWR wants to hear from you – right now! As long as you have a passion for videogaming, anyone can be a record-breaker. It costs nothing and you could earn yourself a GWR certificate. You may even be in the book next year...

PRACTICE MAKES PERFECT

You wouldn't turn up at a sports competition without having done any training – and the same should be true for Guinness World Records attempts. The more you practise your attempt, the higher your chances of success.

READ THE RULES

Your application will be processed within six weeks. If the record exists already, you'll be sent our official guidelines or, if we like your idea for a new record, we'll compile rules for it. Many concepts are turned down at the application stage so don't take it personally – GWR will explain why it was rejected. Take a close look at previous *Gamer's Editions* and GWR's website to see the kinds of thing we like, then try again!

MAKE AN APPLICATION

The first step on your journey to becoming a record-breaker is to visit **www. guinnessworldrecords. com**. Hit "Set a record" to find out how the process works, what your options are and to register an account. Let us know by email which gaming record you'd like to attempt.

MEET THE RECORD HOLDERS

Record holders come from all over the world – and to prove it, proud owners of GWR certificates often send us photographs that illustrate the love for gaming that has led to them conquering their favourite games. Will you join the GWR hall of fame?

LONGEST VIDEOGAME MARATHON

Okan Kaya (Australia) played *Call of Duty: Black Ops II* for 135 hr 15 min 10 sec in Waterloo, New South Wales, Australia, from 13 to 19 November 2012.

GREATEST AGGREGATE TIME PLAYING *GOD* OF *WAR: ASCENSION*

"Milliejacqueson" (USA) had played *GoW: Ascension* for 1,326 hr 30 min as of 25 March 2014. For more on *GoW*, turn to p.100.

MAKE YOUR ATTEMPT

Once you reach a point where you feel you can prepare no more, you're ready to take on the record. Ensure you have everything in place that's required to meet the guidelines – you will need a decent-quality video recorder, witnesses and anything else that we've told you in the guidelines to gather for your claim.

GWR CHALLENGERS

You can make an attempt to set a record right now. Visit **www.guinnessworldrecords.com/ challengers**, pick the record you want to beat and follow the instructions for supplying video evidence. If it's a videogame record attempt, you'll have to make sure that GWR can see every moment of play. You'll soon hear from us – adjudications are made every week.

SEND YOUR EVIDENCE

When filming videos to supply as evidence, do a trial run to make sure that the lighting is right and any obstructions are taken care of. Just a bit of preparation will ensure your potential new record isn't missed or rejected because of technical issues. Package up all the evidence and send it to GWR for assessment. Then, simply wait…

FRAME YOUR CERTIFICATE!

Congratulations! Those who have beaten a record will be sent an official certificate to show off to their mates. If you're very lucky, you may even be one of the fortunate few to make it to these pages next year. And if you're not successful? Don't despair: you can always give it another shot. There's no limit to the number of attempts you can make.

1,000

or more applications reach GWR every week – so bear with us while we get through them all.

FASTEST SKELETON RUN (*MARIO & SONIC WINTER OLYMPICS*)

On 16 February 2014, Shawn Alvarez (USA) set a time of 65.05 sec in the Skeleton Run event on *Mario & Sonic at the Olympic Winter Games*.

FASTEST 100% COMPLETION OF *CRASH BANDICOOT*

"WHiPCPL" (Denmark) finished *Crash Bandicoot* in 1 hr 15 min 33 sec on 11 April 2014. For more on the game itself, see p.52.

www.guinnessworldrecords.com/gamers

GRAND THEFT AUTO MANIA

As *Gamer's Edition 2014* went to press, *GTA V* was released worldwide with, above, a fan at a US midnight store-opening getting a bear hug from *GTA* senior animator Michael Peterson. Rockstar's open-world phenomenon became – deep breath – the **best-selling game in 24 hours** (11.21 million copies), the **fastest entertainment property to gross $1 billion** (£625 million) and the **highest-grossing game in 24 hours**, generating the **highest revenue by an entertainment product in 24 hours** ($815.7 million; £511.8 million). For more on *GTA*, see pp.166–69.

TOKYO GAME SHOW

A total of 270,197 people attended the Tokyo Game Show in 2013 – the largest number in the event's history. The show, open both to industry professionals and members of the public, recorded more than 100,000 visitors on each of its public days for the first time. Some 352 exhibitors from 30 countries descended on the Japanese capital to show off almost 1,000 games, including *Knack* (above), *Dead or Alive 5*, *Wolfenstein: The New Order* and *Driveclub*.

LET THE GAMES BEGIN

The start of the autumn traditionally heralds a plethora of new releases, and 2013 was no different. *Angry Birds Star Wars II*, *Wii Party U*, *LEGO Marvel Super Heroes* (pictured) and *Battlefield 4* arrived in stores, while *GTA Online*'s launch on 1 October was fraught with glitches. Players encountered repeated problems in connecting to the game servers and Social Club. Rockstar offered *GTA* players $500,000 of in-game currency as compensation.

THANK YOU FOR THE *DAYZ*

Indie survival-horror title *DayZ* was released on 16 December 2013 in alpha stage via Steam. Its terrifying zombie-apocalypse scenario was surely the perfect piece of post-Christmas-lunch entertainment. *DayZ* remained the No.1 game in the Steam chart for two weeks, selling 172,500 copies in its first 24 hours.

NINTENDO DIRECTLY

At a Nintendo Direct press conference in February 2014, company president Satoru Iwata announced that Little Mac would be joining the *Super Smash Bros.* character roster, while *Mario Kart 8* (see pp.132–33) would also welcome seven new faces in the shape of the Koopa Kids.

DISKINECTABLE

Despite sluggish early global sales of the Xbox One, Microsoft insisted it was standing by the Kinect, even though its inclusion in the package meant the console was costing around $100 (£59) more than the PS4. A Microsoft marketing chief described Kinect as "integral to the Xbox One experience". In May 2014, three months later, Microsoft ditched the Kinect from the package and slashed the price of the console from $499 (£429) to $399 (£349).

2014: MOST ACCLAIMED

The critics couldn't get enough of *The Last of Us: Remastered*, Naughty Dog's PS4 version of the 2013 hit that scooped more than 200 Game of the Year awards (see pp.112–13). *The Last of Us: Remastered* received an average critics' score of 95.74% on gamerankings.com. *Dark Souls II* on the Xbox 360 was in second place with 90.33%, followed by platformer *Guacamelee! Super Turbo Championship Edition* on the PS4 with a round score of 90%.

2014: WORST-RATED

At the foot of the acclaim table is *One Piece: Romance Dawn* on the 3DS, with a lousy 42.71% score from the critics ("A weak game that mangles its beloved source material," said IGN). *Yaiba: Ninja Gaiden Z* is close behind on 44.18%, and the PS4 version of *Daylight*, with just 47%, shows that it hasn't been entirely a bed of roses for Sony in 2014.

GAMER GATHERING

On 7 September 2013, a total of 491 gamers in Tampere, Finland, set the record for the **largest gathering of people dressed as videogame characters**. The successful attempt was organized by the Tampereen Särkänniemi theme park, which includes an *Angry Birds* Land. Games represented among the 491 participants included *Minecraft*, *Super Mario Bros.*, *The Legend of Zelda* and *Assassin's Creed*. A year earlier, Tampereen Särkänniemi attempted to break the previous record of 470, but fell short.

EUROGAMING

The biggest gaming event in Europe, the sixth annual Gamescom trade fair welcomed 350,000 visitors in Cologne, Germany, over five days in August 2014. As well as giving European gamers, journalists and industry pros the chance to try out the latest games, the event also showcased some exciting premieres. Among the new titles that made waves were PS4-exclusive *Alienation* (above), the episodic action-adventurer *Life is Strange*, Xbox-exclusive *ScreamRide* (from the team behind the *RollerCoaster Tycoon* series), and *The Tomorrow Children*, a post-apocalyptic sci-fi yarn for the PS4.

Life Goes On

Stikbold!

THE PAX 10 2014

The 2014 PAX (Penny Arcade eXpo) Prime show was held in Seattle, Washington, USA, from 29 August to 1 September. The entire enterprise is organized by the people behind the *Penny Arcade* web comic. Every year, 50 industry experts select the best indie games in an influential list known as the PAX 10. The 2014 games are: *Duet*, *Flickers*, *FRAMED*, *Life Goes On*, *Mushroom 11*, *Nova-111*, *Poöf vs the Cursed Kitty*, *Skullduggery!*, *Stikbold!* and *The Counting Kingdom*.

BANNED!

Construction and political sim *Tropico 5* was banned by Thailand's military government in August 2014. Although the country's *de facto* leader, General Prayuth Chan-ocha, has not explained the decision, *Tropico 5*'s distributors believe the game, in which the player assumes the role of dictator El Presidente and runs an island state, might be a little too close to the bone for Thailand's military rulers. General Chan-ocha seized power in a coup in May 2014.

CRIMECRAFT

The British government's chief adviser on intellectual property asked ministers to consider passing a law to criminalize the theft of valuable in-game items. The proposed law would land thieving gamers the same criminal sentences as people who steal in real life. Mike Weatherley MP (above), a *World of Warcraft* fan, told Buzzfeed, "If you've spent £500 building up your armed forces and someone takes them away online, I guess you can feel hard done by and you want your £500 back."

DICTATING THE AGENDA

The former dictator of Panama, Manuel Noriega (inset), sued Activision in July 2014 after a character based on him appeared in *Call of Duty: Black Ops II* in 2012. Noriega, currently serving a lengthy jail sentence, was leader of Panama from 1983 to 1989, and formerly served as a CIA informant. In *Black Ops II*, Noriega helps the American intelligence agency capture a terrorist before turning on them. The legal case filed in 80-year-old Noriega's name claims that he is portrayed in the game as a "kidnapper, murderer and enemy of the state" who commits "numerous fictional crimes". He is also referred to as "old pineapple face".

2014: BEST-SELLERS

Watch_Dogs on the PS4 topped the 2014 sales chart (as of August 2014) with sales of 2.3 million, closely followed by *Mario Kart 8* on 2.2 million and *Titanfall* in third place with 2 million. *YouKai Watch 2: Ganso and Honke* on the 3DS was in fourth place with 1.78 million units – sales that are all the more impressive when you consider that the game is exclusive to Japan. The Xbox 360 version of *Minecraft* comes just below with sales of 1.71 million units.

In July 2014, actor **Lindsay Lohan** announced she was suing Take-Two Interactive and Rockstar Games, claiming that her image was used to create a character based on her in *GTA V*. Lohan says that her permission was not sought before the character Lacey Jonas was devised for the blockbusting 2013 release.

Sony revealed that they turned down the new **Access** subscription system for EA Games, opting instead to expand PlayStation Plus, which they say has seen an increase in membership of 200% since the launch of the PS4. EA Access is instead available on the Xbox One at $4.99 a month (£3.99 in the UK).

In April 2014, the Swedish government launched **"Democreativity"**, an initiative to spread notions of peace, love and democracy through a new videogame. The idea is to encourage suggestions for games in which there are no winners and losers, but in which "alliances, collaboration and exploration" are triumphed. More than 500 people from 126 countries have submitted their ideas for the game. Check out the site at **www.democreativity.com** for gaming peace and love.

Also from Sweden comes the news that a father made the extraordinary decision to take his two gamer kids to a **war zone** to put them off playing shooters such as the *Call of Duty* series. Journalist Carl-Magnus Helgegren wanted to show his sons Leo, 11, and Frank, 10, the reality of war, so he took them to Israel and Syria in August 2014.

> **"***GTA V, The Last of Us***, new consoles and the rapid growth of mobile games – for so long a niche interest, gaming became bigger than ever in 2014."**
>
> **CRAIG GLENDAY**
> EDITOR-IN-CHIEF, GWR

CHARTING A NEW PATH

Amy Hennig, the creative director and writer of the *Uncharted* series, left Naughty Dog after 10 years of service to join Visceral Games and EA. Hennig, who was leading the *Uncharted 4* team for the PS4, has become the creative director of the new *Star Wars* game. Industry veteran Hennig's first job was as a designer on Atari title *Electrocop* in the 1980s, before she became a regular creator of NES and SNES games.

VIRTUALLY READY

In March 2014, Sony officially announced the prototype for Project Morpheus, a virtual reality (VR) system for the PS4. The hardware had been in development for more than three years and is now being used by game designers. For more Morpheus, turn to pp.188–89.

Facebook, meanwhile, completed its purchase of the Oculus Rift VR kit in July 2014 for $400 million (£239.5 million) in cash, $1.6 billion (£958 million) in Facebook stock, and a further $300 million (£179 million) subject to Oculus meeting certain financial targets. After decades of console conflicts between Sony, Microsoft, Nintendo and Sega, "Oculus Rift vs Project Morpheus" potentially heralds the first VR war. Release dates are yet to be revealed…

GAME CHANGER

In 2006, Nintendo released the Wii, the family-friendly home console that brought motion control to the masses. Seven years and 101 million sales later, production of the original version of Nintendo's most successful ever console ceased in Japan and the EU. We take a look at the life of the Nintendo Wii.

2006 For many years, home consoles competed for supremacy based on processing power and sheer graphical grunt, but in 2006 Nintendo bucked that trend with the release of the Wii, which focused on simple graphics and gameplay. Nintendo's aim was to produce a console that would shake up the games market by providing a family-oriented alternative to Sony's PS3 and Microsoft's Xbox 360, the consoles of choice for dedicated gamers.

The Wii launched with a simple but highly innovative controller. The Wii Remote, or "Wiimote" (left), featured a simplified button layout, intuitive pointer and motion controls, and a familiar television remote styling.

2008 The Wii Wheel was released with *Mario Kart Wii*, and also sold separately. Although it doesn't do anything other than house the standard remote, it adds a fun sideways steering dynamic to driving games.

The Wii was an instant success, leading to worldwide stock shortages during its Christmas 2006 launch period.

2007 The Wii Balance Board (right) and Wii Zapper (far right) followed in 2007. *Wii Fit* was the first title to make use of the board, while the zapper was a container for the remote used in shooter games.

TOP 5 WII SUPER-SELLERS

5: New Super Mario Bros. Wii: 27.44 million
The superstar plumber took the Wii by storm in 2009 with this, the 14th *Super Mario* title, reinforcing the Wii's primary focus on social gaming.

4: Wii Play: 28.81 million
This collection of nine party mini-games came bundled with a Wii Remote, giving gamers an additional controller for multiplayer action. It is the **best-selling party videogame**.

3: Wii Sports Resort: 32.37 million
The game that really showed off the more refined control of the MotionPlus peripheral, which came bundled with it. It featured 12 different sports.

2: Mario Kart Wii: 34.53 million
The sixth entry in the mighty *Mario Kart* series raced ahead of all the competition on every platform to become the **best-selling kart racing game**.

2011 The Wii Family Edition was released in a bundle with *Wii Sports* and the 80-mini-game *Wii Party*. It was a reconfiguration of the original console but sacrificed GameCube support (and controllers) for a slimmer frame. And it was designed to sit flat, rather than upright.

Wii™

WHY WII?

Code-named "Revolution" during its development period, in April 2006 Nintendo unveiled the name "Wii" to the bemusement of some gamers. But there was reasoning behind the apparently curious decision. As well as crossing language barriers to communicate the uncomplicated nature of the console to a global audience, the name was also supposed to promote inclusiveness (Wii as in "we"), while the distinct "double-i" spelling aimed to conjure images of two people standing next to one another.

2009 Three years after the Wii's launch, Nintendo released its MotionPlus device that plugged into the bottom of the Wiimote and further enhanced its motion-control capabilities. The Wii's motion control blazed a trail for the Sony Move and Microsoft Kinect (although motion-control games on the PS and Xbox consoles weren't as popular).

2012 The Wii Mini, in resplendent red, first landed on shelves in 2012. As the title suggests, it's a scaled-down version of the Wii with fewer features (for instance, it has no connectivity, so is dependent on disc games).

2010 The MotionPlus device was built into the new breed of Remotes – Remote Plus (left) – launched in a bundle with *Wii Sports Resort*.

2014 In a sign suggesting that Nintendo is keen to move on, in early 2014 President Satoru Iwata announced plans for a new console to arrive as early as 2015.

2012 With such enormous sales, the Wii was always going to be a tough act to follow. Sure enough, the Wii U (below), released in 2012, has sold just 6.45 million units, well short of Nintendo's expectations. As a result, some developers have been cautious about producing new titles for the console.

New Super Mario Bros. U (2012) is the **best-selling Wii U title**, having shifted 4.16 million units.

1: *Wii Sports*: 82.03 million Bundled with the majority of Wii consoles, this collection of golf, boxing, baseball, tennis and bowling is the **best-selling videogame** of all time – see p.104.

AWARDS ROUND-UP

E3 GAME CRITICS AWARDS 2014

Best of Show: *Evolve*

Best Original Game	No Man's Sky
Best Console Game	Evolve (pictured above)
Best Handheld/ Mobile Game	Super Smash Bros. for 3DS
Best PC Game	Tom Clancy's Rainbow Six: Siege
Best Hardware/ Peripheral	Oculus Rift
Best Action Game	Evolve
Best Action-Adventure Game	Batman: Arkham Knight
Best RPG	Dragon Age: Inquisition
Best Fighting Game	Super Smash Bros. for Wii U
Best Racing Game	The Crew
Best Sports Game	NHL 15
Best Strategy Game	Sid Meier's Civilization: Beyond Earth
Best Social/Casual/ Family Game	Mario Maker
Best Online Multiplayer	Evolve
Best Independent Game	No Man's Sky
Special Commendation for Innovation	No Man's Sky

GAMESCOM 2014 AWARDS

Game of the Year: *Evolve*

Most Wanted Consumer Award	Super Smash Bros. for Wii U
Best Console Game: Sony PlayStation	The Evil Within
Best Console Game: Microsoft Xbox	Evolve
Best Console Game: Nintendo Wii	Splatoon
Best Role-Playing Game	Risen 3: Titan Lords
Best Action Game	Evolve
Best Simulation Game	Theatrhythm Final Fantasy: Curtain Call
Best Sports Game	PES 2015
Best Family Game	LittleBigPlanet 3
Best PC Game	Evolve
Best Mobile Game	Super Smash Bros. for 3DS
Best Social/Casual/ Online Game	LittleBigPlanet 3
Best Online Multiplayer Game	Evolve
Best Hardware	Oculus Rift DK 2 (Oculus VR)

GOLDEN JOYSTICK AWARDS 2013

Game of the Year: *Grand Theft Auto V*

Best Gaming Moment	Far Cry 3's "The Definition of Insanity"
Best Gaming Platform	Steam
Best Handheld Game	Assassin's Creed III: Liberation
Best Indie Game	Mark of the Ninja
Best Mobile/Tablet Game of the Year	XCOM: Enemy Unknown
Best Multiplayer	Payday 2
Best Newcomer	The Last of Us
Best Online Game	World of Tanks
Best Visual Design	BioShock Infinite
Hall of Fame	Call of Duty
Innovation of the Year	Oculus Rift
Lifetime Achievement	Ken Levine
Most Wanted	The Witcher 3: Wild Hunt
Studio of the Year	Naughty Dog
YouTube Gamer Award	The Yogscast

INDEPENDENT GAMES FESTIVAL 2014

Seumas McNally Grand Prize: *Papers, Please* (right)

INDEPENDENT GAMES FESTIVAL

Audience Award	The Stanley Parable
Best Student Game	Risk of Rain
Excellence in Audio	DEVICE 6
Excellence in Design	Papers, Please
Excellence in Narrative	Papers, Please
Excellence in Visual Art	Gorogoa
Nuovo Award	Luxuria Superbia

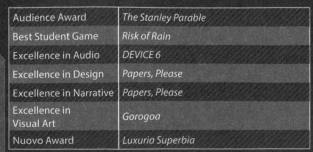

10TH BRITISH ACADEMY GAMES AWARDS

Best Game: *The Last of Us*

Neil Druckmann accepts the award for Best Story (*The Last of Us*).

Action and Adventure	*The Last of Us* (pictured below)
Artistic Achievement	*Tearaway*
Audio Achievement	*The Last of Us*
British Game	*Grand Theft Auto V*
Debut Game	*Gone Home*
Family Game	*Tearaway*
Game Design	*Grand Theft Auto V*
Game Innovation	*Brothers: A Tale of Two Sons*
Mobile/Handheld	*Tearaway*
Multiplayer	*Grand Theft Auto V*
Original Music	*BioShock Infinite*: James Bonney, Garry Schyman
Performer	Ashley Johnson (Ellie), *The Last of Us*
Sports	*FIFA 14*
Story	*The Last of Us*: Bruce Straley, Neil Druckmann (pictured above)
Strategy and Simulation	*Papers, Please*
Young Game Designers/ Game Concept	*Tomatos Role*: Rhianna Hawkins
Young Game Designers/ Game Making	*AlienX*: Adam Oliver
BAFTA Fellowship in 2014	Rockstar Games
Ones to Watch	*Size DOES Matter*: Mattis Delerud, Silje Dahl, Lars Andersen, Trond Fasteraune, Nick La Rooy

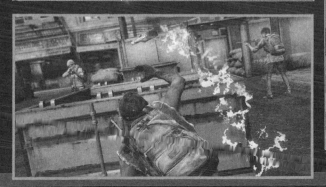

D.I.C.E. AWARDS 2014

Game of the Year: *The Last of Us*

Adventure Game	*The Last of Us*
Casual Game of the Year	*Plants vs. Zombies 2*
Downloadable Game of the Year	*Brothers: A Tale of Two Sons*
Family Game of the Year	*Super Mario 3D World*
Fighting Game of the Year	*Injustice: Gods Among Us*
Handheld Game of the Year	*The Legend of Zelda: A Link Between Worlds*
Mobile Game of the Year	*Plants vs. Zombies 2*
Online Game of the Year	*World of Tanks*
Outstanding Achievement in Animation	*The Last of Us*
Outstanding Achievement in Art Direction	*The Last of Us*
Outstanding Achievement in Game Direction	*The Last of Us*
Outstanding Achievement in Gameplay Engineering	*Grand Theft Auto V*
Outstanding Achievement in Original Music Composition	*BioShock Infinite*
Outstanding Achievement in Sound Design	*The Last of Us*
Outstanding Achievement in Story	*The Last of Us*
Outstanding Achievement in Visual Engineering	*The Last of Us*
Outstanding Character Performance	Ellie, *The Last of Us*
Outstanding Innovation in Gaming	*The Last of Us*
Racing Game of the Year	*Forza Motorsport 5*
Role-Playing/Massively Multiplayer Game of the Year	*Diablo III*
Sports Game of the Year	*FIFA 14*
Strategy/Simulation Game of the Year	*XCOM: Enemy Within*

14TH ANNUAL GAME DEVELOPERS CHOICE AWARDS

Game of the Year: *The Last of Us*

Best Audio	*BioShock Infinite*
Best Debut	The Fullbright Company (*Gone Home*)
Best Design	*The Last of Us*
Best Downloadable Game	*Papers, Please*
Best Handheld/ Mobile Game	*The Legend of Zelda: A Link Between Worlds*
Best Narrative	*The Last of Us*
Best Technology	*Grand Theft Auto V*
Best Visual Art	*BioShock Infinite*
Innovation Award	*Papers, Please*
Lifetime Achievement	Ken Kutaragi

GAMING COLLECTIONS

For some gamers, just playing a game isn't enough. The passion can drive them to hunt out every iteration and affiliated piece of merchandise in the quest to amass the most comprehensive collection – a quest that for some of our record holders turns into a lifelong enterprise. They can end up sharing their home with hundreds, if not thousands, of objects, but for these hardcore fans it's a small price to pay to say they've been there, played that and got the T-shirt… And the mug. And the cuddly toy. And the… well, you get the idea…

LARGEST COLLECTION OF...

VIDEOGAMES

Although Michael Thomasson (USA) has 10,607 games, as verified in 2012, he is currently hoping to sell them to raise funds for his family. He has previously built up and sold two other sizeable collections.

VIDEOGAME MEMORABILIA

Lisa Courtney (UK) really took her favourite franchise's motto – "Gotta catch 'em all!" – to heart, having amassed 14,410 Pokémon items as of 14 October 2010. After trips to Japan she has often shipped new acquisitions home in crates.

GAME SCREENSHOTS

Rikardo Granda (Colombia) had taken 17,000 images from Rondo of Blood, as of September 2012. The 1993 entry in the Castlevania series was only released in Japan, although it later appeared on the Wii's Virtual Console.

SILENT HILL MEMORABILIA

Whitney Chavis (USA) has been collecting Silent Hill memorabilia ever since the survival-horror series began in 1999 and now has 342 items, as verified on 24 July 2014.

STREET FIGHTER MEMORABILIA

Clarence Lim from Ontario, Canada, had 2,723 items based on Capcom's Street Fighter, as of 29 June 2014. Clarence even met his wife through the

game and treasures the copy of the Capcom 25th anniversary documentary I Am Street Fighter that features her.

SUPER MARIO MEMORABILIA

It's quite possible that there's no greater fan of Mario than Mitsugu Kikai from Tokyo, Japan. As of 15 July 2010, he owned 5,441 Super Mario-related objects including toys, posters and even a full-size Mario outfit.

XBOX GAMES

Neil Fenton (UK) owns 814 PAL-region Xbox games, as counted in Rainham, Essex, UK, on 16 June 2014.

LARGEST COLLECTION OF
TOMB RAIDER MEMORABILIA

Rodrigo Martin Santos (Spain) had 2,383 distinct *Tomb Raider* items as of 21 April 2014. "I became a fan when I was nine years old," says Rodrigo, who has spent 10 years collecting the memorabilia. One of his favourite objects is a sketch drawn by Toby Gard, from the team that created Lara Croft. He also has special affection for the original costume used by Rhona Mitra, the live-action model for *Tomb Raider II*, as well as a Lara statue with roses ("probably the most difficult to get – there are less than 50 in the world") and a movie poster signed by the whole cast, including Angelina Jolie.

The Electronic Entertainment Expo, better known as E3, turns 20 in 2015. This annual gathering of the great and the good of gaming has become a hugely significant and influential event in the gaming calendar. We take a look at why E3 is the centre of the gaming universe – and run down some of the most important announcements from its first 19 years.

E3 2014 was held in the Los Angeles Convention Center. Nintendo's stand was as popular as ever, sharing details of the new open-world *Legend of Zelda* game planned for the Wii U, and *Super Smash Bros. for Nintendo 3DS* and *Wii U*, both hotly anticipated by fans.

What is E3 all about?

E3 is devoted to showcasing the newest videogames and hardware. It is one of the largest global gaming conventions and it is where developers, publishers, press and investors gather to celebrate games and reveal the future of electronic entertainment in stage presentations and with hands-on gameplay. Major trailers from E3 can count their YouTube audiences in the millions.

Who goes and what happens there?

Everyone who has a passion for videogames attends E3 to be one of the first people to test out demos of new games and hardware. The major companies such as Sony, Microsoft, EA and Ubisoft also compete with each other to put on the best press conferences. E3 is a reliable taste-maker, predicting what is going to be big in the coming year in gaming.

What made the E3 2014 headlines?

Indie games were a huge hit at E3. Among these were the platformers *Ori and the Blind Forest* and *Apotheon* (which is flavoured with Greek mythology), plus the procedurally generated universe of *No Man's Sky*.

Virtual reality also hogged the limelight, with Sony inviting attendees to try out the Project Morpheus headset on three games, and the Oculus Rift, bought by Facebook in 2014, was also on show.

E3 2015

The 2015 expo will be held on 16–18 June 2015 at the Los Angeles Convention Center in Los Angeles, USA.

Sony's Project Morpheus headset at E3 in 2014.

FPS *Evolve* – with the predatory Goliath monster (below) in person at E3 – was the talk of the town, scooping four critics' awards.

GWR AT E3

GWR's Annie Nguyen was on hand to present certificates to Twitch (above) for the **most concurrent viewers of a gaming live-streaming service** and **most participants on a single-player online game** – for more on Twitch, turn to pp.130–31. Square also received a certificate (below) for the **longest-running JRPG series** – *Dragon Quest* (26 years).

5.9 million
unique views of 2014's live day-one E3 events were recorded on Twitch.tv.

405,029
people watching the day-one E3 livestream concurrently on Twitch.tv.

48,900
industry professionals, investors, journalists and retailers present.

200
countries represented by attendees to the show.

100
exhibitors displaying their videogames, hardware and new concepts.

E3 HISTORY

1995: Hello, Sony
The first E3 welcomed 50,000 guests to witness the Japanese tech giant entering the home-console market by announcing the PlayStation. It wasn't such a rosy event for Nintendo, however, whose Virtual Boy was announced with much fanfare, only for it to flop by selling fewer than 800,000 units.

1996: The magic number is 64
If 1995 proved a downer for Nintendo, 1996 was an altogether better party: the N64 and its flagship launch title *Super Mario 64* were star attractions.

1998: Of its time
The Legend of Zelda: Ocarina of Time for the N64 was shown to the world for the very first time. By now, E3 was very much the epicentre of gaming and it attracted 70,000 guests.

Sega launched the Dreamcast in 1999.

1999: Double-six
The sixth-generation consoles arrived, with Sega's Dreamcast making its US debut and Nintendo announcing the "Dolphin" console that would be renamed as the GameCube when it was launched.

2000: Sega's samba
At the unveiling of the PS2, few in the conference hall would have guessed that it would go on to become the **best-selling console** of all time, with worldwide sales of 157.68 million. Sega, meanwhile, showcased *Samba de Amigo*, a music game controlled with motion-sensitive maracas.

Sony launches the PlayStation 2 in 2000.

2001: Enter Microsoft
There was a welcome for Nintendo's GameCube and Microsoft's first foray into home consoles, the Xbox. Unfortunately, Microsoft's announcement show was full of hitches, including games repeatedly blacking out.

Microsoft announced the Xbox 360 in 2005.

2005: Triple action
An epic year. In the first E3 to air on TV, Sony took the opportunity to show off its brand new PlayStation 3 (although it wasn't playable). Nintendo blew the lid on the "Revolution" – which would later become the Wii. Finally, Microsoft didn't want to be left out of the next-generation party, so they announced the Xbox 360.

***Wii Fit* debuted in 2007.**

2007: Scaled down
New rules on attendees saw invitees only allowed into a new, downsized version of the event now called E3. A crowd of 10,000 saw trailers for *Halo 3* and *Halo Wars*, the debut of *Wii Fit* and Wii peripherals, and the fifth editions of both *Gran Turismo* and *Resident Evil*.

2009: Bulking up
Having been at a smaller scale for the previous two years, E3 defied the worldwide recession and expanded again, with more exhibitors and over 40,000 attendees. Games to be showcased included *Super Mario Galaxy 2* and a surprise unveiling of *Final Fantasy XIV*. IGN awarded best platforming game of E3 to *LittleBigPlanet* on the PSP.

2010: Motion-controlling
The Legend of Zelda: Skyward Sword wowed the audience, while the Microsoft Kinect, until then known as Project Natal, was showcased along with Sony's equivalent, the PlayStation Move.

2012: Nothing to see here
E3 was as revealing for what it didn't show as for what it did – despite much anticipation, there was, in the end, nothing to show from Sony or Microsoft when it came to new consoles.

In 2013, Sony won the press conference battle.

2013: Eighth generation
After revealing the PS4 and Xbox One earlier in the year, Sony and Microsoft used E3 to showcase new games for their latest consoles, among them *Ryse: Son of Rome*, *Dead Rising 3*, *DriveClub*, *Knack* and *Killzone: Shadow Fall*.

GAMING FIRSTS

The first computer game was John Bennett's *NIM*, a graphic-less, logic-based strategy game that demonstrated computing at the Festival of Britain in 1951. The first videogame was A S Douglas's *OXO*, a 1952 noughts and crosses game. But it was the 1970s that ushered in four decades of milestones, starting with 1972's first home console, the Magnavox Odyssey.

1970s

FIRST CONSOLE PERIPHERAL
Ralph Baer, the man behind the Magnavox, also created the realistic-looking light gun that came with the *Shooting Gallery* game for the Odyssey in 1972. Some 80,000 units were sold of this innovative gaming rifle – which even needed to be cocked after each shot.

FIRST PUZZLE GAME
Although it never drew as many coins as Atari's other arcade hits, 1973's *Gotcha* was a two-player cabinet that saw gamers chasing each other through ever-changing mazes.

FIRST GAME LAWSUIT
The massive success of Atari's *Pong* spawned many imitators. The makers of two of these imitators, Allied Leisure Industries and Midway Manufacturing, took part in the first gaming lawsuit. In a complaint filed on 19 October 1973, Allied claimed that Midway had copied the designs of the printed circuit boards for their game. The two companies reached an out-of-court settlement in 1974.

FIRST ACTION-ADVENTURE GAME

The wonder of *Adventure* is that it exists at all. At a time when adventure games were text-only, it was released in 1979 for the Atari 2600, despite its tiny memory. The gameplay involved exploring castles and rooms to locate keys and items to progress through the game. The graphics were primitive – the player was represented by a square cursor – but it was revolutionary for bucking conventions such as scoring and it sold 1.3 million copies.

FIRST GAME TO USE REAL-WORLD PHYSICS
Asteroids (1979) involved the player jetting around in a spaceship to pulverize lumps of rock in space, with momentum making the job harder. It was a commercial hit and, although *Tennis for Two* from 1958 also used physics-based technology, it was displayed on an oscilloscope, confined to a US lab, so was in practical terms a videogame prototype.

1980s

FIRST CONSOLE RPG
Written in 1981, *Advanced Dungeons & Dragons: Treasure of Tarmin* was released in 1983 for the Intellivision. Although there had been other arcade-style *Dungeons & Dragons* videogames before it, *Treasures of Tarmin* presented its world as a solid 3D maze and was the first to use recognizable role-playing features such as variable player statistics.

FIRST FEMALE CHARACTER IN A VIDEOGAME

According to creator Toru Iwatani (Japan), 1980's original *PAC-Man* was designed to appeal primarily to women. Two years later, the addition of a hair bow and lipstick turned *PAC-Man* into *Ms. PAC-Man*, released by Bally Midway in the USA.

FIRST VIDEOGAME WORLD CHAMPION
Ben Gold (USA) won the North American Video Game Olympics at the Twin Galaxies Intergalactic Scoreboard in Ottumwa, Iowa, USA, on 8–9 January 1983. These, the **first videogame world championships**, were broadcast on ABC's *That's Incredible!* television programme on 21 February 1983. Competitors played *Frogger*, *Millipede*, *Joust*, *Super PAC-Man* and *Donkey Kong Jr.*

FIRST CONSOLE TO USE A GAMEPAD
Home gamers used paddle controllers until Atari popularized four-way joysticks, but the first gamepad was 1983's Famicom – later the NES (Nintendo Entertainment System). Atari's 7800 controller followed, with a gamepad under its removable joystick.

FIRST OPEN-WORLD VIDEOGAME
Elite allowed gamers of 1984 to become space pilots who were free to travel anywhere in the galaxy. This was the open world of the game, where interstellar merchants traded in goods ranging from commodities to risky contraband.

FIRST CONSOLE TO PLAY CD-ROMS
A hit in Japan, the PC Engine (also known as TurboGrafx-16) launched in 1987 and was closer to arcade-quality games than its competitors. A CD-ROM peripheral was added in 1989.

FIRST KARAOKE GAME
Arriving as a peripheral that plugged into the Nintendo Famicom's cartridge slot, Bandai's Japan-only *Karaoke Studio*, from 1987, had its own microphone and 15 songs. It was shortly followed by two expansion cartridges.

FIRST LIVE-ACTION MOVIE BASED ON A VIDEOGAME

Super Mario Bros. was released in 1993 with Bob Hoskins as Mario and Dennis Hopper as King Koopa – both sharing the record for the **first Oscar-nominated actor to star in a videogame-licensed film.** Hoskins later called the film his worst job and greatest regret.

FIRST PERSON TO PLAY A VIDEOGAME IN SPACE

Russian cosmonaut Aleksandr Serebrov played *Tetris* on the *Mir* space station in 1993. "Like all cosmonauts, I love sport," wrote Serebrov. "My particular favourites are football and swimming. During flight, in rare minutes of leisure, I enjoyed playing Game Boy."

FIRST PLAYSTATION GAME TO SELL OVER 1 MILLION UNITS

Released in 1995, *Tekken* was an instant hit. The *Tekken* series is now the **best-selling fighter franchise without crossovers**, with 36.3 million sales as of 20 June 2014.

FIRST 64-BIT GAME CONSOLE

The Nintendo 64 was released in 1996 in the fifth generation of consoles. Atari's earlier Jaguar had 64-bit architecture, but with two 32-bit RISC processors and a 16/32-bit Motorola 68000, it wasn't a true 64-bit machine.

FIRST 3D STEALTH GAME

Tenchu was released in Japan on 26 February 1998, preceding the better-known *Metal Gear Solid* by seven months. It was released in the West as *Tenchu: Stealth Assassins.*

FIRST BACKWARD-COMPATIBLE HANDHELD CONSOLE

The Game Boy Color was launched in October 1998 and allowed gamers to play original Game Boy and Game Boy Pocket titles.

FIRST GAME TO USE RAG-DOLL PHYSICS

"Rag-doll physics" is the effect applied to polygonal game character deaths that are generated by algorithms rather than manual programming. In 1998, *Jurassic Park: Trespasser* was the first title to introduce the rag-doll concept to gaming.

FIRST 128-BIT GAME CONSOLE

Despite being Sega's fifth machine and the **first sixth-generation console** in 1998, the Dreamcast was more of a nightmare. After the device managed sales of only 10.6 million, Sega abandoned hardware and stuck to games.

FIRST GAME ON THE COVER OF *TIME* MAGAZINE

In November 1999, *Time* was taken over by *Pokémon* at the height of its success. The magazine interviewed creator Satoshi Tajiri and a child psychologist about what the phenomenon meant.

FIRST ONLINE 3D FIGHTING GAME

The first 3D fighter to offer an online gaming mode was *Mortal Kombat: Deception*, released in 2004 as the sixth instalment in the series. The game offered PlayStation 2 and Xbox players one-on-one fighting between two players over the net in addition to two more sedate mini-games – *Puzzle Kombat* and *Chess Kombat*.

FIRST HD CONSOLE

Microsoft's Xbox 360 hit the shelves on 22 November 2005, almost a year before Sony's PS3, which also supported HD. In the end, the two consoles shifted almost the same number of units worldwide – 82.63 million (Xbox 360) and 83.01 million (PS3), as of 18 August 2014.

FIRST US PRESIDENTIAL CANDIDATE TO USE IN-GAME CAMPAIGN ADVERTISING

Billboards featuring candidate Barack Obama appeared in *Burnout Paradise* in autumn 2008, followed by ads in a number of other EA games in 10 key swing states. Obama carried the majority of those states and returned to in-game advertising for his successful re-election campaign of 2012.

FIRST SPORTS GAME FOR KINECT

Kinect Sports, released on 4 November 2010, was compatible with the Kinect, the **fastest-selling gaming peripheral.** The Kinect sold an average of 133,333 units per day in its first 60 days on sale, from 4 November 2010 to 3 January 2011 – a total of 8 million units. By 2013, over 24 million Kinects had been sold.

FIRST CONSOLE GAME TO SUPPORT STEAM

The arrival of *Portal 2* on the PS3 in 2011 was the first time Valve's Steam platform for PCs and Macs was made available to console players.

FIRST MOBILE GAME SERIES TO REACH 1 BILLION DOWNLOADS

On 9 May 2012, Rovio (Finland) announced its *Angry Birds* series had racked up a total of 1 billion downloads across all its titles. By spring of 2014, this figure had doubled and the game even had several dedicated parks and attractions around the globe.

SPEED-RUNS

Anyone who has finished a favourite game after many hours of playing will know the sense of anticlimax that follows. One way of getting around it is to finish it again – but faster. Then find all the bugs and glitches that allow you to do it even quicker and, before you know it, you'll be hosting your own speed-running Twitch channel.

MOST MONEY RAISED BY SPEED-RUNNING

Many players like to complete games in record time just for the thrill of it, to find and exploit glitches or to experience the satisfaction of planning the best possible route through all of its challenges. Then there is Games Done Quick – the expert gaming group who organize speed-running events for charity. The first of their 2014 speed-run marathons, named "Awesome Games Done Quick", ran from 5 to 11 January and raised $1,031,189 (£626,238) for a cancer charity.

FIRST PERSONALIZED HIGH-SCORE TABLE

Gamers have been trying to beat each other's scores ever since 1979, when Atari's *Asteroids* introduced initials into its high-score table.

FASTEST COMPLETION OF *METROID PRIME*

William "Pirate109" Tansley (UK) completed *Metroid Prime* in 1 hr 7 min on 29 August 2011. William's attempt was logged on Speed Demos Archive, the resource founded in 1998 by Nolan "Radix" Pflug, merging with another site and initially dedicated to *Quake* runs. *Metroid Prime* was the next game added, in 2003. YouTube and Twitch.tv now provide more places for speed-runners to show their stuff.

FASTEST COLLABORATIVE *DOOM* SPEED-RUN

An anonymous group of gamers ran the four levels of the original *Doom* separately as "Doom Done Quicker" in 16 min 5 sec on 10 December 2000. Six years earlier, in November 1994, UK *Doom* fanatic Simon Widlake (UK) set up the COMPET-N website to support completing *Doom* and its sequel as quickly as possible. COMPET-N had a very specific focus, but the general speed-running concept spread online, although for a long time there was no other dedicated community site for logging fast feats.

FASTEST COMPLETION OF...

Game	Time	Holder(s)	Date	Notes†
*Bastion** (right)	14 min	"Vulajin"	26 Dec 2013	PC
*BioShock Infinite**	1 hr 57 min 57 sec	"FearfulFerret"	29 Apr 2014	
*Castlevania**	11 min 48 sec	"kmafrocard"	15 Dec 2013	
*Dead Space 2** (right)	2 hr 14 min 40 sec	"Sahail Tenshouha"	27 Oct 2013	PC, "Hardcore" difficulty
*Dead Space 2**	2 hr 25 min 51 sec	Craig "osey889" Kean (USA)	27 May 2013	Xbox 360, "Casual" difficulty
Devil May Cry	58 min 27 sec	Wesley "Molotov" Corron	17 Jun 2005	100%, "Normal"
Dragon Quest	4 hr 47 min 36 sec	Eric "Lhexa" D'Avignon	23 Sep 2011	10 segments, US NES
Dragon Soul raid (*World of Warcraft*)	1 hr 11 min 36 sec	Stars Guild (Chinese Taipei)	12 May 2012	
*E.T.: The Extra-Terrestrial**	53 sec	"DSmon"	19 Jul 2013	
Fable	1 hr 37 min	David Arnold	2 Aug 2010	
Gears of War 2	3 hr 56 min 48 sec	"zzDAZZLEzz" (Canada)	19 May 2013	
Gothic (right)	5 min 56 sec	"LordSaradoc"	8 Mar 2014	
Half-Life 2	1 hr 27 min 51 sec	"SourceRuns" team	6 Jul 2013	
*Jak and Daxter: The Precursor Legacy**	1 hr 12 min 19 sec	"Bonesaw577"	3 Dec 2013	
*Metal Gear Solid**	1 hr 7 min 56 sec	"TheSlade"	19 Jan 2014	"Extreme" difficulty; glitches
Metal Gear Solid: The Twin Snakes	1 hr 3 min 7 sec	Caleb Hart	30 May 2011	GameCube
Metal Gear Solid V: Ground Zeroes	3 min 54 sec	"CrumandMimalmo"	24 Jun 2014	
*Metal Gear Solid 2: Sons of Liberty**	1 hr 37 min 37 sec	Cody Miller (USA)	12 May 2007	PS2, "Extreme" difficulty
*Mirror's Edge** (right)	57 min 23 sec	David "Weatherproof" Streeter (USA)	23 Sep 2011	
*Ninja Gaiden Black**	1 hr 55 min 5 sec	Josh Mangini (USA)	25 Oct 2006	
Pikmin 2 (pictured)	3 hr 10 min	Charles Griffin	25 Sep 2009	128 segments
Pokémon Y	3 hr 52 min 45 sec	"iMAX1UP"	28 Feb 2014	
Resident Evil	1 hr 2 min 30 sec	"PopovAmiral" (France)	16 Oct 2013	PS2
Resident Evil 4	1 hr 34 min 26 sec	"blaze8876"	23 Apr 2013	PC
Sonic the Hedgehog	15 min 5 sec	Charles Griffin	1 Aug 2008	
*Spelunky**	1 min 55 sec 353 nanosec	"Pibonacci" (Germany)	14 Jul 2014	
*Super Mario Bros. 2**	8 min 32 sec	Chris "cak" Knight (USA)	12 Jun 2013	NES
*Super Meat Boy**	18 min 24 sec	John De Sousa (USA)	5 Dec 2013	PC
Super Metroid	41 min	Brandon Moore (USA)	10 May 2010	NTSC
*VVVVVV**	13 min 56 sec	Jared "FieryBlizzard" Klein (USA)	16 Jun 2013	
*We Love Katamari** (right)	1 hr 5 min 31 sec	Tom Batchelor (USA)	25 Dec 2005	

* Single-segment run; †all attempts made on easiest level unless stated otherwise; nationalities given where known

FROM PRIMETIME TO PIXELS

Developers have long tuned in to television for inspiration, and for good reason. TV's most successful shows are defined by memorable characters, compelling visuals and addictive storylines – the same elements essential for a blockbuster game. And it's starting to work both ways now, with videogames influencing TV…

The crossover can be traced back to the arcade halls of the 1970s, where *Fonz* – a re-branded version of Sega's *Moto-Cross* game – gave *Happy Days* fans a chance to cruise along with main character and epitome of cool Arthur "The Fonz" Fonzarelli. Later spin-offs such as *Popeye*, *The Three Stooges* and Japan's *Cosmo Police Galivan* also brought arcade-goers closer to their small-screen icons, while beefing up ratings and video sales for their respective shows.

TV stars of the 1980s moonlighted on virtually every console. As well as colourful adaptations of *Looney Tunes* and Disney shows, the decade saw gamers helping cat-loving aliens fix their spaceships in *ALF*, saving towns from intergalactic invasions in *Fester's Quest*, and going full throttle for *KITT* justice in adventure-driving NES title *Knight Rider*.

From gimmick to genre
From the 1990s onwards, TV spin-offs transformed into a genre all of their own. Retail shelves buckled under the weight of games based on hit programmes *The X-Files*, *Star Trek: The Next Generation* (and later *Deep Space Nine* and *Voyager*), *Home Improvement*, *Law & Order* and *Lost*. Even old-school classics were dusted off and digitized for a new shot at fame, such as *The Adventures of Rocky and Bullwinkle and Friends* and *The Dukes of Hazzard: Racing for Home*. Granted, some games fell short of critical acclaim and many failed to trouble bestseller lists, but for aficionados, the opportunity to play alongside their TV heroes was more than enough reason to come back for repeat plays.

The new wave(length)
The collaboration between TV and videogames has reached new heights in recent years.

VIDEOGAME OF THRONES

Just as *The Walking Dead* writer Robert Kirkman played a critical role in the development of *The Walking Dead: The Game*, Telltale's upcoming *Game of Thrones* is forging ahead with support from franchise insiders, including the PA to George R R Martin.

In 2012, Telltale Games' *The Walking Dead: The Game* episodic series, based on AMC's undead TV hit (which itself is based on Robert Kirkman's comic books), resurrected the point-and-click genre and became one of the most acclaimed games based on a television series.

Its success gave Telltale the clout to bring HBO's *Game of Thrones* series (based on George R R Martin's *A Song of Ice and Fire* books) to gamers in a similar fashion. And the hits keep coming. Games such as *South Park: The Stick of Truth*, *The Simpsons: Tapped Out* and multiple titles based on current

hit shows *Adventure Time*, *Family Guy*, *CSI* and many others prove the audience for TV tie-ins remains alive and well. Mobile developers have also caught on, leading to app spin-offs such as *Family Guy: The Quest for Stuff*.

Crossing over
Today, the lines between the small screen and the console continue to blur, with one influencing the other and vice versa. *Defiance* offers sci-fi followers a persistent MMO shaped by the TV show of the same name, while *Quantum Break*, scheduled for a 2015 release, aims to create a hybrid TV-videogame that

TV TIMES
While gaming's relationship with TV began as long ago as 1976, the quality threshold for these spin-offs was something of a moot point until fairly recently. For every *South Park: The Stick of Truth* or *The Walking Dead*, there are several *American Gladiators* and *Murder, She Wrote*s – spin-offs that didn't quite make the grade.

Here we take a look at some of the games that have spun off from hit TV shows of their day, starting with the cult American sitcom *Happy Days*.

Happy Days (1974–84)

Popeye the Sailor (1960–62)

Knight Rider (1982–86)

Fonz (1976): The coolest man on TV had the existing motorbike game *Moto-Cross* re-hashed, re-named and released in arcades by Sega.

Popeye (1982): The spinach-loving sailor first became a TV star in the 1960s, and when a new series launched in 1978, this arcade title soon followed.

Knight Rider (1988): "The Hoff" once fought crime as Michael Knight, and he and his AI car *KITT* chased down baddies in the NES spin-off title.

its developers have called a "revolutionary entertainment experience".

As *The Super Mario Bros. Super Show!* attests, the relationship also goes both ways. There have been numerous cartoons based on franchises including *Sonic the Hedgehog*, *Pokémon* and *Super Mario*. In 2013, Microsoft announced that Steven Spielberg's Amblin Entertainment are to produce a series based on *Halo* (see right).

Virtual future

So where to from here? With the advance of virtual reality technology in the form of

HALO GOODBYE?

In May 2013, Microsoft announced that Hollywood legend Steven Spielberg (right) had signed up to produce a *Halo* TV series.

It seemed that the team behind the then-unreleased Xbox One had pulled off a real coup, the idea being that Spielberg's TV series would be released at the same time as *Halo 5: Guardians* in 2015.

Microsoft staked a lot on the *Halo* TV show. It was due to be the flagship series for the Xbox Live network in its bid to compete with Netflix and other streaming services. But in July 2014 Microsoft announced that Xbox Entertainment Studios would close by the end of the year. The news came as Microsoft shed 18,000 jobs, mostly from its Nokia mobile phone division.

Facebook's Oculus Rift and Sony's VR headset, code-named Project Morpheus, the boundaries between what we watch and what we play may soon be erased entirely. The "interactive TV show", once a derided sub-genre, might well make a comeback as producers of games and TV series work closer together to create intertwining, immersive entertainment.

Who hasn't dreamed of becoming part of their favourite cast, or playing

along to a show's weekly adventures? Soon, we may be all powering up and tuning in for our very own primetime roles.

SYFY *DEFIANCE*

Trion Worlds' *Defiance* launched in April 2013 for PC, PS3 and Xbox 360. A third-person shooter MMO, it became free2play in 2014. The game is a collaboration between Trion Worlds and the TV channel Syfy and became the **first videogame and TV show to directly influence one another**, the idea being that the TV characters' struggles are then played out inside the game.

The Addams Family (1964–66)

Home Improvement (1991–99)

Star Trek: TNG (1987–94)

The X-Files (1993–2002)

Fester's Quest (1989): The TV show inspired by Charles Addams' kooky family appeared 20 years later in this NES overhead shooter.

Power Tool Pursuit! (1994): Tim Allen's sitcom was unexpectedly made into a SNES platformer. Weapons included nail guns and chainsaws.

Future's Past (1994): Every *Star Trek* television series has made the jump to gaming. This adventure game was Captain Picard's first spin-off.

The X-Files Game (1998): The sci-fi show was a huge hit so it's little wonder it got its own game. An interactive movie, it required seven PC disks!

THE WALKING DEAD

It's rare for a game to receive as much attention and acclaim as the TV show on which it is based, but Telltale Games' *The Walking Dead* episodic games have certainly not just ridden on the coat-tails of the hit series. They have been lauded and successful in their own right.

The success is largely down to the collaboration between the games' developers and *The Walking Dead* creator Robert Kirkman. The monthly comic books – written by Kirkman and drawn and designed by Tony Moore and Charlie Adlard – began in 2003 and are still going strong. Their simple premise follows the trials and particularly gruesome tribulations of a group of zombie apocalypse survivors on a dangerous, ravaged Earth.

The games tell an original story set within the world painted by the TV show and comic books, led by protagonist Lee Everett and his young ward Clementine.

The five episodes that make up the first season of the game have sold over 17 million – making *The Walking Dead* the **best-selling episodic videogame**. Reviews were as strong as sales, and the game won several 2012 Game of the Year awards.

The Dukes of Hazzard (1979–85)

24 (2001–10)

The Sopranos (1999–2007)

The Office (2005–13)

Racing for Home (1999): When the good ol' boys' show hit the PlayStation we got a chance to drive General Lee, Daisy's Jeep and more.

24: The Game (2006): Jack Bauer fever was at its height when this third-person shooter, revolving around terrorist attacks in LA, came to the PS2.

Road to Respect (2006): Another PS2 exclusive, this gangster adventure voiced by many of the original cast received poor reviews.

The Office (2007): Two years after the US sitcom launched, the Dunder Mifflin team came to PC as bobblehead characters. The game did not prove as popular.

DAVE FENNOY
Videogame voice actor

American Dave Fennoy is a videogame acting stalwart whose credits include *Bayonetta*, *Skylanders* and *DotA 2*. He is also the voice of *The Walking Dead: The Game*'s main protagonist Lee Everett. So what's it like to help bring one of the biggest TV shows in history to gamers? GWR went to the source…

Were you a fan of *The Walking Dead* [*TWD*] before you took up your role as Lee?

I was familiar with the show, and knew it was created from Robert Kirkman's comic-book series, but I had not watched the show until the audition arrived on my desk. Needless to say, I began watching the show and reading the comics and have become a big fan.

How did you prepare for the role?

By finding out as much as I could about the character. That, and watching the TV show and reading the comics to understand the tone and feel of the *Walking Dead* universe.

How successful do you think the game was at capturing that tone?

It did a great job at capturing the feel and spirit of the *Walking Dead* show and comics. Part of the genius of Robert Kirkman is that he created a world that can accommodate many stories of numerous people trying to survive zombies – and each other.

What was your most memorable scene? [Spoiler alert!]

The most memorable was Lee's goodbye to Clem. The head writer, Sean Vanaman, told me during the recording of Episode 3 that Lee was going to die in the end, and my initial reaction was not good. I thought it didn't make sense to kill off the hero, not to mention the fact that it would mean I wouldn't be in the second season! However, the scene when Lee says goodbye to Clem was magical. It touched players all over the world, and the truth is I ended up in tears while I was recording the scene. I think it made Episode 5 more special.

What would be your next dream role?

Since playing Lee, Greg Miller from IGN's *Up at Noon* and fans of the *Walking Dead* games and show have been tweeting Robert Kirkman and AMC to get me on the show as the character Ezekiel [from the comics] because I look just like the character with my dreadlocks. And yes, I'd love to play Ezekiel on the show, just as long as they don't cast Siegfried and Roy's tiger!

Lost (2004–10)

The Simpsons (1989–)

Adventure Time (2010–)

South Park (1997–)

***Via Domus* (2008):** This was the third of seven games based on the ABC show, set 17–21 days after the plane crash. Critics were largely unimpressed.

***Tapped Out* (2012):** This iOS and Android city-builder, set after Homer triggers a nuclear meltdown, is the 27th title based on the much-loved cartoon.

***Explore the Dungeon Because I Don't Know!* (2013):** Second game from the Emmy-winning show with Finn and Jake saving the Candy Kingdom.

***The Stick of Truth* (2014):** This critically acclaimed RPG in which you play the new kid on the block sold over a million copies on the PS3, PC and X360.

50-40

MOST PROLIFIC DEVELOPER OF TOY VIDEOGAMES

As of 19 June 2014, developer TT Games had released 20 titles under the LEGO® brand. These include LEGO-themed adaptations of *Star Wars*, *The Lord of the Rings*, DC Comics, Marvel Comics, *Indiana Jones* and *The Hobbit*, pictured here. TT Games owns Traveller's Tales and TT Fusion, and is now a subsidiary of Warner Bros. Interactive Entertainment. The early LEGO games developed by TT were so successful that they inspired Warner Bros. to buy out the company in 2007. TT's contract with LEGO is set to end in 2016, and no announcement has yet been made on a possible extension.

JUST DANCE

Summary: It's fun, it can keep you fit, and President Obama plays it with his daughters. Six years on, *Just Dance* remains the undisputed champion of limb-waving boogie battles.

Publisher: Ubisoft
Developer: Ubisoft
Debut: 2009

BEST-SELLING DANCE VIDEOGAME SERIES

The ever-popular *Just Dance* is firmly entrenched in boogie wonderland with total franchise sales of 46.78 million across all formats as of 11 June 2014. The series' popularity has been boosted by successful launches in South Korea and Japan, where versions specifically tailored to those markets have shifted more than 1 million units.

Just Dance's biggest rival, *Dance Dance Revolution*, has been on the dancing scene since 1998, but lags behind with sales of 21.52 million.

235,871,193
tracks played in *Just Dance 2014* from its launch in October 2013 until 22 April 2014.

FIRST GAME WITH PLAYER-CHOREOGRAPHED DANCE ROUTINES

The "Just Create" mode in *Just Dance 3* for the Xbox 360 allows players with a Kinect to video themselves performing moves that they have created. They can then use this video to challenge friends to copy their choreography, or simply share routines online.

BEST-SELLING GAME AFFILIATED TO A MUSIC ARTIST

The "King of Pop" still reigns supreme. *Michael Jackson: The Experience* – a *Just Dance* spin-off – has sold 6.08 million copies worldwide. Dance games affiliated to a particular artist or band have become on-trend in recent years. Other popular titles include *The Black Eyed Peas Experience* (0.86 million sales) and *ABBA: You Can Dance* (0.72 million).

BEST-SELLING DANCE GAME

Just Dance 3 is the most successful dance videogame ever, with a total of 12.41 million games sold globally for the Wii, PS3 and Xbox 360 combined. The series' most recent incarnation, *Just Dance 2014*, has sold 4.83 million copies. At E3 2014, Ubisoft announced two new titles for its hit franchise – *Just Dance 2015* and *Just Dance Now*, a free mobile game.

LARGEST ONLINE VIRTUAL DANCE BATTLE

These days, you don't need to hook up with a flashmob for group dancing insanity. With the "World Dance Floor" mode in *Just Dance 2014*, you can do the same thing from the comfort of your own living room. It was in that mode, and game, that the biggest online virtual dance battle took place – 66,101 gamers connected for simultaneous festive rump-wiggling on Christmas Day 2013.

MOST POPULAR DANCE GAME TRACK

The video of the *Just Dance 4* routine for One Direction's "What Makes You Beautiful" had 22,969,161 YouTube views as of 14 July 2014 – the most for any song featured in a dance game. The British boyband also holds a host of non-gaming records, including the **highest debut by a UK group on the US singles chart**, achieved when "Live While We're Young" debuted at No.3 on 20 October 2012.

▶▶FIRST VIDEOGAME RECOGNIZED AS AN OFFICIAL SPORT

Just Dance may be the dancing queen for now, but Konami's pioneering *Dance Dance Revolution* still boasts a host of records, starting with its recognition as an official sport. On 9 December 2003, the Norwegian Dancing Association registered the game as a sport under the name "machine dancing". The *DDR* series went on to claim another significant first when *Dance Dance Revolution Hottest Party* became the **first full-body motion dancing game** upon its release on 25 September 2007. Using a Wiimote and dance mat, it tracks players' movements in both the upper and lower body.

▶▶LONGEST-RUNNING DANCE GAME SERIES

Dance Dance Revolution started life on 21 November 1998, and its most recent release, *Dance Dance Revolution Pocket Edition*, was released on 7 October 2013. This span of 14 years 10 months

16 days comfortably lands it the record – and that's well over twice the length of *Just Dance*'s life span.

▶▶MOST CRITICALLY ACCLAIMED DANCE GAME

DDR may have the stamina, and *Just Dance* might be the most popular, but gaming critics have other ideas. The highest-rated dance game is Xbox 360-exclusive *Dance Central 3*, with a GameRankings score of 86.88%. In fact, *Dance Central* occupies three of the top five spots in the most acclaimed dance games list, despite the series' three games only selling 5.73 million units worldwide.

MOST *JUST DANCE* APPEARANCES BY ONE ARTIST

With nine songs featured across the franchise as of 19 April 2014, the most prolific artist in the *Just Dance* series is US singer Katy Perry. For *SingStar Dance*, it's fellow American Britney Spears – but with a far more meagre three songs.

BEST-SELLING THIRD-PARTY WII SERIES

The majority of titles for Nintendo's consoles, such as *Super Mario* or *Zelda*, are designed by their own development team. This record category, however, recognizes the achievements of developers other than Nintendo. Total sales of 40.55 million make *Just Dance* the most successful third-party series on the Wii, and Ubisoft can also lay claim to the **best-selling third-party Wii game**, with more than 9.92 million copies of *Just Dance 3* shifted worldwide.

PARTY TIME!

For a while, gamers couldn't move for novelty instrument controllers, but – particularly now that we've hit the eighth generation of consoles – the rhythm gaming fad is fading. However, there are still party games that we can't resist loading up when we get together.

Look out for Cru-el-la De Vil

GIVE US A BREAK

Tony Hawk developer Neversoft got the *Guitar Hero* gig from the third title on, after co-founder Joel Jewett admitted they played the game in breaks from coding skate games.

SHORTEST *SINGSTAR* SONG

The *101 Dalmatians* song "Cruella de Vil" clocks in at a mere 1 min 7 sec on *SingStar: Singalong with Disney* on PS2, making it the shortest of all *SingStar* tracks. At the other end of the scale is "Koi Mil Gaya" by Kuch Kuch Hota Hai from *SingStar Bollywood*. At a lung-busting 7 min 43 sec, this is the **longest** *SingStar* **song**.

BEST-SELLING BAND-SPECIFIC SEVENTH-GENERATION GAME

The Beatles: Rock Band has sold 4.05 million copies across all platforms as of 13 August 2014, beating the likes of *Green Day: Rock Band* and *Guitar Hero: Aerosmith*. Themed Rickenbacker and Gretsch guitars, a Höfner bass and a Ludwig drum set launched alongside *The Beatles: Rock Band*, the Wii version of which is the **best-selling band-specific game on a single platform**, with sales of 1.69 million as of 13 August 2014. The same game is also the **most critically acclaimed band-specific videogame**, with a GameRankings score of 89.83% from 57 reviews.

Gaming with Wii controllers...

BEST-SELLING PARTY GAME

Wii Play has sold 28.81 million copies, according to VGChartz. It consists of nine mini-games, including a shooting range (pictured inset), fishing and billiards. The Wii is also home to the **best-selling physical fitness game**, *Wii Fit*. The game, which sold 22.69 million copies, was bundled with the Wii Balance Board to perform activities such as yoga, aerobics and strength training. *Wii Fit* is the sixth-best-selling game on the Wii overall.

BEST-SELLING KARAOKE GAME SERIES

According to VGChartz, *SingStar* had sold 21.18 million copies across the dozens of editions released for PlayStation since the series began back in 2004. When it comes to the **best-selling band-specific karaoke game**, the winner takes it all – it's *SingStar ABBA* (left), with sales of 2.25 million units on the PS2 and PS3.

BEST-SELLING WII U PARTY GAME

Nintendo Land has sold 3.09 million copies and is second only to *New Super Mario Bros. U* – the overall **best-selling Wii U game**. The virtual amusement park benefited from being bundled with the Wii U and features 12 mini-games based on Nintendo favourites such as *The Legend of Zelda*, *Metroid* and, of course, *Mario*.

FIRST CONSOLE KARAOKE GAME TO USE A PHONE APP AS A MICROPHONE

Celebrating its 10th birthday as a PlayStation series in 2014, *SingStar* is to be launched on PS4 with innovative new features including an app for singing into smartphones rather than using the standard microphone accessory. As of 14 August 2014, the **best-selling *SingStar* track** is "Let Her Go" by Passenger, while previous record holder Carly Rae Jepsen is at No.4 with "Call Me Maybe".

8 centuries 81 years 15 days 17 hr 31 min
total time played on *Rocksmith* as of 13 August 2014.

FOR THE WIN

DJ HERO 2

To unlock Deadmau5 as a playable character in *DJ Hero 2*, enter "Open the Trap" under Retail Cheats in the Options menu.

FIRST "NO GRAPHICS" PARTY GAME

Part of the Kickstarter-funded *Sportsfriends* on PS3 and PS4, *Johann Sebastian Joust* is played without the need to look at a screen and is solely controlled by the PlayStation Move. The idea of the mini-game is to keep the controller still while bumping other players. As J S Bach's Brandenburg concertos play at a slow tempo, up to seven players must try to knock the others out of the game. The tempo increases and gamers can make bigger movements.

FIRST RHYTHM GAME TO GENERATE $1 BILLION

Guitar Hero III: Legends of Rock is the first rhythm game to generate $1 bn (£650 m), as announced by publisher Activision in January 2009.

The **longest *Guitar Hero World Tour* marathon** was set by Simo Piispanen (guitar), Aku Valmu (bass), Jaakko Kokkonen (vocals) and Simo-Matti Liimatainen (drums) when they unleashed an epic jam of 24 hr 2 min at gaming event Assembly Winter 2009 in Tampere, Finland, on 21 February 2009.

NBA 2K

Summary: The franchise got a fresh look and revamped features such as My Career for its 2013 outing on the new console generation. EA's *NBA Live* is never far behind as a competitor series.

Publisher: Sega/2K Sports
Developer: Visual Concepts
Debut: 1999

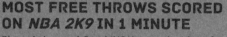

MOST CONSECUTIVE FREE THROWS SCORED ON *NBA 2K9*

Blaine Griffin (USA) scored 15 consecutive throws on *NBA 2K9* at the NBA All-Star Jam Session in Phoenix, Arizona, USA, on 15 February 2009.

The **most three-point shots made in *NBA 2K9* in 1 minute**

6

Jay-Z songs on the soundtrack for *NBA 2K13*. The superstar also served as executive producer.

MOST FREE THROWS SCORED ON *NBA 2K9* IN 1 MINUTE

Phoenix Legend Goad (USA) scored with 18 free throws in Indiana, USA, on 20 January 2014. He was matched dunk for dunk less than a month later by Tristen Geren (USA) in Fredericksburg, Texas, USA, playing on 16 February.

is 26, by Chad Heathcoat (USA) playing against other Jam Session fans at the same event on 12 February 2009.

MOST ASSISTS PLAYING *NBA 2K11*

Barak Yakovi (USA) made 23 assists at the 2K Sports booth during the All-Star Jam Session in Los Angeles, USA, on 18 February 2011.

The **most points scored playing Michael Jordan in *NBA 2K11*** is 51, by Burtland Dixon (USA) at the same event. In real life, His Airness held five GWR

titles as of June 2014, including the **highest point-scoring average in an NBA career**, with 30.1 (32,292 points in 1,072 games). Jordan also set the **highest point-scoring average in NBA play-offs**, with 33.4.

FOR THE WIN

DEFENDING IN *NBA 2K14*

You don't always need to attack. In *NBA 2K14*, get into defence for a while, choose taller players and spend time understanding the controls. By blocking balls and perfecting timing jumps, you will gain a better grip on games.

YOUNGEST PROFESSIONAL GAMER

"Lil Poison", aka Victor De Leon III (USA), was born on 6 May 1998 and just two years later picked up a Dreamcast controller to play *NBA 2K*. In 2005, aged seven, the gaming prodigy signed his first Major League Gaming deal for *Halo*.

▶▶FIRST VIDEOGAME TO FEATURE A NATIONAL ANTHEM

The US "Star-Spangled Banner" rang out in *Double Dribble* in arcades in 1986. On its NES port, the cinematic presentation was retained to include cutscenes and speech. The title refers to dribbling, when a player stops and restarts or uses two hands.

▶▶FIRST GAME SOUNDTRACK TO REACH PLATINUM STATUS

An *NBA Livestyle 2003* music CD was bundled with *NBA Live 2003* – the first year that EA used in-game soundtracks with a mix of new and established acts. In March 2003, six months after its release, it was confirmed as having sold over 1 million copies, likely thanks to artists on the CD such as Snoop Dogg.

MOST GAME COVER APPEARANCES BY A BASKETBALL PLAYER

Allen Iverson (USA) played for four teams in the NBA between 1996 and 2010, including a decade-long stint with Philadelphia 76ers. From 1999 to 2003, the shooting guard and point guard was the cover star for five *NBA 2K* games: *NBA 2K*, *NBA 2K1*, *NBA 2K2*, *NBA 2K3* and *ESPN NBA Basketball*.

BEST-SELLING BASKETBALL VIDEOGAME FRANCHISE

The Sega/2K Sports *NBA 2K* series is top of the list of b-ball franchises. It has sold 37.24 million copies since its debut in 1999, edging closest rival, EA's *NBA Live* (see **longest-running basketball videogame series**, right), which has sold a total of 33.54 million copies. *NBA Live 15*, set for a late 2014 release, looks ready to build on the success of the series and to make up for a break in production from 2009 to 2013.

▶▶LARGEST BASKETBALL VIDEOGAME DATABASE

The 2014 *World Basketball Manager* had more than 12,500 players, 1,400 managers, 194 nationalities and 972 clubs and national teams. The database is maintained entirely by the game's loyal fanbase.

▶▶LONGEST-SERVING VIDEOGAME ANNOUNCER

All fans of the original 1993 *NBA Jam* remember the catchphrases of Tim Kitzrow, whose ebullient "Boom-shaka-laka!" and "He's on fire!" defined the game. He reprised his role for the 2003 Acclaim version and again in 2010 – an overall span of 17 years.

▶▶FIRST MOBILE PHONE GAME WITH AN NBA LICENCE

Flick NBA Basketball was released for iOS devices in 2009. It featured players from all 30 NBA teams in a set of five mini-games that tested touch-control skills.

▶▶LONGEST-RUNNING BASKETBALL VIDEOGAME SERIES

EA's *NBA Live* franchise began more than two decades ago with *NBA Live 95*. There have been 17 entries in total, including *NBA Live 14*, making it also the **most prolific basketball videogame series**. Its competition includes *NBA 2K* (15 editions), while *NCAA Basketball* first appeared in 1998 (under the name *NCAA March Madness*) and ran until 2009.

EURO HEROES

Basketball videogames traditionally concentrated on the American national league until *NBA 2K14* broke the mould. The game includes 14 teams officially licensed from Euroleague basketball playing against the more recognizable NBA clubs.

Summary: Split seconds separate PlayStation's *Gran Turismo* and Xbox's *Forza Motorsport* as driving sims – your choice of game is likely to come down to which system you own.

Publisher: Sony
Developer: Polyphony Digital
Debut: 1997

MOST EXPENSIVE VIRTUAL CAR

While the Jaguar XJ13 Chrome Line from *Gran Turismo 6* can be acquired by progressing through the game, there is an alternative for drivers with cash as well as gas to burn. Players can pay out a real-world total of $196 (£119) in micro-transactions to get the keys to the Jag.

LONGEST CHART RUN FOR A RACING GAME

Gran Turismo 5 spent 155 weeks in the VGChartz Top 75 rundown, including its final week of 9 November 2013. The sixth entry in the series took the top spot a month later. As of 30 July 2014, *Gran Turismo 6* had notched up its 33rd week in the chart.

MOST SUCCESSFUL VIRTUAL-TO-REALITY COMPETITION

Players of *GT6* took part in the sixth instalment of the GT Academy competition, hoping to become a real-life racing driver for Nissan. Since its inception in 2008, there have been four million entrants. For more on this record-breaking competition, turn to pp.40–41.

LONGEST-SERVING DESIGNER OF A RACING FRANCHISE

The producer of the *Gran Turismo* series, Kazunori Yamauchi (Japan, see right), was the lead designer on 16 of the games from the core series to its spin-offs, over a period of some 21 years. He also created two *Motor Toon Grand Prix* titles.

MOST COURSES IN A *GRAN TURISMO* GAME

With 86 courses to choose from, *GT6* beats its immediate predecessor in the series by 26 tracks. Including all games in the series and repeated appearances of tracks, there are 335 courses in *Gran Turismo*.

FASTEST LAP OF "LAGUNA SECA"

Tommy Lee (Canada) set a time of 59 sec on *GT5*'s "Laguna Seca" on 3 July 2013. The **fastest lap of Laguna Seca by a team of two** was 1 min 38.20 sec set by by Callum McGinley and Olajide Olatunji (both UK) sharing the buttons on one controller on 8 August 2013.

BEST-SELLING NON-KART RACING GAME

Gran Turismo 3: A-spec has recorded total sales of 14.98 million copies, but while the race track ace may take pole position in its own class, in overall racing fun terms it lags well behind *Mario Kart* – for the lowdown on Nintendo's genre-killer, see pp.132–33. *A-spec* is also the **best-selling PS2 racing game** and, were it not for *Grand Theft Auto* instalments *San Andreas* and *Vice City*, it would be the highest-selling game on the platform overall.

5 years of development that went into the original *Gran Turismo*, released in 1997.

KAZUNORI YAMAUCHI

Before becoming the president of Polyphony Digital and designer of the *Gran Turismo* series, Yamauchi worked on *Motor Toon Grand Prix*, released for the PlayStation in Japan. Far from displaying the realistic elements that have made *GT* so famous, *Motor Toon Grand Prix* showcased the cartoon style suggested by its title. Yamauchi-san has gone beyond the virtual with the success of *Gran Turismo* – he is also a professional racing driver, having competed in real races, including the 24 Hours of Nürburgring.

BEST-SELLING PS3-EXCLUSIVE GAME

Gran Turismo 5, released in 2010 – some six years after the previous main entry in the series – has sold 10.90 million copies. This figure is higher than any individual entry in the *Forza Motorsport* and *Need for Speed* series – its main rivals for scope and ambition – making *GT5* the **best-selling racing game on an HD console**. Petrolheads hungry for more *NfS* action should race to pp.134–35.

▶▶MOST COMPLEX CAR MODELS IN A VIDEOGAME

There are 1,000,000 polygons (discrete 2D shapes used to build objects) for every car in *Forza Motorsport 5*. The roster of gorgeously realized vehicles includes (clockwise from top left) a 1952 Ferrari 375, a fearsome Hummer H1 Alpha from 2006, F1's highly successful Lotus Type 49 from 1967 and the 1956 Ford F-100 truck. *Forza 5* is also the **fastest-selling Xbox racing game**, with sales of 1.3 million from 22 November 2013 to 18 February 2014. This figure is all the more remarkable for representing a third of all Xbox One owners.

▶▶MOST PARTICIPANTS IN A RACING RELAY

Emulating the 24 Hours of Le Mans endurance race, in which cars have to keep going for the full period, 49 gamers played GT's close simulator competitor *Forza 5* on the same console at Audi City Berlin in Germany on 5 June 2014. Each player was allowed a 30-second pause between changeovers.

▶▶FIRST RACING SIMULATOR TO RESPOND TO HEAD MOVEMENTS

Forza 4 primarily used the Kinect to track the movements of a player and reflected them in the game. This enabled drivers to reduce blind spots, checking mirrors with just a minor movement of the head, and to increase visibility when using the bonnet-cam view.

LONGEST RACETRACK IN A VIDEOGAME

The oval test track Special Stage Route X, released as DLC for *Gran Turismo 5* and *Gran Turismo 6*, is 30.28 km (18.8 mi) long, with two 11-km (6.8-mi) straights. The longest real-life track featured in the series is the Nordschleife from Nürburgring, in *Gran Turismo 4*, *Gran Turismo PSP* and – at 20.83 km (12.94 mi) – in *Gran Turismo 5*. The real-world Nürburgring is the world's **longest motor-racing circuit**, with its two main circuits creating a combined length of 25.95 km (16.12 mi).

FASTEST CAR IN A VIDEOGAME

The Red Bull X2011 in *GT6* is an impressive vehicle, as shown in a YouTube video featuring the in-game car speeding along at 622 km/h (386 mph). With a 1,635-hp engine, the car was first seen in *GT5*. Its creation was a result of a collaboration between Kazunori Yamauchi and Adrian Newey, F1 engineer and chief technical officer for Red Bull Racing. The design brief focused solely on speed and ignored all the regulations faced by real-world racing.

INSIDE THE GT ACADEMY

Many gamers have entertained the idea that enough practice on the virtual track would stand them in good stead for real-life racing. It wasn't until the GT Academy's creation that we saw just how close to reality was that dream of putting down the controller and donning the driving gloves...

The legendary Silverstone racing circuit in England, a former airfield that first hosted a motor-racing event in 1948.

The GT Academy programme began in Europe in 2008 as a collaboration between Sony, Polyphony Digital (developers of the *Gran Turismo* games) and Nissan Europe. The structure remains the same as it was then: first of all, thousands of *Gran Turismo* players are assessed in online time trials.

Each country's finalists then battle it out in special race pods throughout a series of live elimination rounds, with the very best virtual drivers invited to a Race Camp at the Silverstone circuit in the UK, where they switch a PS3 for a real Nissan sports car.

In 2008, there were over 25,000 online applicants across Europe who posted lap times in the initial online event. All of them were aiming to become their country's finalist, thus securing a spot in the GT Academy with fellow winners from seven other territories.

The eventual winner of the inaugural Academy, 23-year-old Spaniard Lucas Ordóñez, outclassed thousands of adversaries not just by consistently outpacing them in *Gran Turismo*, but by transferring those skills to the track and demonstrating his supremacy inside a real racing car.

His triumph made him the **first person to transfer from virtual to real-life racing**.

"The major difference between *Gran Turismo 5* and the real thing is the G-force," Lucas tells GWR. "The game is very close to reality with parameters such as tyre wear, racing lines – even curbs are accurately recreated. The one that's difficult to recreate, even in a full-on simulator, is the G-force. You have to be really physically fit to deal with that."

GT Academy competitors at the wheel in special *Gran Turismo* Race Pods at Silverstone.

Spot the difference? *Gran Turismo 5* in-game graphics of the driver controls in an ARTA Garaiya and (top) the real-world equivalent.

Online qualification for the 2014 GT Academy took place in *Gran Turismo 6*, the latest game in the series.

Ordóñez has gone on to compete in the legendary 24 Hours of Le Mans three times, finishing second in class in 2011 for Signatech Nissan. He came third in class at the Dubai 24 Hour in 2012, and competed for Nissan GT Academy Team RJN in the Pro-Am class of the FIA GT Series in 2013. Not bad for a gamer who was getting his racing thrills exclusively from videogames just six years ago.

Since it began, the GT Academy has only grown in popularity. In 2008, it began with 25,000 applicants and by 2014 had recorded a total of 4 million entrants, making it the **most successful virtual-to-reality competition**.

From the PS3 to F1? The Red Bull X2011 and Sebastian Vettel from *Gran Turismo 5*. The GT Academy has not produced an F1 driver – yet.

More than 120 million people have tuned in to watch the latter stages of the competition on TV, and the programme has expanded beyond Europe to the USA and Russia. But perhaps even more impressive than the growing scale of the competition are the achievements of its alumni – most

notably the 2011 victor and **youngest GT Academy winner**, Jann Mardenborough.

Jann was 19 when he won the Academy. Now aged 22, the Briton competed in GP3 in 2014 – just two categories below Formula One – and is taking part in an intensive development programme with Red Bull, after just two years of racing. The toughest aspect of making the jump to real life, he tells us, is "where to look! In the game you're staring at a flat screen, so it's pretty

easy to take in all the information. The racing line, the braking zones and the apexes are all presented very accurately. In the game your eyes barely move. The instructors at Silverstone taught me where to look on a racetrack, looking as far ahead as possible. If I'm on a straight, I'll be focusing on the next corner and where I want to apex, so I position my eyes accordingly. It's the same for braking and accelerating – I'm immediately focusing on the next challenge."

There's no denying the natural talents of the individuals who make their way through the ranks of the GT Academy to a real-life racing circuit, but the programme also demonstrates that all your practice in *Gran Turismo* might very well be making you a better racing driver. And there's always the next GT Academy to put that theory to the test, of course...

Jann Mardenborough, the **youngest GT Academy winner**, now competes in GP3 in the UK and his aim is to be an F1 driver. He raced at the Goodwood Festival of Speed in 2014.

Britain's Jann Mardenborough gets in some karting practice before one of his first pro races – the Dubai 24 Hour in 2011.

"The new generation of gaming steering wheels give you really good feedback through the wheel, but they can't replicate what you feel through your other senses as you go through Eau Rouge [at Belgium's Circuit de Spa-Francorchamps] or a similarly demanding corner." – Lucas Ordóñez

✳ 43 WORLD OF TANKS

Summary: Taking eSports by storm with its military commanders and battle tanks, this free2play has won praise for its fair approach to in-game fees.

Publisher:
Wargaming.net
Developer:
Wargaming.net
Debut: 2010

▶▶ MOST DAMAGE CAUSED IN *WORLD OF WARPLANES*

World of Warplanes was in development as its tank-based sibling was being released. *WoW* took flight in 2013, with *World of Warships* due in 2014. As of 1 July 2014, *WoW* pilot "Kluszkov" had doled out the most damage to enemy aircraft, with 7,714,653 points.

FIRST TANK WARFARE MMO VIDEOGAME

There is a landscape that is perpetually at war, where the only vehicles in sight are tanks – lots of tanks, of all shapes and sizes. This is the – literally – earth-shaking *World of Tanks*, which became the first MMO to focus solely on caterpillar-tracked combat when it rolled out in Russia on 12 August 2010 and Europe and the USA in 2011.

FOR THE WIN

PLAY LIKE A PRO

Watch in-game replays of the best players before asking to team up. Your win rate will increase, you'll learn the best tactics, and you'll find helpful advice from seasoned players.

MOST PLAYERS ON ONE MMO SERVER SIMULTANEOUSLY

Located in Moscow, Russia, the RU2 server for *World of Tanks* played host to a record-breaking 190,541 battle commanders on 21 January 2013. A year later, the Russian cluster of servers (of which RU2 is one part) collectively entertained 1.1 million players concurrently according to the game's developer.

DMITRY "LEBWA" PALASCHENKO

Natus Vincere (Na'Vi)
World of Tanks team

Na'Vi won Wargaming.net's *World of Tanks* League Grand Finals in April 2014. We asked Dmitry what it's like being part of the team that collectively won $110,000 (£64,000).

What attracted you to *World of Tanks*?
We have fun with our friends while playing, and we find satisfaction by participating in tournaments. Being engaged year-round, we boost our revenue as professional gamers. Money is a powerful incentive, but eSports is also a basis for social interaction. *World of Tanks* is pushing the pro component forward.

What is it like to compete in Wargaming.net's tournaments?
Each game and tournament is a priceless lesson for us, and full of memorable moments. The Grand Finals competition was probably the most emotional one. We are thankful for the opportunity to play at this tournament and thrilled to hold the title of world champions.

What advice would you give for those hoping to play at a competitive level?
Organize your day and devote enough time to playing, but know your limit. Train with your team-mates and alone; that way, you'll be prepared for a variety of situations you may encounter in combat. It's also very important not to overwhelm yourself with training materials and guides. Give yourself time to relax and believe in your team. Together, you can pull up trees.

75,000,000
registered accounts on *World of Tanks*, according to Wargaming.net as of January 2014.

WORLD OF ESPORTS

Wargaming.net invested $2.5 m (£1.4 m) in its first eSports *World of Tanks* league in 2013. More than 200,000 gamers played in tournaments, watched by millions of fans online. *WoT* has been predicted to make $506 m (£305 m) in revenue during 2014.

MOST DAMAGE CAUSED IN *WORLD OF TANKS*

"SamJax" held the top spot on the *WoT* leaderboards as of 22 July 2014, with a total of 118,623,520 points. The **greatest win/loss ratio in *World of Tanks*** was set by "theqx", who held a 93.84% ratio on the game's Russian servers as of 25 April 2014, according to data from Wargaming.net. The US region followed with "BOBK_33RU" on 89.90%.

MOST BATTLES FOUGHT IN WORLD OF TANKS

"SIMURQ" has played *WoT* a staggering 136,750 times, beating European region gamer "EvilJoe" (124,308 battles) and the US server champ "Definder" (105,112 battles).

TANKS FOR THE MEMORIES

Wargaming.net's report for 2013 listed 780 million tank commanders destroying 22 billion vehicles in a total of 976 million battles.

MOST BATTLES FOUGHT IN WORLD OF TANKS: XBOX 360 EDITION

Xbox owners got their own version of the PC favourite in early 2014. And gamers wasted no time in getting stuck in with their base-capturing and tank-destroying antics. By July of the same year, "REVERENDMAX" had fought 22,343 battles to rise to the top of the leaderboards, using medium tanks for 35% of those fights.

FRAG MOVIE — Хорошая Арта - Мертвая Арта
Frag Movie. Хорошая Арта - Мер...

СТРИМ — с общего теста 0.9.2
Стрим с общего теста патча 0.9...

ФАНОВЫЙ СТРИМ — СО ЗРИТЕЛЯМИ!
Фановый Неадекватный Стрим...

КОРИЧНЕВЫЙ АД — СТРИМ-ШОУ
Беспощадное стрим-шоу "Корич...

НАГИБАТОРСКИЕ ПОЗИЦИИ 6
Нагибаторские Позиции на карт...

НЕ ГОВНО! — ОБЗОР T7 COMBAT CAR
НЕ ГОВНО! (Обзор T7 Combat Car)

MOST POPULAR WORLD OF TANKS CHANNEL

The *"World of Tanks*: Jove [Virtus.Pro] fan channel on YouTube had 1,456,152 subscribers as of 22 July 2014. It is run by a representative of the Russian eSports group Virtus. Pro, who took second place to Na'Vi in the 2014 League Grand Finals and scooped almost $100,000 (£58,000) as a prize. Team manager Sergey Pisotsky revealed, "We train about 20 hours in a week and we do not use mods at all."

> "In *World of Tanks* you only live once, so you have to always be aware of your surroundings. It's a thinking game where strategy and skills determine success."
>
> **MICHAEL ZHIVETS**
> PRODUCER, *WORLD OF TANKS*

▶▶MOST AIRCRAFT DESTROYED IN WORLD OF WARPLANES

"Suzukizuki" has taken out 27,276 planes in the course of playing 16,058 games – winning 67.23% of fights.

Staying with the air ace Wargaming.net release, the **greatest win/loss ratio in World of Warplanes**, according to the developer, was set by US pilot "CrayolaCrayon", with 90.81% as of 25 April 2014. In second place lies "Dark IIIuSH4k4", with 87.16% on the Russian servers.

The **most battles fought in World of Warplanes**, meanwhile, are the 18,821 aerial skirmishes that "Maverick9333" engaged in, flying the most nimble fighters and winning 47.77% of battles.

MOST SUCCESSFUL FREE2PLAY MMO

Free2play games rely on in-game purchases (also known as microtransactions) to replace income generated by games funded by subscription. *World of Tanks* has the highest average revenue per user for a free2play, earning $4.51 (£2.64) per player, according to a March 2014 report by SuperData. Overall, the **most revenue generated by a free2play MMO** is $957 million (£560 million) for SmileGate's 2007 game *CrossFire*. It has a bigger user base (although per head they spend less than *WoT* gamers) and so earns more.

RED DEAD REDEMPTION

Summary: This epic open-world action-adventure Western was a massive hit for Rockstar and is widely considered one of the seminal games of the seventh generation.

Publisher: Rockstar
Developer: Rockstar
Debut: 2010

MOST CRITICALLY ACCLAIMED WESTERN ACTION-ADVENTURE

As of 14 July 2014, the PS3 version of *Red Dead Redemption* is the Western-themed RPG with the highest critical rating on GameRankings, with a score of 94.66%. "Rockstar have produced nothing less than the finest recreation of the Wild West on a console," said the *Daily Telegraph* newspaper.

BIGGEST POKER CHEAT IN *RED DEAD REDEMPTION*

Cheating at poker in *Red Dead Redemption* is par for the course. Donning the Elegant Suit allows John Marston to hide an

FOR THE WIN

COLLECT THOSE COINS

There are advantages to being a good guy. If you max out your reputation as a paragon of the Old West, a nun will approach you with a gift of a holy cross. Wear this item and you'll be blessed in combat, making most enemy bullets miss you.

FASTEST COMPLETION OF *RED DEAD REDEMPTION*

It took many decades for the Western Frontier to be tamed in real life, but dedicated speed-runner "Steve50013" managed it somewhat quicker in a record-breaking *Red Dead Redemption* play-through on 21 February 2013. He galloped through the entire game in just 5 hr 57 min 27 sec, skipping cutscenes but otherwise completing the story in one sitting. He certainly earned a glass of soda at the saloon.

extra card and therefore dupe opponents. The biggest cheat of them all is "LordSunQuan", who, according to Rockstar's Social Club, has been caught cheating a total of 64 times. The **most successful poker player in *Red Dead Redemption***, meanwhile, is Australian gamer "OZREG", who has played 64,302 hands and won 27,745 of them, netting a cool $599,252 (£350,000) in the process. However, "OZREG" managed to lose $670,290 (£391,400) along the way, rather confirming the old saying that gambling is only a mug's game...

MO COWBOY

Prior to the game's launch, Rockstar organized a moustache contest with the Movember charity, which raises awareness of men's health issues. Canadian Charles Leece had his moustache selected by Rockstar and his likeness immortalized in *Red Dead Redemption*.

BEST-SELLING WESTERN-THEMED GAME

With its worldwide sales of 11.98 million, *Red Dead Redemption* is comfortably the best-selling videogame set in the American Wild West. Cowboy John Marston and his loyal steeds took the seventh generation by storm, and although standalone zombie DLC *Undead Nightmare* proved popular, *RDR* fans are longing for a formal sequel. *RDR* is itself a belated sequel to 2004's *Red Dead Revolver*.

▶▶FIRST 3D OPEN-WORLD WESTERN VIDEOGAME

Before *Red Dead Redemption* there was *Gun*, released by Activision in 2005 for the Xbox, PlayStation 2 and Nintendo GameCube, and the first Western-themed videogame to offer a free-roaming 3D Wild West environment to explore. It was later released for the Xbox 360 and PlayStation Portable. Just like *RDR*, *Gun* allowed players to hunt wild animals, play poker and earn their reputation as either a lawless bandit or an honourable sharpshooter. The game was developed by Neversoft, the studio behind the *Tony Hawk* and *Guitar Hero* titles, and starred Thomas Jane (star of *The Punisher*) as lead character Colton "Cole" White.

Big Blue River crossing
May 15, 1848
Press SPACE BAR to continue

▶▶LONGEST-RUNNING VIDEOGAME

First developed on an HP 2100 minicomputer in 1971 by three teachers to help children understand frontier life, the educational Western adventure *The Oregon Trail* has been remade and released for multiple platforms to the present day.

The **longest-running Western series** is *Lucky Luke*, with 10 releases across 28 years. The titular star of the series is a quick-shooting sheriff, star of his own hugely successful Belgian comic strip, too.

AAARRGGHHHH!

In *Red Dead Redemption*, listen out for a particularly memorable scream during gunfights. It's the famous Wilhelm scream, the **most common sound effect in film**. The screech was first recorded in 1951 Western *Distant Drums*, although the actor remains unknown. It was later named after Private Wilhelm, a character killed in 1953 film *The Charge at Feather River*. The scream was added to the Warner Bros. studio sound library and has appeared in some 225 movies since. It's often used as an in-joke by directors, and has popped up everywhere from *Star Wars* to *Indiana Jones* and *The Lord of the Rings*.

FOR THE WIN

SECRET PHRASES

Go to the **Options** menu in *RDR* and you'll be able to enter secret phrases to activate cheats. But using cheats means you won't be able to save your game or earn Achievements or Trophies unless you reboot. Here are some of the best phrases and what they offer:
• **I WISH I WORKED FOR UNCLE SAM** – no bounty or wanted level
• **WE NEED GUNS JOHN!** – unlocks all weapons
• **HE GIVES STRENGTH TO THE WEAK** – invincibility
• **I'M DRUNK AS A SKUNK AND TWICE AS SMELLY** – gets John drunk

▶▶FIRST LIVE-ACTION GUN GAME

The first live-action game (though not videogame) to utilize light-gun play was Nintendo's *Wild Gunman* in 1974, which used still photographs instead of moving graphics. Players shot at images of cowboys projected on to a digital display. The **first live-action light-gun arcade game**, meanwhile, was *Mad Dog McCree*, released in 1990.

Summary: The awesome spectacle of combat sets fighting games apart. *Mortal Kombat* may not have been the first, nor is it the overall biggest seller, but this classic franchise is *your* pick of the fighters.

Publisher: Midway/ Time Warner
Developer: Midway/ NetherRealm
Debut: 1992

BEST-SELLING XBOX 360 FIGHTING GAME

Mortal Kombat has sold 1.85 million copies, according to vgchartz.com. *UFC 2009 Undisputed* has recorded sales of 2.03 million, but is classed as a sports game.

FIRST GAME TO FEATURE "JUGGLING"

"Juggling" in fighting games is a little more violent than keeping a few balls in the air. It's all about knocking a helpless opponent skyward and keeping them airborne with follow-up hits and was first seen in the debut *Mortal Kombat*.

FASTEST SINGLE-SEGMENT, "VERY HARD" COMPLETION OF *ULTIMATE MORTAL KOMBAT 3*

Nick Mathews (USA) completed the arcade version of *Ultimate Mortal Kombat 3* in an impressive 8 min 28 sec at the Galloping Ghost Arcade in Brookfield, Illinois, USA, on 27 April 2013. His character of choice in the 1995 classic was cyber-ninja Smoke and he didn't lose a single round – not even when faced with the ultimate boss challenge in the shape of Shao Kahn!

FOR THE WIN

SUPER METER

In the 2011 reboot of *Mortal Kombat*, it's tempting to burn your whole Super Meter on the bone-shattering and spectacular X-rays. Wiser fighters may find that it helps to win in the long run by conserving the bar for combo-interrupting Breakers and Enhanced Special Moves.

21,014,446 views for the first episode of YouTube live-action series *Mortal Kombat: Legacy* (USA, 2011).

MOST "LIKED" FACEBOOK FIGHTING GAME PAGE

Mortal Kombat's home on Facebook had 5,279,587 "likes" as of 3 July 2014. The page is updated with news, polls and artwork like this teaser of 2015-slated *Mortal Kombat X* (main picture). Behind it in "likes" sit *Tekken* with 3,224,705 and *Street Fighter* with 1,901,047.

WHO YA GONNA CALL?

John Tobias, the co-creator of *Mortal Kombat*, was an artist for *The Real Ghostbusters* comic-book series, a spin-off of the legendary movies. He was still just 19 when he was hired by Midway's owner to work on the arcade game *Smash T.V.*

LONGEST ONLINE WINNING STREAK IN *MORTAL KOMBAT*

Gamer "WaTaDaaah GER" had an unbroken streak of 384 online wins of the 2011 game by 23 June 2014. The Xbox 360 record also tops the PS3 chart. Were these wins followed by some gruesome Fatalities? We'd be surprised if "WaTaDaaah GER" didn't pull off a coup de grâce or two. Above, Cyrax launches an energy net at Sektor.

HIGHEST-GROSSING FIGHTING GAME MOVIE ADAPTATION

Having pulled in a staggering $122,195,920 (£71.7 million) worldwide since its release in 1995, as of July 2014, the videogame-inspired *Mortal Kombat* is without doubt king of the fighter game movies. Its arch-rival *Street Fighter*'s 1994 adaptation is just behind with $99,423,521 (£58.4 million).

▶▶LONGEST-RUNNING FIGHTING GAME SERIES

While losing out at the movies, *Street Fighter* has been providing the strongest competition to *Mortal Kombat* ever since its release in 1987, winning generations of fans. Second entry *Street Fighter II: The World Warrior* remains one of the most influential fighting games, introducing combos and featuring a huge roster of playable characters. In 2014 the series celebrated 27 years with *Ultra Street Fighter IV*, first released in Japanese arcades in April.

▶▶MOST POPULAR STREET FIGHTER CHARACTER

Ryu arrived as a lead with the first *Street Fighter* arcade game and he remains a favourite for fans. In a poll conducted by Capcom in February 2013, Ryu received 18,740 votes and a 5.9% share across more than 60 characters. His status was confirmed by a dorkly.com poll in 2014 when Ryu hit No.1 again with 338,517 votes out of the 423,147 cast.

MOST POPULAR *MORTAL KOMBAT* CHARACTER

Dorkly.com asked its readers to name their favourite fighter in the *Mortal Kombat* series. A total of 919,134 votes were cast over the course of the December 2013 poll, with Scorpion accounting for 762,881 of them. Not bad for one of the least stealthy looking ninjas in gaming. Second and third were Sub Zero II and Raiden, with Taven least popular, the *Mortal Kombat: Armageddon* fighter coming 66th.

▶▶LONGEST MARATHON ON A FIGHTING GAME

Anthony "AJ" Lysiak (USA) played *Street Fighter X Tekken* for 48 hr exactly at Game Emporium in Garrettsville, Ohio, USA, on 4–6 May 2012, also the **longest marathon on *Street Fighter X Tekken***.

▶▶BEST-SELLING 3D FIGHTING GAME

Tekken 3 has sold 7.16 million units worldwide. The 1998 game was the last appearance of the series on the PlayStation and was highly rated by critics.

▶▶BEST-SELLING FIGHTING GAME SERIES (INCLUDING CROSSOVERS)

Street Fighter has sold 38.54 million units including crossovers such as *Marvel vs. Capcom* alongside the main series. This excludes the non-fighting likes of *SNK vs. Capcom: Card Fighters DS*. The **best-selling fighting game series (excluding crossovers)** is *Tekken*, with 36.30 million units.

VIDEOGAME VOGUE

"Clothes make the man. Naked people have little or no influence on society." So said American author Mark Twain, and although he died long before videogames were invented, his adage certainly applies to the heroes and villains of modern consoles.

Building a gaming character isn't all about weapons, vehicles and witty banter. What they wear speaks volumes about who they are. We take a look at some of the classic clothes of gaming. Strike a pose!

Salvador
Borderlands 2's "pint-sized" badass plumps for a punky look, complete with a bulging T-shirt that screams "rage".

Dante
Edging ahead of his twin brother Vergil, the *Devil May Cry* mercenary brings a gothic style to proceedings, with striking details on his boots, belt and gloves.

Lara Croft
The adventurous archaeologist's brown shorts, tight top and all-action boots are nothing short of iconic.

Johnny Gat
So cool he could do with an hour in the sauna, the *Saints Row* star shows that looking slick can be achieved with just a fitted dark suit, shades and a bright shirt.

Lightning
The protagonist of *Final Fantasy XIII* loves her buckles. The "thigh satchel" is a particularly brave fashion choice.

Princess Zelda
Not likely to trouble any of the major fashion weeks, Zelda opts for a traditional – if rather bright – flowing, elegant dress befitting a royal.

Prince of Persia
Simple, rugged and effortlessly chic, the Prince successfully fuses dandy and warrior styles.

Arno Dorian
In a series dripping with fashion triumphs (*Assassin's Creed*), it's hard to pick a winner, but Arno and his cape-coat rule.

Raiden
The *Mortal Kombat* legend isn't just a dab hand at fighting and teleportation – he knows how to turn heads with his sartorial style, too. The room-to-manoeuvre jumpsuit is trendy, but it's also handy for stretching those legs in combat.

Zack
The *Dead or Alive* DJ is famous for his vast array of wild costumes. In *DoA 5*, pictured here, his wardrobe includes full disco inferno outfit, complete with platform shoes and white gloves.

COSTUME PLAY

The significance of gaming characters' clothes, costumes and accessories is aptly demonstrated by the popularity of cosplay. No gaming convention is complete without an army of enthusiasts dressed up as Link, Lightning or Lara (among many others). The very best cosplayers are notable for meticulous attention to clothing detail and the commitment with which they make their replica costumes.

King of All Cosmos
A star of the *Katamari Damacy* series, the eccentric King raises the costume bar by several notches with this extravagant number that wouldn't have looked out of place in the court of Queen Elizabeth I.

GUESS THE HEADGEAR

Which gaming heroes do these belong to? Turn to page 211 for the answers.

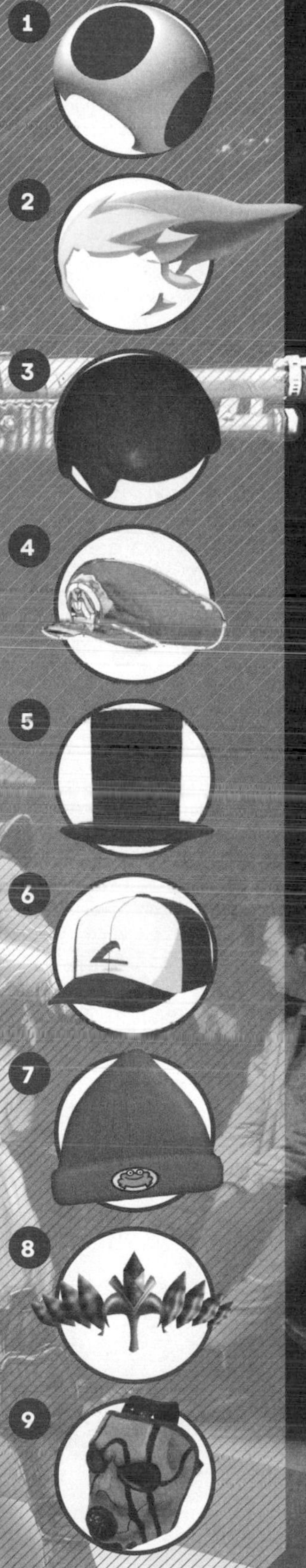

1
2
3
4
5
6
7
8
9

MOST PROLIFIC VIDEOGAME SERIES BASED ON A TOY

Since LEGO® first entered the gaming scene with *LEGO Island* in 1997, the series had produced 59 games as of 10 June 2014. This includes titles produced for LEGO's *Bionicle* franchise, numerous entertainment licences, mobile games and sporty spin-offs. Developer TT Games has released 20 titles under the LEGO brand, making them the **most prolific developer of toy videogames** (see p.30).

Summary: The brick-building sensation was launched in 1932. It made its gaming debut 65 years later, quickly becoming a mainstay of multiple genres from MMOs to action-adventure.

Publisher: Various
Developer: Various
Debut: 1997

WELL PLAYED!

The name "LEGO" derives from the Danish "leg godt", which means "play well".

FIRST VIDEOGAME-INSPIRED LEGO SET

On 1 June 2012, *Minecraft Micro World: The Forest* became the first videogame-inspired LEGO set to be commercially released when it was made available via the brick-maker's CUUSOO website. CUUSOO is a site created by the LEGO Group in 2008 to give aspiring LEGO builders a forum to showcase ideas for potential LEGO sets. Those that receive enough public votes, and pass LEGO's review, are released for sale with the original creator earning a portion of the royalties.

MOST CRITICALLY ACCLAIMED GAME BASED ON A TOY

LEGO Star Wars II: The Original Trilogy for PC, based on the *Star Wars* films *A New Hope*, *The Empire Strikes Back* and *Return of the Jedi*, is the highest-rated game based on a toy line. The sci-fi brick venture holds an 86.83% review score on GameRankings.com across a total of 21 reviews. *Skylanders Swap Force* on the Xbox 360 ranks second with a score of 84.68%. For more on *Skylanders*, see page 144.

BEST-SELLING SUPERHERO GAME

LEGO Batman: The Videogame is the best-selling videogame based on a superhero, batting off the opposition with a cool 12.63 million copies sold as of 10 June 2014. By comparison, *Batman: Arkham City* has sold 9.94 million copies. *LEGO Batman*'s success also makes it the **best-selling game based on a DC Comics character**. The sequel, *LEGO Batman 2: DC Super Heroes*, stars 28 villains from all corners of the DC Comics universe – the **most villains in a Batman videogame**. These baddies can be unlocked in the character roster once found or fought by the player. While *LEGO Batman 2* offered a gargantuan Gotham City hub environment, it was *LEGO City Undercover: The Chase Begins* that became the **first open-world videogame on the 3DS**. It was released exclusively on Nintendo's handheld console on 21 April 2013, and is set two years before the events of *LEGO City Undercover*.

THE FAMILY WAY

LEGO likes to keep it in the family – it is now owned by the grandson of its founder.

BEST-SELLING LEGO VIDEOGAME

LEGO Star Wars: The Complete Saga is the best-selling title of the LEGO franchise, with sales of 14.06 million. It is also the **biggest-selling *Star Wars* game** overall (*Angry Birds Star Wars* has been downloaded over 50 million times, but it's a free app). On top of all that, the Wii version of *The Complete Saga* boasts the **first virtual lightsabre in a videogame**, courtesy of the Wiimote. The force is definitely with LEGO.

MOST PLAYABLE CHARACTERS IN AN ACTION-ADVENTURE VIDEOGAME

LEGO Marvel Super Heroes packs in 180 heroes, villains and sidekicks from the Marvel universe, and allows players to create over a billion unique characters through its hero customizer system. Pictured here are Wolverine, Iron Man, Captain America and Hulk.

5,164
virtual LEGO pieces used to create Sandman in *LEGO Marvel Super Heroes*.

SUPER STUDS

Most LEGO games contain a bonus level that challenges players to earn 1,000,000 studs by investigating objects and smashing and building everything in sight.

RAREST TROPHY FOR *LEGO HARRY POTTER: YEARS 5–7*

LEGO games include meta-game achievements that encourage players to interact with characters (aka "minifigures") in fun and creative ways. In *LEGO Harry Potter: Years 5–7* for the PS3, the "What if?" trophy requires players to defeat every version of Harry Potter with Lord Voldemort. As of 25 April 2014, only 7.1% of players had completed this dark task.

Even trickier is the **rarest PC achievement for *LEGO: Lord of the Rings***, which is called "Delved too greedily". This requires players to collect more than 10,000,000,000 studs, and as of 28 April 2014, only 2% of gamers had unlocked the rich achievement on Steam.

FOR THE WIN

RED-BRICK CODES

Secret codes can be tapped into the "Enter Code" section (under "Extras"). For *Lego Batman 2: DC Super Heroes*, some of the most helpful include 2X Stud Multiplier (74EZUT), Extra Hearts (4LGJ7T), Gold Brick Finder (MBXW7V) and Regenerate Hearts (ZXEX5D). Get tapping.

Summary: Naughty Dog invented this series of fruity platformers before handing over control to various others. The most recent release was in 2008; rumours abound of a new title for the PS4.

Publisher: Various
Developer: Various
Debut: 1996

BEST-SELLING PLATFORMER SERIES ON THE PLAYSTATION

Crash Bandicoot was introduced to the world as Sony attempted to create a mascot for its fledgling PlayStation in a similar style to Sega's Sonic and Nintendo's Mario. *Crash* found resounding success on the original PlayStation, selling 21.53 million copies of the first three *Crash Bandicoot* games before the series switched hands and went multi-platform.

BEST-SELLING PLAYSTATION KART RACING GAME

Not content with having a hit PS-exclusive platformer series on its hands, in 1999 Sony launched *Crash Team Racing*, a *Bandicoot* spin-off. It did the business, and with total sales of 4.79 million, it's top dog when it comes to karting games on the original PlayStation.

▶▶MOST CRITICALLY ACCLAIMED 3D PLATFORMER FOR PS2

PS2 classic, and third game in the series, *Ratchet & Clank: Up Your Arsenal*, has a GameRankings rating of 91.54%, ranking it in the top 25 PS2 games overall.

FIRST WESTERN VIDEOGAME TO SELL 1 MILLION UNITS IN JAPAN

Naughty Dog's final *Crash* game, *Crash Bandicoot 3: Warped*, sold 1.42 million copies. It was the first western release to cross the 1-million mark in Japan. Crash's third outing is joined by *Crash Bandicoot 2* as the only two western titles in Japan's top 20 PS chart.

MOST GAMES OF ONE SERIES IN THE PS GLOBAL TOP 10

In the all-time PlayStation top 10 sales chart the *Gran Turismo* and *Final Fantasy* franchises each have two entries. The *Crash Bandicoot* series rules, however, with three appearances. *Crash Bandicoot 2: Cortex Strikes Back* claims the No.5 spot with 7.58 million copies sold, *Crash Bandicoot 3: Warped* is at No.7 with 7.13 million copies sold, and the game that started it all – *Crash Bandicoot* – is at No.8 with a respectable 6.82 million.

MARIO WHO?

So the portly plumber may hold the record for **best-selling kart racing game** with *Mario Kart Wii*'s astonishing 34.53 million sales, but it's all about Crash when it comes to non-Nintendo racing. PlayStation's original kart-off is king with over 4 million copies of *Crash Team Racing* sold worldwide since launch (see record above). The *Bandicoot* spin-off sees Crash, Coco and company screeching around tracks, breaking crates of Wumpa fruit and desperately avoiding explosive TNT as they quest for karting glory in the shape of shiny trophies.

▶▶FIRST GAME WITH CRACK PROTECTION

Crash and Spyro have long been linked, starting with the purple fire-breather's role in a hidden demo within *Crash Bandicoot 3: Warped*. The third entry in the *Spyro* series, *Year of the Dragon*, was the first game to feature an anti-piracy protection system that thwarts hackers from cracking the game.

FASTEST 100% COMPLETION OF *CRASH BANDICOOT*

The speed-run record for a 100% completion of the first *Crash Bandicoot* was set by Danish gamer "WHiPCPL" in just 1 hr 15 min 33 sec on 11 April 2014. As for a non-100% speed-run, the **fastest completion of *Crash Bandicoot*** was accomplished by gamer Trent "CaneofPacci" Lowry in a distinctly speedy 45 min 17 sec, with every jump and spin available to watch on his Twitch channel. Trent says he is aiming for the 100% speed-run record next.

WHAT CHEEK

Due to the fact that 3D platforming – revolutionary for 1996 – means you see little more than the back of Crash for the majority of the game, the original *Crash Bandicoot* was jokingly nicknamed the "Sonic's ass game" by its creators Jason Rubin and Andy Gavin during development.

▶▶MOST GUNS IN A PLATFORM SERIES

Ever since run-and-gun classics such as Konami's *Contra* and the *Metal Slug* series, platformers and shooters have comfortably shared the same game space. The *Ratchet & Clank* franchise is the most trigger-happy platformer, with a mighty 122 standard weapons utilized throughout. But this total rises to at least 420 when all upgrades and variants are taken into account.

FOR THE WIN

THE FATES OF ROO AND BRIO

Want to find out what happened to Crash's foes after he beat them in the original game? It's no mean feat, but earn every gem and key then head to the Great Hall for a full lowdown on the future careers of Ripper Roo and Nitrus Brio.

▶▶BEST-SELLING PLATFORMER FOR PS4

Mark Cerny, executive producer and designer of multiple *Bandicoot*, *Ratchet & Clank* and *Spyro the Dragon* games, has a legendary Sony platforming CV. Taking his expertise into the eighth generation, Cerny directed PS4 launch title *Knack*. A shape-shifting creature who can change his size and body matter by absorbing relics, Knack can transform from an unassuming little thing into an enormous wrecking machine. As of 26 June 2014, *Knack* was top of the PS4 platformers, with sales of more than 1.08 million.

▶▶MOST PROLIFIC 3D PLATFORM SERIES

PlayStation platforming and *Crash Bandicoot* may go together like cheese and macaroni, but there's another long-running PS-exclusive platform series that has shifted more than 23 million units since its debut in 2002. *Ratchet & Clank* has turned out 14 games, with a 15th for the PS4 announced at E3 2014. Ratchet the Lombax mechanic and Clank the tiny robot also hold the record for the **first episodic 3D platform series**, which began with *Quest for Booty*, a PSN spin-off from 2007 retail release *Ratchet & Clank Future: Tools of Destruction*.

Summary: Having become one of PlayStation's most recognizable franchises, *LBP* retained its quirky, home-made charm along the way. Players can still use their old levels in the third edition.

Publisher: Sony
Developer: Media Molecule/Various
Debut: 2008

MOST "HEARTED" *LITTLEBIGPLANET* LEVEL

The best-rated community level is "Little Dead Space", made by Darknessbear. Starring *Dead Space*'s Isaac Clarke, the level involves players investigating

MOST PLAYER-CREATED LEVELS IN A VIDEOGAME

A staggering 8,786,985 *LittleBigPlanet* levels had been made by fans as of 9 June 2014. Growing at a rate of 5,000 a day – that's 200 every hour – the community's expansion shows no sign of slowing down. *LittleBigPlanet PS Vita* alone has more than 166,487 fan-made creations ready to sample. The series passed the 8-million milestone on 1 July 2013.

Sony game characters (Joel and Ellie are from *The Last of Us* and Delsin Rowe is from *InFAMOUS: Second Son*), and are also drawn from sources as diverse as DC superheroes and the Muppets, plus *BioShock* and *Mass Effect*.

LONGEST MARATHON PLAYING *LITTLEBIGPLANET 2*

David Dino, Lauren Guiliano and Sean Crowley (all USA) played *LittleBigPlanet 2* for 50 hr 1 min. The marathon took place in the Sony Style PlayStation Lounge in New York City, USA, from 17 to 19 January 2011 and was organized by publishers Sony to celebrate the launch of the second game in the series.

the dark interior of the USG *Ishimura* from EA's terrifying survival horror. "Hearted" by 290,212 players as of 24 June 2014, "Little Dead Space" has been played more than 2 million times since it was first published in November 2008.

▶▶MOST BAFTAS FOR A HANDHELD GAME

Media Molecule has more than one crafty classic to its name, as the PS Vita exclusive *Tearaway* showed. A hit with critics, it was nominated for eight awards at the 2014 BAFTAs and won three – for Artistic Achievement, Mobile & Handheld and Family.

MOST DOWNLOADABLE COSTUMES FOR A PLATFORM GAME

With more than 340 costume downloads for *LittleBigPlanet*, there's no shortage of ways to personalize Sackboy or Sackgirl. The costumes come from

SACKING YELLOWHEAD

A character called YellowHead was originally destined to be the lead role in *LittleBigPlanet*. Eventually, he was redesigned to become the Sackboy we know and love, but you can still earn a YellowHead costume in *LittleBigPlanet* and he even appears in *Tearaway*. Players can scoop a trophy by having their picture taken with him.

BEST-SELLING PLATFORM SERIES ON PS3

With 5.45 million copies sold of *LittleBigPlanet* and 3.13 million of *LittleBigPlanet 2*, Sackboy has faced off competition from the *Ratchet & Clank* and *Sonic the Hedgehog* franchises. Not to be left out, *LittleBigPlanet PS Vita* is the **best-selling PS Vita platform game**, with 0.72 million copies sold.

> "The death animations... they were really fun to do."
>
> **FRANCIS PANG, MEDIA MOLECULE** ARTIST ON CREATING SACKBOY

▶▶ MOST IN-HOUSE LEVELS IN A 2D PLATFORMER

Super Meat Boy has a total of 307 different stages and, while Media Molecule's *LittleBigPlanet* may have a few million more user-created levels (see left), those included in *Super Meat Boy* were all created by independent developer Team Meat.

KART BOOST

United Front Games, developer of the customizable *ModNation Racers*, partnered with Media Molecule for *LittleBigPlanet Karting*. If you want to get a head start on your opponents, hold down **drift** and **accelerate** together until GO! appears, then take your finger off **drift** and you'll boost ahead.

196,318 user-created tracks have been uploaded in *LittleBigPlanet Karting*.

FASTEST COMPLETION OF RAYMAN LEGENDS

"FearfulFerret" (USA) completed an any-percentage run in 1 hr 26 min 10 sec on 27 January 2014. "The game is very difficult to do well," he notes of the popular platformer, "because the end is so brutal." On 7 December 2013, "EnsgMaster" recorded the **fastest completion of *Rayman Origins*** with a time of 53 min 40 sec. The secret was discovering a sequence break that skips much of the game.

ANOTHER PLANET

Announced at E3 for a November 2014 release on the PS4, *LittleBigPlanet 3* introduces new characters into Sackboy's folksy world. Alongside Toggle are, above left and right, Swoop and Oddsock – all are playable characters with unique skills to help players get through levels.

Summary: When it comes to musclebound monsters pretending to thump the stuffing out of each other, one series is the undisputed king of the ring. *WWE 2K* has been top dog for over 10 years.

Publisher: THQ/2K Sports
Developer: Yuke's
Debut: 2000

FIRST STEREOSCOPIC 3D WRESTLING GAME

THQ's *WWE All Stars*, released across multiple platforms in 2011, became the first wrestling game to benefit from stereoscopic 3D when it arrived on the 3DS. Console versions of the game included 13 WWE stars available as DLC.

BEST-SELLING COMBAT SPORTS GAME

With more than 7.32 million copies sold across six console formats as of 30 July 2014, *WWE SmackDown vs RAW 2008* is the best-selling combat sports title of all time. The PlayStation 2 version (whose name is sometimes shortened to *WWE SvR 2008* or *SvR '08*) is the top performer, shifting an impressive 2.34 million units. The PS2 also hosts the **best-selling combat sports game on a single format**, *WWF SmackDown! 2: Know Your Role*, with sales of 3.2 million.

MOST WATCHED *WWE 2K14* MATCH

The wrestling match with the most spectators in *WWE 2K14* is the YouTube video of Hulk vs Red Hulk, with 4,203,086 views as of 30 July 2014. Record holder and uploader Marcus Garlick created both superhero combatants himself, but let the AI decide upon the result of the match – and it is Red Hulk who wins with a suitably enormous bear hug.

MOST DOWNLOADED USER CREATION IN *WWE 2K14* (PS3)

The most downloaded user-created wrestler in *WWE 2K14* on the PS3 is "Curtis Axel", created by "GaMeVoLt" and downloaded 21,189 times as of 18 April 2014. Axel appeared in *WWE '12* under his previous alias of Michael McGillicutty, but was strangely omitted from *2K14's* official roster by Yuke's.

"GaMeVoLt" is a prominent figure in the creative WWE community. For this particular model, he adjusted an Xbox 360 version originally made by a collaboration of Twitter users.

FIRST WWE GAME WITH ONLINE MULTIPLAYER

WWE SmackDown! vs. Raw used the PS2's Network Adaptor to allow players to compete online

MOST PROLIFIC DEVELOPER OF COMBAT SPORTS VIDEOGAMES

With 79 commercially released combat sports titles, including the *WWE* series, *Rumble Roses* and *UFC Undisputed*, Japanese company Yuke's is the most prolific developer of games in the genre. They are most famous for their *WWE 2K* games, which were originally called *WWF SmackDown!* and then *WWE SmackDown!* before becoming just *WWE*, and, most recently, *WWE 2K*.

BEST-SELLING WRESTLING GAME SERIES

With total sales of 55.73 million across all of Yuke's WWF and WWE games, the name-changing series is top of the heap.

MOST ARENAS IN A COMBAT GAME

There are a grand total of 46 arenas in *WWE 2K14*, including the official arenas for every TV show and pay-per-view event in the WWE calendar, as well as accurate recreations of every WrestleMania. In addition to utilizing those provided by Yuke's, players are also able to generate up to 50 of their own using a variety of "create-an-arena" tools.

LONGEST-RUNNING ANNUAL COMBAT GAME SERIES

Yuke's *WWE 2K* wrestling franchise (originally titled *WWF SmackDown!*), which published its 15th game in 14 years on 29 October 2013, is the annual combat series with the longest legs. Pictured above is artwork from *WWE 2K15*, due for late 2014 release and starring, from left, Bray Wyatt, Hulk Hogan and Roman Reigns. *2K15* will be the first official *WWE* game to be released on the Xbox One and PS4.

in "One-on-One" or "Bra and Panties" matches (in which the competitors strip).

►►LARGEST ROSTER IN A COMBAT SPORTS VIDEOGAME

If you prefer your combat sports a little more rough, ready and kicky, then mixed martial arts (MMA) are probably more up your street. Yuke's are behind *UFC Undisputed 3*, a game with a mighty 162 fighters. It features 147 playable MMA fighters on disc, with a further 15 available as downloadable content.

MAGNIFICENT 7

Only seven of the 90+ on-disc current-era characters in *WWE 2K14* had never appeared in the series before: Seth Rollins, Roman Reigns, Dean Ambrose, Titus O'Neil, Darren Young, Aksana and Kaitlyn.

39,210,000
copies of *WWE SmackDown! vs Raw* games sold between 2002 and July 2014.

FIRST FEMALE WWE SUPERSTAR CHALLENGE WINNER

The annual WWE Superstar Challenge started in 2003, bringing together the top WWE wrestlers to compete against one another on the official videogame. US wrestler AJ Lee (born April Jeanette Mendez, above) defeated Mark Henry in the final match of a 16-person knockout tournament on 30 March 2012 in Miami, Florida, USA, to become the first female victor.

The winner of the **most WWE Superstar Challenge** events is Shelton Benjamin (USA), with four victories.

LONGEST ABSENCE FROM WWE GAMES

The longest time spent away from appearing in official WWF and WWE games is an epic 16 years 4 months, achieved by "Macho Man" Randy Savage (aka Randy Poffo, right). After appearing in the Game Gear release *WWF Raw* in November 1994, the Macho Man wouldn't feature in official wrestling federation games again until *WWE All Stars*, released in March 2011. Tragically, Randy died in May 2011 after suffering a massive heart attack while driving. He was 58.

SIMULATIONS

A genre of gaming that's as diverse and as wide-ranging as life itself, sims task the player with managing everything from the controls of an aircraft to the day-to-day running of a city. Here, to illustrate the variety on offer, we explore four major sims sub-categories: life, construction, business and transport.

UTOPIA

The **first simulation videogame** is recognized as being *Utopia* by Don Daglow. Released in 1981 for the Intellivision, its object was to manage an island, its people, food and natural disasters while fending off aggressors.

Prison sims *Hard Time* proves that any aspect of life can be made into a sim. This darkly funny jail sim challenges you to "juggle the physical and mental demands of prison life"!

LIFE

From dog sims to god sims, what can be more taxing than life itself? This category of simulation puts you in control of a pet, an individual human, an ecosystem or even an entire world, and lets you play god. The genre began in the 1980s with the likes of god-sim *Utopia* (1981) and "artificial life game" *Little Computer People* (1985), and has evolved and expanded to cover topics as varied as dating (*Girl's Garden, True Love, Boyfriend Maker*), pets (*Petz, Tamagotchi, Nintendogs*), biology (*Spore, Creatures*) and society (*The Sims, Animal Crossing*).

Road-building sims Laying down roads and streets is a key part of most city-building sims, but in *Road Construction Simulator* by Excalibur (see right) this is the sole aim of the game, tasking you with placing traffic cones, driving a steam roller and repairing potholes!

CONSTRUCTION

The aim of this sims sub-genre is building, whether it's a pinball machine, a roller-coaster, a city or a government. There are inevitable crossovers between the sims sub-genres, of course, but here the ultimate objective is the construction of a functioning system that must survive the myriad challenges that real life throws up. Although pre-dated by *Utopia* (see above), the daddy of such games is considered to be 1989's *SimCity*, with later titles such as *Caesar, Tropico* and *Civilization* blending the genre with real-time strategy.

NINTENDOGS

With global sales of 24.6 million, Nintendo's DS dog sim is, as of 29 August 2014, the second-best-selling game for the console overall (behind *New Super Mario Bros.*) and the **best-selling sims game** of all time.

THE SIMS

The **best-selling sims series** ever is *The Sims* (2000–present). According to vgchartz.com, the 101 titles in the franchise have sold more than 74.89 million units. The best-selling game in the series remains the 2000 original, *The Sims*, with sales of 11.23 million.

PINBALL CONSTRUCTION SET

Before there was *SimCity* there was Bill Budge's *Pinball Construction Set* – the **first "builder" videogame**. Released in 1983, *PCS* allowed players to make their own virtual pinball machine, opting where to place flippers and bumpers. Will Wright, the man behind the *SimCity* and *The Sims* games, credits *PCS* as a major influence on his work and acknowledges the title as a foundational game for the sims genre.

SIMCITY

The **first city-building game** was Maxis' *SimCity* in 1989, devised by sims legend Will Wright. It went on to secure records for the **most prolific sims series** (with more than 130 games in the franchise) and the **best-selling city-building game series**, selling over 18 million copies. The most successful title – the **best-selling *SimCity* game** – is *SimCity 2000*, shifting 4.23 million copies.

BUSINESS

It's not all fun and games: sims can plunge you into the cut and thrust of running a company, be it a lemonade stand, a farm, a theme park or an intergalactic courier company. Such "tycoon" computer games can be traced back to the 1960s, when graphics didn't need to be sophisticated (or present at all); today, business sims are as visually exciting as they are economically challenging, placing you at the centre of industries as diverse as oil and gas, railways, dinosaur parks, skate parks, fast food, coffee, Hollywood, hospitals, casinos…

FARMVILLE

At the height of its popularity in the spring of 2010, *FarmVille* – the **most popular farming sim** – was being played by 83.8 million people every month. According to Zynga, more than 400 million people have played *FarmVille* and *FarmVille 2* (see pp.140–41 for more on the runaway success of this billion-dollar game).

Babysitting sims

No business is too small for a sim: the DS' *Imagine: Babysitters*, for example, puts you in charge of feeding, nursing and dressing babies.

STREET CLEANING SIMULATOR

One for fans of quirkier sims, the **first street-cleaning sim** requires you to operate a firm that keeps the roads free from leaves and dirt. Excalibur (UK) – the **most prolific publisher of consumer simulation games** – also created garbage-truck and chemical-spillage sims.

FLIGHT SIMULATOR

The **best-selling** – and **longest-running** – **flight sim series** is *Microsoft Flight Simulator*, which has sold over 22 million copies since its first incarnation on the Apple II back in 1980. With sales of 5.12 million, the Windows 95 edition is the single **best-selling flight sim title** ever.

WING COMMANDER

The *Wing Commander* series is both the **best-selling** and **longest-running space combat simulator** of all time, selling 5 million units in total to date. Very much a combat crossover, the cinematic sci-fi series struck the right balance between flight simulation and dog fighting, and effectively established the space-combat genre. *WC* also saw variable success beyond gaming as a feature film, TV series, collectible card game and action-figure range.

TRAINZ

With a total of 16 releases across two publishers as of April 2014, the *Trainz* franchise is the **most prolific train simulator series**. Created by train and model-train enthusiasts, the series boasts 650,000 registered users.

Trucking sims

Combining vehicle and business sims is *18 Wheels of Steel* by ValuSoft, which has grown from the 2002 original to a seven-game series. The aim? To deliver cargo safely and efficiently across the country.

SHIP SIMULATOR

The **first ship sim**, *Ship Simulator 2006*, put gamers behind the wheel of various watercraft, from river taxis to the ill-fated RMS *Titanic* (pictured). The following year, developer VSTEP produced *Ship Simulator Professional* for the maritime training market – proof that sims can have real-world applications beyond just gaming.

VEHICLES

Planes, trains, automobiles and boats are the typical subjects for vehicle and transport sims, putting the gamer behind the wheel or yoke to not only control the vehicle but often to win a race or engage in combat. Again, there is much crossover with other sims and other genres of gaming, but key to vehicle sims is realism in terms of both the graphics and the gameplay; the purest flight sims, for example, task you with micromanaging every aspect of the cockpit, be it in a Sopwith Camel, a Boeing 777 or a Space Shuttle.

COUNTDOWN

40-31

FASTEST COMPLETION OF *MASS EFFECT 3* MULTIPLAYER MATCH ON "PLATINUM" DIFFICULTY

The fastest completion time for all 10 enemy waves in a *Mass Effect 3* multiplayer contest on the hardest "Platinum" difficulty, with a full team of four players, is 6 min 43 sec. This impressive time was set on 13 May 2013 by players "cricketer15", "d_nought", "dunvi" and "Payn3zz" on the Firebase Jade map. The "Platinum" setting was introduced in July 2012, and is so difficult that even Bioware's *Mass Effect* development team struggled to beat it, according to game producer Mike Gamble.

Summary: Late to the mean streets of the open-world action-adventure genre, the series made up for it by bringing swag bags of attitude, style and technical polish to the party.

Publisher: THQ/Deep Silver
Developer: Volition
Debut: 2006

SAINTS TRIBUTE

Saints Row IV is dedicated to Michael Clarke Duncan, who played Benjamin King in the first game and was set to reprise the role. Sadly, Duncan died while *SR IV* was in production, having only recorded the end credits cast singalong version of Biz Markie's "Just a Friend". In the game, the track fades out, leaving just Duncan's voice as a tribute.

77

minutes of original music in *Saints Row IV*, according to the developer's own figures (that also mischievously claimed the game's production required the consumption of 124,800 cans of drink and 1,506 pizzas).

MOST POPULAR *SAINTS ROW* USER-CREATED CHARACTER SKIN

Saints Row allows gamers to create their own characters, and thousands of budding artists share their creations with the game's community. The most popular of these – as measured by "likes" – is a rather cheeky copy of *GTA IV*'s player character Niko Bellic (above left), by gamer "navydude37", which had received the thumbs-up from 186,929 players as of 27 April 2014. The most popular character skin as measured by the number of times it has been queued for use, however, is a version of Marvel's wise-cracking mercenary Deadpool (above right), designed by "Chief08cool" and downloaded to play in the game by 28,689 gamers.

MOST EXPENSIVE VIDEOGAME PACKAGE

ONLY 1 AVAILABLE

In keeping with the game's tongue-in-cheek approach, the "Super Dangerous Wad Wad Edition" of *Saints Row IV* came in at $1 million (£580,000) and featured appropriately over-the-top goodies. The fee included a Toyota Prius and a Lamborghini Gallardo, membership of the écurie25 supercar club, a day of spy training, a "hostage rescue" experience, a trip into space with Virgin Galactic, plastic surgery, a personal shopper and spending spree, seven nights for two at the Jefferson Hotel in Washington, USA, a stay in the Royal Suite at the Burj Al Arab in Dubai, UAE, a replica Dubstep Gun (above right) – oh, and a copy of *Saints Row IV*.

LONGEST STUNT JUMP IN *SAINTS ROW: THE THIRD*

Stunt jumps are available in the second and third *Saints Row* games. Digital daredevil Jacob Burcar (USA) recorded a leap of 5,028 m (16,496 ft) from one of *SR III*'s ramps in February 2012. How did he do it? He drove a two-seater Emu car on to the helipad at the top of the Saints casino skyscraper (both car and casino fully upgraded) and covered the back of the vehicle with sticky Satchel Charges. With a friend in the passenger seat, Burcar then drove at full turbo off the ramp and the roof, and detonated the charges for an additional boost. Both players threw more Charges out of the windows, the explosives detonating beneath and behind the car and keeping it airborne. In this way, the acrobatic pair were able to "fly" across the entire map until they eventually ditched in the ocean.

FIRST VOICE ACTOR CAMEO IN A GAME

Few game voice actors become celebrities in their own right – but that's certainly not the case with Nolan North (USA). The former holder of the record for **most prolific game voice actor** (a title currently taken by US actor Steve Blum) is best known for playing *Uncharted*'s Nathan Drake and *Assassin's Creed*'s Desmond Miles. *SR IV* vocal options include "Nolan North Voice" (with appropriately amusing dialogue).

> "A group of people came up with a dragon, which you could ride and could breathe fire on the enemies, and they got a crude prototype working."

JIM BOONE, SENIOR PRODUCER, VOLITION, ON IDEAS FROM THE DEVELOPER'S "AWESOME WEEK" BRAINSTORM THAT DIDN'T MAKE *SAINTS ROW*

▶▶FIRST USER-GENERATED CONTENT CREATOR FOR AN OPEN-WORLD CONSOLE VIDEOGAME

Standing alongside *Saints Row* and *Grand Theft Auto* is the urban action-adventure game with attitude (and superpowers): *inFAMOUS*. The second game in the series was the first with a user-generated content creator – inspired by Media Molecule's *LittleBigPlanet* (for more on Sackboy and his creators see pp.54–55 and pp.86–87). The *inFAMOUS* user levels returned for the standalone expansion *inFAMOUS 2: Festival of Blood*, but were absent from the third entry *inFAMOUS: Second Son*.

FOR THE WIN

SUPER BALLISTIC MANAPULT

The *Saints Row* games are known for getting pretty crazy, but what's the weirdest vehicle in the series? Professor Genki's Super Ballistic Manapult has to be a contender. This colourful but fragile vehicle, available in the *Funtime!* DLC packs for *Saints Row: The Third* and *Saints Row IV*, features the giant Genki Cannon on the roof and it's this that is the draw. Anybody you run over is sucked into the cannon and can be fired out again at high speed. You can actually load yourself into the cannon, and use the vehicle to access high rooftops.

FASTEST COMPLETION OF *SAINTS ROW IV*

On 24 August 2013, just four days after *Saints Row IV* was released to good reviews in North America, dedicated competitive gamer Matt "BLiTZ" Siegfried (USA) challenged record-chaser "FoxPeace" to a speed-run through the story mode of *Saints Row IV*. Siegfried powered through the high-octane action, completing the game – and getting the "good" ending – in 4 hr 22 min 5 sec.

Summary: There's something rather naughty about much-loved Nintendo mascots knocking each other about. Yet alongside the fun is a very playable fighting series.

Publisher: Nintendo
Developer: HAL Laboratory
Debut: 1999

LONGEST SOLO HOME-RUN IN *SUPER SMASH BROS. BRAWL*

The home-run is a minigame in which players use a bat to whack a sandbag as far as they can after damaging it first. On 12 April 2012, gamer "yy1032" used the Ice Climbers to achieve a distance of 3,838.3 m (12,593.3 ft). The hit was approved by allisbrawl.com on 16 September 2012.

MOST TROPHIES IN A VIDEOGAME

If you need to collect trophies or in-game rewards to make your playing experience complete, *Super Smash Bros. Brawl* is the game for you. It has no fewer than 544 trophies to collect for achievements completed throughout the game, ranging from a simple statue of Mario to a fearsome-looking Metal Gear REX.

HIGHEST EARNINGS IN A *SUPER SMASH BROS.* TOURNAMENT

Playing as Falco on 19 November 2006, Christopher "PC Chris" Szygiel (USA) won $10,000 (£5,150) in the *Super Smash Bros. Melee* Singles National Championship organized by Major League Gaming.

LARGEST *SUPER SMASH BROS.* TOURNAMENT

The Evolution Championship Series, or Evo, is held annually and brings together the best fighting games players to duke it out in the USA. The 13th edition was held on 11–13 July 2014 in Las Vegas and featured 970 "Smashers", up from 709 competitors the previous year. The winner in the singles category for the second year running was Joseph "Mango" Marquez (USA), who took home $5,820 (£3,458). Shown above is 2014's *Super Smash Bros.* for the Wii U and 3DS.

BEST-SELLING FIGHTING GAME SERIES FOR NINTENDO HARDWARE

The first three games in the *Super Smash Bros.* series, including *Melee* and *Brawl*, had sold 24.82 million copies as of 4 August 2014. The Wii U and 3DS versions of the game (main picture below) look set to maintain the popularity of the crossover franchise. Nintendo will launch amiibo figures with the Wii U edition and promise that the 10 figures that kick off the new range will be usable in other titles. For more on the popularity of toys that can be used to interface with games, turn to our feature on pp.144–45.

SMASH IT UP

In late 2014, *Super Smash Bros.* is set to hit handhelds for the first time. Alongside a Wii U edition, a version for the 3DS will debut, marking the first playable appearances by Greninja (*Pokémon*), Little Mac (*Punch-Out!!*), Mega Man (*Mega Man*), Rosalina (*Mario*), Villager (*Animal Crossing*) and the Trainers (*Wii Fit*).

BEST-SELLING FIGHTING GAME

Super Smash Bros. Brawl has sold a total of 12.2 million copies, according to VGChartz. Working with a smaller user base on the 3DS and Wii U, the 2014 editions of *Super Smash Bros.* seem unlikely to overtake the 2008 Wii classic. Coming in distant second place lies *Tekken 3*, with sales of 7.16 million.

MOST KOs IN *SUPER SMASH BROS. BRAWL*

A KO – or knockout – happens in *Super Smash Bros. Brawl* when a character is knocked out-of-bounds on the screen. Klayton Schaufler (USA) went to the GWR Challengers website to register 51 knockouts in *Brawl* on 8 February 2013.

The **most KOs on Super Smash Bros. Melee** was 23, recorded by James "TwisTeD_ EnEmY" Bouchier (Canada), playing in Aberystwyth, UK, on 16 June 2010.

19

Age in years of future *Super Smash Bros.* creator Masahiro Sakurai when he designed his first Nintendo character, Kirby.

HIGHEST-EARNING *SUPER SMASH BROS. MELEE* PLAYER

"SephirothKen", aka Ken Hoang (USA), has accumulated earnings of $28,625 (£17,000) from *Super Smash Bros. Melee*, according to esportsearnings.com. He won his first tournament in 2003 and in total has been champion in 27 competitions. *Melee* was first introduced to the Major League Gaming line-up in 2004 and ran until 2006. It appeared at Evo in 2007, 2008, 2013 and 2014.

STRONGEST CHARACTER IN *SUPER SMASH BROS. BRAWL*

A match-up is a prediction of how two characters will perform in a bout. Smash World Forums published their third annual Match-up Chart on 9 July 2013 and Meta Knight had earned 252 points. His repertoire of "counters" (or characters he is well matched with) include nine soft, 11 hard and two almost unlosable match-ups.

BEST-SELLING GAMECUBE GAME

Selling 7.07 million units, *Super Smash Bros. Melee* is not only the best-selling GameCube title but also the third best selling fighting game of any kind. Its total sales are only fractionally behind *Tekken 3* (7.16 million copies), and in Japan – where it was first released in 2001 – it became the fastest-selling title for the GameCube, shifting more than 360,000 copies in its first week alone.

30% 0% 76% 76%

FOR THE WIN

BRAWL CONTROLLER

Try to avoid using the inefficient Wiimote as your controller of choice, and focus instead on using the Wiimote + Nunchuk – or use the Classic Controller, which offers two Z buttons so that you can choose which hand you want to use when performing grabs. The distance between right-hand buttons and control stick is also reduced.

ᐊ36 PORTAL

Summary: Bending the rules of physics was never such fiendish fun. This first-person puzzler began as *Narbacular Drop*, a project by students who were spotted and taken on by Valve's Gabe Newell.

Publisher: Valve
Developer: Valve
Debut: 2007

FASTEST SEGMENTED *PORTAL* SPEED-RUN BY A TEAM

SourceRuns is a community of speed-runners who focus on Valve titles. A team comprising David "Imanex" Connick (Australia), Nick "Z1mb0bw4y" Roth (USA), Nick "Gocnak" Kerns (USA) and Sullivan "SullyJFH" Ford (UK) mastered glitches, skips and tricks to finish *Portal* in a total time of 7 min 54 sec on 31 December

MOST VIEWED FAN FILM BASED ON A SCI-FI PUZZLE GAME

As of 28 May 2014, the live-action film *Portal: No Escape*, directed by Dan Trachtenberg (USA), had been viewed 14,203,176 times on YouTube since debuting on 23 August 2011. The seven-minute *Portal* tribute stars a woman (played by Danielle Rayne, above) who wakes up with amnesia in a mysterious, high-tech facility. She must overcome her fears, foes and the laws of physics if she hopes to escape.

2013. The record-breaking run, entitled "Portal Done Por", was recorded in 31 segments and smashed the previous record of 8 min 31 sec set on 16 July 2012.

FASTEST COMPLETION OF *PORTAL 2* (CO-OP)

On 15 January 2014, Imanex and Klooger (collectively known as "Klooganex") led

TEACH WITH PORTALS

In June 2012, Valve launched "Steam for Schools", making *Portal 2* and custom puzzle-creation software free through its "Teach with Portals" programme. More than 2,500 teachers brought the joys of Test Chamber creation to students with the suite.

RAREST *PORTAL* ACHIEVEMENT

On the PC version of *Portal*, the "Aperture Science" achievement is given to players who have earned gold medals on all challenges. As of 23 April 2014, only 0.7% of players had added this badge to their virtual collection.

The **rarest *Portal 2* achievement** is "The Talent Show", which tasks PC co-op players with completing the sixth chamber of the "Mobility Gels" co-op course without dropping a single cube. As of 28 May 2014, only 1.6% of PC gamers had managed the feat.

co-op characters ATLAS and P-body through the team challenges in 30 min 32.83 sec (without load times). The speedy team – who promise a "sub-30 incoming" – beat the record held by team "Snernicus" of 33 min 24 sec (without load times).

FIRST CROSS-PLATFORM MULTIPLAYER PUZZLE GAME

Portal 2 co-op mode allows PS3, PC and Mac gamers to play together using Valve's online gaming service Steam as a bridge between the platforms. This was the first time that Steam was made available to PS3 owners, although Xbox 360 owners missed out on the action.

MOST POPULAR FAN-MADE *PORTAL 2* EXPANSION

The "12 Angry Tests" PC map pack by Sebastian "CaretCaret" Evefjord (Sweden) had attracted 353,017 unique subscribers on Valve's Steam Workshop as of 28 May 2014. Sebastian is a games programmer working for Overkill, whose games include the *Payday* series.

FASTEST SINGLE-SEGMENT COMPLETION OF *PORTAL*

Canadian gamer "Blizik" finished *Portal* without resorting to using out-of-bounds areas in 12 min 53.72 sec on the PC version of the game. "Blizik" was 15.63 sec faster than nearest rival "SullyJHF". Unfortunately, there was still no cake.

FOR THE WIN

PORTAL 2 SPEED-RUNNING TIPS

Bunny hop: Jump back and forth instead of walking to gain greater speeds.
Portal boost: Fire while exiting a portal on the ground for momentum.
Object boost: Grab and jump off in-game objects to reach new heights.
Peek-a-portal: Move fast between forming portals for new perspectives.
Out-of-bounds: Use glitches and exploits to navigate routes outside of normal game boundaries.

RARE GROOVES

Certain areas of *Portal 2* contain a musical score generated in real time, based on the player's action. According to lead composer Mike Morasky, one of the pieces of music will only repeat every 76,911 years 125 days 7 hr 56 min 30.3 sec.

FASTEST COMPLETION OF *ANTICHAMBER*

Antichamber is an indie platform puzzler developed by Alexander Bruce, based on mind-bending geometry in the *Portal* style. On 5 December 2013, Jadon "Pallidus" Wylie collected all 120 signs in a time of 12 min 24.19 sec.

FASTEST-SELLING PUZZLE GAME ON A SEVENTH-GENERATION CONSOLE

Portal 2 was launched on 19 April 2011 and sold 910,175 copies within its first week alone. By June 2014, it had sold a total of 4.06 million units.

FASTEST SINGLE-SEGMENT COMPLETION OF *PORTAL 2*

On 8 June 2014, *Portal* speed-running specialist Alex "Znernicus" Thieke beat his own record by finishing *Portal 2* in 1 hr 6 min 23 sec. Alex shaved 57 sec off the time he had set on 14 May 2014. He uses *Portal 2 Live Timer* to record accurate in-game split times.

Summary: PAC-Man is the Japanese gaming legend that keeps on giving. In addition to starring in dozens of his own games, he has appeared in titles as varied as *Mario Kart* and *Street Fighter X Tekken*.

Publisher: Namco/
Bally Midway
Developer: Namco
Debut: 1980

FIRST ANIMATED TV SERIES BASED ON A VIDEOGAME

American animation studio Hanna-Barbera, most famous for *The Flintstones*, *Scooby-Doo* and *The Smurfs*, produced the *PAC-Man* animated series. The first episode aired on 25 September 1982. It ran for two series and followed PAC-Man and wife Pepper.

FIRST VIDEOGAME MASCOT

Before Mario, Sonic, Lara and Sackboy, there was PAC-Man. The pizza-shaped waka-waka hero quickly became synonymous with gaming after the release of the original arcade game, and remains an icon recognizable to millions, to be found on everything from T-shirts to coffee mugs.

FIRST VIDEOGAME FAMILY

Before the Mario brothers came along in 1983, PAC-Man had already established the first videogame family. Following the breakout success of the original *PAC-Man*, American licensee Bally Midway released a series of unofficial spin-off games. *Ms. PAC-Man* (released 13 January 1982) proved so successful that Namco eventually adopted it as an official release, but the same cannot be said of unofficial titles *Baby PAC-Man* (1982) and *Jr. PAC-Man* (1983), which, along with *Professor PAC-Man* (1983), contributed to Namco eventually severing all ties with Bally Midway.

MOST VIEWED *PAC-MAN* VIDEO

In April 2009, renowned French prankster Rémi Gaillard uploaded a video of himself dressed in a full-size PAC-Man costume being chased by cohorts dressed as ghosts in a supermarket, on a golf course and at other locations. The clip is the most viewed *PAC-Man* video on YouTube, with 45,831,671 views as of 18 August 2014.

▶▶FIRST VIDEOGAME TO USE MULTIPLE LIVES

Two years before *PAC-Man*, there was *Space Invaders*. The first arcade game to take the world by storm proved to be influential in several ways. We may take gaming re-incarnations for granted nowadays, but it was *Space Invaders* in 1978 that introduced the concept of multiple lives. Pesky enemies that fire at us are now also par for the course, but this was the **first game to have targets that could fire back**. The game raked in over $600 million (£300 million) from 100,000 arcade units in its first year alone.

Paying tribute to the iconic game, the **largest piece of Space Invaders artwork** (left, below) measured 150 m² (1,614.59 sq ft) and was created in chalk by street artists Leon Keer and Remko van Schaik (both Netherlands) at the EPFL campus in Lausanne, Switzerland, on 17 March 2014.

MOST COSTLY *PAC-MAN* GAME

To celebrate the 30th anniversary of the game's release, Google unveiled a *PAC-Man*-inspired Google Doodle on 21 May 2010. This interactive banner used the same graphics and gameplay as the original arcade version. Visitors to Google.com played the doodle for nearly 500,000,000 hours, which – based on the average office worker's salary – is estimated to have cost businesses £85 million ($122 million) in lost productivity!

FIRST PERFECT SCORE ON PAC-MAN

Billy Mitchell (USA) scored a perfect 3,333,360 points on *PAC-Man* on 3 July 1999. He achieved this in 5 hr 30 min exactly. An arcade legend, Billy was selected as one of the 10 most influential gamers of all time by MTV in 2006.

HIGHEST SCORE ON *PAC-MAN CHAMPIONSHIP EDITION DX*

The greatest score achieved on *PAC-Man Championship Edition DX* is 530,920 points by Michael Sroka (USA) in Farmington Hills, Michigan, USA, on 22 August 2013. *Championship Edition DX* was released on the Xbox Live Arcade and the PlayStation Network in 2010.

MOST POPULAR *PAC-MAN* SONG

"PAC-Man Fever", a pop song by US group Buckner & Garcia, featured original sound effects from the game. It was a massive success, selling more than 2.5 million copies upon its release in 1982. The single, which appeared on an album of the same name, reached No.9 on the *Billboard* Hot 100 chart in March 1982. The album contains 10 songs, each about a different arcade game, including *Frogger*, *Donkey Kong*, *Centipede* and *Defender*.

FIRST VIDEOGAME FOR ANDROID PHONES

PAC-Man, released on 23 September 2008, became the first title on Android smartphones. The game retailed for $9.99 (£5.43) but was offered free to owners of flagship Android handset the HTC Dream (aka T-Mobile G1). Players were able to control the little yellow pill-popper by swiping the phone's touch screen, tilting the handset or using the trackball.

BEST-SELLING ARCADE MACHINE

No arcade game before or since has beaten *PAC-Man*'s sales of more than 400,000. In his book *The Video Game Explosion: A History from Pong to PlayStation and Beyond*, author Mark J P Wolf states that "one study estimated that it had been played more than 10 billion times during the twentieth century". *PAC-Man* certainly raked in hundreds of millions of dollars – one quarter at a time.

SUPER PAC BROS.

Super Smash Bros. for Nintendo 3DS and Wii U, set for a late 2014 release, is the first in the series to feature PAC-Man (main picture). *Smash* creator Masahiro Sakurai revealed that Nintendo legend Shigeru Miyamoto originally wanted PAC to feature in *Super Smash Bros. Brawl* in 2008.

COMMERCIAL BREAK

As the gaming industry has become bigger and more lucrative, so the advertising campaigns around new titles are ever more dazzling. The promo is now an art form in itself, from classic full-page ads in glossy magazines to city-wide billboard blitzes accompanied by trailers that wouldn't disgrace a blockbuster movie.

Sega in the USA
The Sega Genesis, the US version of the Mega Drive, was launched in 1989 as the company began its head-to-head with Nintendo. A later advert boasted, with the slightly laboured pun, "We do what Nintendon't".

Conquering console
The Atari 2600 was released in 1977 and gained popularity through building up a library of entertaining titles. The marketing campaign focused on the number of games: they were simple, but the novelty of being able to play more than one title by switching cartridges helped Atari win the early console wars.

Supersonic spin cycle
Nobody was left in any doubt that Sonic would be a speedy hedgehog. His adverts run over several pages – on the first is the slogan "Get ready for the sonic boom", with just a ghostly trail underneath, leading to the two pages with the "BOOM" and our blue hero scattering exciting screenshots.

As seen on TV
Game trailers in primetime slots may now be the norm, but advertising videogames on TV was once unheard of. Sega was the first gaming company to take the big step of using TV adverts when it promoted its space shooter *Zaxxon* in 1982. The commercial focused on *Zaxxon*'s unique feature: it was the **first videogame with an isometric viewpoint display**.

Hurricane kicker
Street Fighter II was the game that changed everything in terms of its playability, but the magazine ad for the home version of the 1988 debut looks the part. It introduces gamers to the idea of a roster of distinct characters.

Manic Monday
The launch of legendary arcade fighter *Mortal Kombat* for home consoles was one of the biggest game events of the early 1990s. Featuring just the bare minimum of text and omitting screenshots entirely served only to underline how much anticipation there was for the title. Every gamer knew what was coming.

SUPER MARIO GALAXY

GET READY FOR MARIO'S GREATEST ADVENTURE!

Brace yourself for Mario's biggest jump of all – a leap into space! Super Mario Galaxy takes Mario on a gravity-defying adventure into the great beyond. New suits bring new powers, while the unique Wii Remote controls immerse you in the game like never before! Mario's back – and he's better than ever.

THE LAST OF US

KILL, OR BE KILLED. IF ONLY IT WERE THAT SIMPLE.

18

FROM THE CREATORS OF UNCHARTED

COULD YOU BE THE LAST OF US?

THELASTOFUS.COM   OUT JUNE 14TH

PS3

Super Mario delivery
The email announcing the arrival of *Super Mario Galaxy* "in Earth shops" in 2007 featured linked content. Those who clicked through were greeted by the sight of no less a figure than the Nintendo president himself, Satoru Iwata, in an exclusive interview with the game's developers.

Bank balance
Money appears to be no object when it comes to booking big names to promote games. British actress Dame Helen Mirren, for example, was reportedly paid £500,000 ($800,000) – the **largest fee paid for an appearance in a videogame advert** – for promoting *Wii Fit* on TV in 2010.

Last but not least
Sony ran a major campaign across all media for *The Last of Us*, including a striking clip in which a gamer in his room transforms into Joel. The print ads maintain the desolate, immersive atmosphere of the game's premise.

Three's company
Rockstar upped the ante on videogame advertising by commissioning giant murals hand-painted on to the side of the Figueroa Hotel in Los Angeles, California, USA, near the location of E3. Other games companies have followed suit, promoting the likes of *Skyrim* and *Final Fantasy XIII*.

Bang up to date
By the start of this century's second decade, gaming was truly a multi-billion-dollar business, reflected in the enormous advertising budgets for new releases. Rockstar's *Red Dead* campaign used bold and direct posters and billboards that appeared on train and underground stations worldwide.

On the trail of Zelda
Trailers are fast becoming the new adverts, with eagerly awaited E3 spots frequently logging views in the millions when uploaded to YouTube. Zelda and father Robin Williams (left) teamed up for a series of *Ocarina of Time* adverts.

WE ARE ALL CONNECTED

WATCH DOGS

Hack's the way to do it
Potential punters can indulge in a little Aiden Pearce-style hacking with QR codes in the *Watch_Dogs* campaign. The codes give access to extra content and competitions.

HALF-LIFE

Summary: Still much loved, the 1990s classic was the first step on Valve's journey from hopeful start-up to today's big gaming beast, valued at approximately $2.5 bn (£1.4 bn).

Publisher: Valve/Sierra
Developer: Valve/Gearbox
Debut: 1998

MOST POPULAR STEAM TECHNOLOGY DEMONSTRATION

Half-Life 2: Lost Coast is an extra level that is primarily used by Valve as a showcase for the high-dynamic-range-rendering capabilities of its Source engine. It had 12.77 million owners on Steam, according to arstechnica.com, as of April 2014, which makes it the third most-owned game on Steam

FIRST GAME TO FEATURE A GRAVITY GUN

Half-Life 2's Gravity Gun can be used to fire almost any object as a projectile, its distance dependent on its weight. This realistic depiction of Newtonian physics is possible through the game's sophisticated Havok engine, which takes into account such factors as the mass, gravity and friction of each object.

HARDEST STEAM ACHIEVEMENT IN *HALF-LIFE 2: EPISODE TWO*

To complete "Get Some Grub", players don't just have to get *some* grubs – they have to squish all 333 of them in *Episode Two* in one play-through. Only 2.3% of the game's owners had managed it as of 5 August 2014.

1,121,024
likes on Facebook for *Half-Life 2*, as of 5 August 2014.

– although the same statistics revealed just 2.1 million people have actually played the game.

FASTEST COMPLETION OF *HALF-LIFE*

On 20 October 2012, Max "coolkid" Lundberg recorded a single-segment run of 36 min 58 sec on the PC version of *Half-Life*. His game was set on "Hard" difficulty. He went on to be one of the members of the fastest team to complete the game (see opposite page).

By comparison, the **fastest completion of *Half-Life* on the PlayStation 2** is 1 hr 6 min 6 sec by Fabrizio "Superfrizzio" Rossebastiano on 7 November 2010. His single-segment run was also achieved on the "Hard" difficulty setting.

HIGHEST-RATED SHOOTER BY *PC GAMER*

No game has received a rating higher than 98% in the US edition of *PC Gamer* magazine. *Sid Meier's Alpha Centauri* was the first of only three games to ever receive the honour, followed by *Half-Life 2* and subsequently *Crysis*. In 2010, readers of the magazine voted *Half-Life 2* the best videogame of all time.

> "We were a single-player videogame company that could have been really successful just doing *Half-Life* sequel after *Half-Life* sequel, but we collectively said, 'Let's try to make multiplayer games'."

GABE NEWELL, CEO OF VALVE, JANUARY 2014
BREAKING THE HEARTS OF *HALF-LIFE* FANS WHO HAVE BEEN HOPING SINCE 2007'S *EPISODE 2* FOR *HALF-LIFE 3*…

▶▶FIRST GAME WITH OCULUS RIFT SUPPORT

Team Fortress shares co-creator Robin Walker with *Half-Life 2* and *Half-Life: Counter-Strike*, among his many other Valve games. *Team Fortress 2* was first released in 2007 and support for the Oculus Rift VR headset was added to the free2play shooter in March 2013.

Oculus

▶▶MOST EXPENSIVE VIRTUAL HAT

Custom hats are prized in *Team Fortress 2*. "Burning Flames Killer Exclusive" is classic journalist's headgear that was sold on 7 March 2014 for 300 Earbuds. In *TF2*'s economy, an Earbud was then worth around $36 (£21) in real money – the hat went for approximately $10,820 (£6,430). The seller said, "I know the undisputed best unusual hat in *TF2* will go to someone who will appreciate it just as much as I did."

MOST CRITICALLY ACCLAIMED PC GAME

Half-Life 2 has an average rating of 95.48% on GameRankings. Only a PC compilation is rated higher – Valve's own *The Orange Box*. Even here, there's no escaping *Half-Life 2*, as it's in the *Box* alongside two other Valve titles, *Team Fortress 2* and *Portal*.

IVAN A NEW NAME

When Gordon Freeman was first drawn by concept artist Chuck Jones, he had a full beard, a bulky spacesuit and a flat-top haircut, leading to the nickname "Ivan the Space Biker". In his final form, "Freeman" was in part a homage by Valve founder Gabe Newell to physicist and mathematician Freeman Dyson.

FASTEST TEAM COMPLETION OF *HALF-LIFE*

Team "Quadrazoid" completed *Half-Life* in "Hard" mode in 20 min 41 sec on 12 April 2014. The members were "quadrazid", "Crash Fort", "coolkid", "pineapple", "YaLTeR", "Spider Waffle" and "FELiP". They took around four years to plan the run, making it in 317 segments and employing various tools and automated keyscripts to give the team extra abilities.

Half-Life 2: Episode One.

TOP 5 MOST COMPLETED STEAM ACHIEVEMENTS IN *HALF-LIFE 2: EPISODE TWO*

"Acid Reflex"
Kill an Antlion Worker: **74.5%** of players

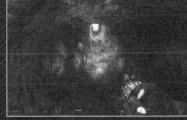

"Into the Breach"
Defend the mineshaft from the Antlions with Griggs and Sheckley: **67.6%**

"Twofer"
Overcome two Antlion Guards outside the White Forest: **61.4%**

"Meet the Hunters"
You and Alyx have to survive the Hunters' car ambush: **59.6%**

"Gunishment!"
Destroy the Combine Autogun in the junkyard – a grenade does the trick: **58.2%**

Summary: Shepard's story is told over three games of remarkable depth and scope. It concludes with one of multiple endings based on the choices that players make earlier in the game.

10,000,000,000 enemies killed online by gamers using *Mass Effect 3*'s multiplayer co-op mode.

Publisher: Microsoft/EA
Developer: BioWare
Debut: 2007

FOR THE WIN

KINECT WITH *MASS EFFECT 3*

Xbox 360 owners will know that their edition of *ME3* allows Kinect voice commands to control many of the game's menu options. But there is also a secret instruction included in the game as an Easter egg that lets players swiftly swap to the shotgun by shouting "Boom stick" at the console.

FASTEST COMPLETION OF *MASS EFFECT 2*

Dustin "Hokorippoi" Hanks sped through *ME2* in 2 hr 2 min 15 sec on 31 March 2013. Hanks completed the game in a single-segment run, on "Casual" difficulty, without DLC. This is all the more impressive when you consider that the average completion time for the game is more than 37 hours.

MOST POPULAR *MASS EFFECT* SINGLE-PLAYER CHARACTER CLASS

According to BioWare's own statistics, the Soldier class is the most popular, with more people playing as a Soldier in *Mass Effect 2* than all the other classes put together. The trend continued in *ME3*, with 43.7% of players opting for a character skilled with guns rather than any of the game's more unusual powers. Gamers are good souls deep down: 64.5% of them play as Paragons rather than as Renegades.

MOST ADVANCED CHARACTER IMPORT SYSTEM

Mass Effect 3 allows gamers to import more than 1,000 of their decisions from the first two games. Importing character details affects players' abilities, how others treat their character and how the adventure will turn out. The *Mass Effect* series fully exploited the idea of carrying over player decisions: actions in the first game had reverberations into the third.

FIRST PERSON NAMED AFTER A *MASS EFFECT* CHARACTER

On 7 January 2014, Adam and Cheri Rose gave birth to a baby daughter and named her Tali'Zorah. BioWare marked the occasion by tweeting a photo of the baby, saying "Welcome to Earth, Tali'Zorah". Adam Rose said his wife "fell in love with the name Tali'Zorah the instant we met the Quarian being hunted by Fist. She told me back then, 'If we ever have a daughter, I'd love to name her Tali'Zorah. It just sounds so beautiful.'"

MOST POPULAR *MASS EFFECT 3* SQUAD MEMBER

Step forward Liara T'Soni... With 24.1% of *Mass Effect 3* players choosing the game's brave but sensitive scientist, she narrowly beats deadpan sharpshooter Garrus Vakarian, who appeals to 23.8% of players. Spare a thought for poor old Kaidan Alenko, however, who is the choice of just 1.5% of players.

COMMANDER HUDSON

Casey Hudson, director of the *Mass Effect* trilogy, among other BioWare projects, announced his departure from the developer in August 2014. He had been with the company for 16 years, before its acquisition by EA, and reassured fans anxious for news of *Mass Effect 4*: "Development for the next *Mass Effect* game is well underway, with stunning assets and playable builds."

> "We have agreed to tell a story that doesn't relate necessarily to any of the Shepard events... It has to feel like a *Mass Effect* game at its heart, at its core."
>
> **MAC WALTERS, *MASS EFFECT* WRITER**
> ON FUTURE DEVELOPMENTS

FASTEST COMPLETION OF *MASS EFFECT 3* ("INSANITY" MODE)

"SpartanB218" (France) finished *Mass Effect 3* in 3 hr 48 min 48 sec and uploaded the video to YouTube on 24 June 2013. SpartanB218 also speed-runs *Super Mario Sunshine*, but specializes in *ME3*.

FIRST DLC ALTERNATIVE GAME ENDING

Fans ran an effective "Retake *Mass Effect*" campaign that resulted in an "extended cut" to bring clarity to the *Mass Effect 3* ending. The new ending was released in June 2012 with additional cutscenes.

MOST COMPLETED BIOWARE GAME

BioWare is known for epic games, and many gamers struggle to finish them. A comparatively high 56% completed *ME2*, more than the 40% who saw the end of the first in the trilogy and more than the 42% who made it to the finale of *ME3*. BioWare's fantasy RPG *Dragon Age II* was also conquered by just 42% of players.

FIRST MASH-UP TEXTURE PACK FOR *MINECRAFT*

Mass Effect launched Mojang's series of mash-up texture packs for *Minecraft*'s console edition in September 2013. The extensive DLC introduced 36 character skins, a pre-built *ME* world and 22 music tracks. All *Minecraft* blocks and items transformed into their *ME* equivalent. Mash-up packs with *Halo* and *Skyrim* themes followed from Mojang in 2014.

CHARITY PLAY

The *Mass Effect* Cast Cosplay Initiative was a charity event that featured original game actors at the 2014 PAX East games convention in the USA, all wearing replica character costumes. An audience of 10,000 watched a panel – including Kimberly Brooks (Ashley Williams), Rana McAnear (Samara/Morinth), Keythe Farley (Thane Krios) and Luciano Costa (Kaidan Alenko) – discuss the games. More than $6,000 (£3,500) was raised for a children's hospital.

SFX EFFECT

The original title of *Mass Effect* was going to be *SFX*, short for *Science Fiction X*, BioWare's code-name for the project. In the end, they dropped the title because it was the name of a leading sci-fi magazine in the UK – and had been since 1995.

MOST CHALLENGE POINTS IN *MASS EFFECT 3* MULTIPLAYER

"Red Eileen" had amassed 484,645 points in the *ME3* multiplayer as of 7 August 2014. Challenge points are earned by completing in-game tasks such as scoring hits with a particular weapon multiple times. To earn these points it took Red Eileen 4,091 hr 6 min 59 sec on the in-game clock, across 9,815 matches.

GEARS OF WAR

Summary: Epic sold *GoW* to Microsoft in 2014, so the franchise is likely to remain an Xbox exclusive. Iconic former Epic designer Cliff Bleszinski confirmed that he is not involved in the series.

Publisher: Microsoft
Developer: Epic Games/Black Tusk Studios
Debut: 2006

FIRST PLAYABLE FEMALE CHARACTER IN *GEARS OF WAR*

The series is famous for its super-macho action and for its heroes with arms and necks roughly the same size as a small car. It wasn't until *Gears of War 3* and the introduction of Samantha Byrne that the battle against the Locust included a victory for equality. Samantha was a playable Gear voiced by Claudia Black, and later in the game players could also choose Anya Stroud, Queen Myrrah and Bernadette Mataki.

FIRST CONSOLE GAME TO USE THE UNREAL ENGINE 3

The third version of Epic Games' award-winning engine was first used on *Gears of War* and many other developers have since signed up to design games with it. Created in 1998, the engine is now in its fourth iteration and had been the tool of production in 408 games as of July 2014 (including all *Gears of War* games), making it the **most successful videogame engine**.

POWERED BY
UNREAL
TECHNOLOGY

BEST-SELLING THIRD-PERSON SHOOTER SERIES

As of 15 July 2014, the *Gears of War* series had sold 20.19 million units, according to VGChartz. Unusually, its main entries were all released on one platform, the seventh-generation Xbox 360. Most best-selling franchises were launched on older consoles, making *Gears of War* a rare example of a platform-exclusive shooter that has achieved prominence within a single console generation. The second title in the war against the Locust horde, *Gears of War 2*, is the **best-selling TPS game**, with 6.68 million units shifted worldwide.

FASTEST COMPLETION OF *GEARS OF WAR 2* ON "CASUAL" DIFFICULTY

"zzDAZZLEzz" (Canada) set a single play-through record with no restarts of 3 hr 56 min 48 sec on 19 May 2013. The same player repeated the feat with the **fastest single-segment completion of *Gears of War: Judgment* on "Casual" difficulty**, recording 2 hr 25 min 58 sec on 5 May 2013.

FOR THE WIN

LAMBENT CHICKEN EASTER EGG

Here's how to get up-close with a giant Lambent Chicken. In Act One, Chapter One of *Gears of War 3*, raise the lift so that the Raven can land. You will see four tubes on the walls. Walk up to each one and shout into the tube. After you've done the same with each tube, a chicken will jump out. Shoot the chicken and it will turn into a fire-breathing Lambent Chicken.

HIGHEST SCORE ON *GEARS OF WAR 3* MULTIPLAYER

"Imyourpusherman", aka Jakob Patterson (USA), had 1,378 points, as of 17 July 2014, in the Major League Gaming multiplayer arena. Patterson has also earned 15 MLG first-place trophies owing to his *Gears* skills.

The **highest score on *Gears of War: Judgment* multiplayer** was set by "TheInvolving", aka Sahad Soria (Mexico), as of 24 June 2014. Soria topped the MLG professional leaderboard for the game with 1,082 points, gained from 446 wins in the MLG arena. Points in MLG are awarded based on player skill level, so only the best reach the top.

FASTEST COMPLETION OF *GEARS OF WAR* ON "INSANE" DIFFICULTY

"Youkai", aka William Welch, completed a segmented run of *Gears of War* in 1 hr 34 min 57 sec on 12 December 2012. The 46th segment proved particularly challenging and William played this through a mind-numbing 1,108 times before he was satisfied with his performance. Teaming up with fellow veteran speed-runner "Brassmaster", aka Andrew Meredith, he set the **fastest co-op completion of *Gears of War*** on 1 September 2011, when the pair recorded a time of 1 hr 34 min 38 sec.

SAVING PRIVATE CLAYTON'S BACON

The Carmine boys don't fare very well as soldiers in the *Gears of War* series. First, Anthony Carmine dies in the original game, while Private Benjamin Carmine is taken out by a sniper in the second game.

When it came to *Gears of War 3*, Epic Games let fans vote on whether another brother, Clayton (below), would survive. They took mercy on him and so he managed to see through an entire campaign without perishing. Epic later released a clip showing how he might have met his end – accidentally electrocuted by a music player in the bath while eating bacon!

Right: Locust-battling hero Marcus Fenix.

GRUB KILLER

After the first modern zombie outbreak hit a remote Pennsylvania cemetery in George A Romero's 1968 film *Night of the Living Dead*, it was just a matter of time before undead hordes reached our own homes. With the rise of zombie console games in the 1990s, we no longer had to leave the living room to be entertained and terrified by the latest in zombie mayhem. What's more, videogames throw the audience straight into the undead action in a way that films can't.

Matt Mogk is the founder and head of the Zombie Research Society and a regular on AMC's *The Walking Dead* aftershow, *Talking Dead*. Here we asked Matt which zombie games he considers to be the most important of all time…

5) ZOMBIES ATE MY NEIGHBORS
(1993)

Although there have been countless zombie games since *Zombies Ate My Neighbors* hit the scene, only a handful can compete with the fun factor in this goofball horror game. The gameplay obviously includes zombies eating neighbours, but it also features many other non-zombie menaces inspired by films such as *The Texas Chainsaw Massacre*, *Friday the 13th* and even *Little Shop of Horrors*, making this game a veritable homage to cinematic schlock and camp from the 1950s onwards. Squirt guns and tomatoes to fight off the walking dead? Sure, why not?

4) PLANTS VS. ZOMBIES
(2009)

If nothing else, *Plants vs. Zombies* proves that the undead can be inserted into any harebrained game concept and succeed. The simple goal of this tower defence game is to keep the shambling horde

away from your house by strategically placing aggressive, zombie-fighting plants in the way. Who knew that gardening could be so much fun? The cutesy design and easy gameplay contributed to *Plants vs. Zombies'* massive global success, raking in sales of over $1 million (£600,000) in its first nine days on sale. Burn them, shoot them, crush them or blend them up with a lawnmower, the zombie menace just keeps coming!

3) DAYZ
(2013)

Are you sick of the heavy-handed concepts that some zombie games rely on? Do you not want to be forced to go on a quest or find a cure or save your long-lost daughter? Well, then how about no concept at all? *DayZ* (above) throws you into an expansive apocalyptic world with one goal, and one goal only: to survive. There are no tasks to accomplish and no drawn-out storylines. You must scavenge for needed supplies, avoid zombies and other hostile humans, and try to live to see another day. That's it. Much like the *Walking Dead* television series and graphic novels, there aren't winners and losers, only the living and the dead. (For more on *The Walking Dead*, turn to pp.28–29.)

2) *LEFT 4 DEAD*
(2008)

Left 4 Dead (bottom left) features the newest iteration of "zombie" in popular culture. These aren't rotting corpses back from the dead but rather humans infected with a highly contagious sickness that causes them to go violently insane and spread the disease. But what really makes this title stand out is its innovative gameplay, which includes an intelligent reshuffling of valuables and threats that make an old campaign feel fresh again each time it's attempted. The multiplayer functionality is also impressive, but be careful not to shoot your team-mate. Being on the end of friendly fire is a quick way to lose friends… and be left for dead.

1) *RESIDENT EVIL*
(1996)

Resident Evil changed the face of horror gaming for ever (see pp.92–93). With more than 15 games, spin-off films, comics, novels and action figures, *Resident Evil* was instrumental in the revitalization of zombies in film, too. Even George A Romero says that *Resident*

THE ZOMBIE RESEARCH SOCIETY

The Society was founded by Matt Mogk in 2007 as an organization dedicated to the historic, cultural and scientific study of the living dead. Zombie movie legend George A Romero sits on the Society's advisory board. They organize Zombie Awareness Month every year, in which, according to the Society, "supporters wear a grey ribbon to signify the undead shadows that lurk behind our modern light of day… and help spread the word of survival". Usefully, the Zombie Research Society has compiled a top 10 of countries most likely to weather a global zombie pandemic – with Australia at the top of the list, largely because "it has the world's biggest moat surrounding it on all sides".

Evil – and the zombie games that followed it – have driven the popularity of zombies in recent years much more than films. The original *Resident Evil*, the **first survival horror game**, remains the most influential and important zombie game ever made, making it a clear choice for the top spot of my zombie game list.

DOTA

Summary: After two years in beta, the MOBA *DotA 2* was formally released in July 2013. The original *DotA*, a mod for *Warcraft III: Reign of Chaos*, was created by gamer and *WoW* map-maker "Eul".

Publisher: Valve
Developer: Valve
Debut: 2005

MOST CHOSEN HERO IN *DOTA 2*

The Grand Magus Rubick tops datdota's list as the hero picked in the most tournament matches, amassing 3,408 picks in the professional *DotA 2* scene as of 31 July 2014.

MOST KILLS IN A *DOTA* GAME

The most kills obtained by a player in a single *DotA* game is 40, achieved by Natus Vincere's Danil "Dendi" Ishutin (Ukraine) as Templar Assassin on 20 November 2012. Danil is also the holder of the record for the **most assists in *DotA*** – see p.81.

GREATEST AGGREGATE TIME PLAYING *DOTA 2*

As of 31 July 2014, the greatest amount of time spent playing *DotA 2* was 221 days 13 hr 34 min, set by *DotA* obsessive "Sonic". In that time, Sonic played an astonishing 8,817 matches, with Pudge his most frequently chosen hero.

1,748,935,328 pairs of Power Treads purchased by the *DotA 2* player-base.

MOST WINS FOR A *DOTA 2* HERO

Despite being on the receiving end of 2,076 defeats, Rubick also lays claim to the most competitive wins for a hero in *DotA 2* with an impressive total of 2,082.

MOST LAST HITS IN A *DOTA* GAME

Wei Sheng "Chains" Tan (Singapore) of the team First Departure achieved 1,141 last hits in a single competitive game of *DotA 2* on 9 April 2014.

LONGEST COMPETITIVE *DOTA 2* MATCH

With no limits as regards the length of games, *DotA 2* matches can test the patience and stamina of competitors. The longest competitive *DotA 2* match lasted 2 hr 5 min 26 sec and took place at the Fragbite Masters 2014 tournament between teams "4 Friends + Chrillee" and "Team Dog" on 15 April 2014.

HIGHEST-EARNING *DOTA 2* PLAYER

The most prize money earned in *DotA 2* by a single player is £649,873.69 ($1,100,851.71), acquired by Chen "Hao" Zhihao (China) of team "Newbee" (see p.81, top right). Newbee assembled in early 2014 and took first place in The International 4, which featured a crowdfunded total prize pool of £6,464,922 ($10,929,274).

TELEPORTATION SCROLLS

Teleportation scrolls are your friend. In addition to using them to defend a tower under siege, you can double-click a teleportation scroll to return to your fountain quickly.

HIGHEST AVERAGE GOLD PER MINUTE IN *DOTA 2*

DotA gold is earned by killing heroes, creeps and buildings. The most gold accrued per minute by a *DotA* pro player is an average of 565, an achievement shared by Team Zephyr's Corey "Corey" Wright and "Arteezy" from Team Evil Geniuses.

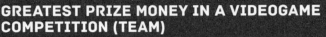

GREATEST PRIZE MONEY IN A VIDEOGAME COMPETITION (TEAM)

Chinese team "Newbee" (inset right receiving their record) scooped a tasty £3,048,970 ($5,028,121) at the fourth annual *DotA 2* competition, The International 4, held at the KeyArena, in Seattle, USA, on 18–21 July 2014. Newbee defeated rival Chinese team "Vici Gaming" to claim the prestigious title.

MOST ASSISTS IN *DOTA*

DotA is a team game, and securing the kill oneself isn't always necessary. The most assists in a single game is 43, by Natus Vincere's Danil "Dendi" Ishutin (Ukraine), as Puck on 11 June 2013.

"Just sitting there and watching people play at the event… it's intense and fun."

CHET FALISZEK
DotA 2 WRITER, ON THE INTERNATIONAL ANNUAL *DotA* TOURNAMENT

FREE TO PLAY

In 2014, Valve produced a low-budget, 75-minute documentary, *Free to Play*, that focused on three pro gamers – including *DotA* record holder Danil "Dendi" Ishutin – as they prepared to compete at The International 2011 in Cologne, Germany.

MOST *DOTA 2* GAME WINS

The most competitive victories by a *DotA 2* player is 476, achieved by Joakim "Akke" Akterhall (Sweden) from "Alliance". Joakim has lost 238 games, with Chen his most chosen hero. The Swede has been with Alliance since October 2012.

BATMAN: ARKHAM

Summary: Batman turned 75 in 2014. The brooding Dark Knight has made a huge impact on gaming, with the *Arkham* titles making us feel more like Batman than ever before.

Publisher: Eidos/ Warner Bros. Interactive
Developer: Rocksteady/ Warner Bros. Games
Debut: 2009

MOST CRITICALLY ACCLAIMED SUPERHERO GAME

With a hugely impressive GameRankings rating of 96.12%, *Batman: Arkham City* on the PlayStation 3 was the most highly rated superhero title as of 8 July 2014. The same game for the Xbox 360 ranks a close second with a score of 93.88%.

▶▶MOST BATMOBILES IN A VIDEOGAME

The upcoming *Arkham Knight* game is justly receiving a lot of attention for its brand spanking new Batmobile, described by *The Guardian*'s gaming critic as "hell on wheels". But the record for most original vehicles from Mr Wayne's underground garage goes to 2013's arcade racer *Batman*, with 10 unique Batmobiles in which to screech around open-world Gotham. Vehicles from *Batman Forever* (USA, 1995), the animated series *Batman: The Brave and the Bold* and *Batman: Arkham Asylum* are all in there, and it features aerial missions with "The Bat" from *The Dark Knight Rises* (USA, 2012).

▶▶FIRST *BATMAN* VIDEOGAME

The original *Batman* was released on the Amstrad and ZX Spectrum in 1986 by Ocean Software. A headache-inducing isometric nightmare, it involved rescuing Robin by collecting Batcraft bits from around the Batcave. The game was also released on other formats such as MSX (a version created by Ocean's own The Hit Squad, shown above).

11,000,000 registered players in *DC Universe Online*.

BEST-SELLING VIDEOGAME BASED ON A COMIC

Rocksteady's *Batman: Arkham City*, the sequel to *Arkham Asylum*, has sold 9.97 million copies worldwide. Like *Asylum*, *Arkham City* integrated stealth elements into its gameplay and included *Star Wars* legend Mark Hamill as the voice of The Joker, a part he has played several times. Follow-up *Batman: Arkham Origins* was developed by Warner Bros. Games Montréal, but the true sequel, *Batman: Arkham Knight*, is the work of original developers Rocksteady. *Arkham Knight*'s scheduled autumn 2014 release has been delayed until 2015.

▶▶FIRST FEMALE SUPERVILLAIN VIDEOGAME

Batman's feline foe became the first female supervillain to star in her own game with the release of *Catwoman* in 2004. It was based on the movie of the same name, which was an epic flop. The game didn't fare much better: it sold just 340,000 copies and was met with critical derision. GameSpot's critic described it as "shoddy".

▶▶FIRST BATMAN VILLAIN INTRODUCED IN A VIDEOGAME

The villainous Sin Tzu (below), from 2003 release *Batman: Rise of Sin Tzu*, was the first official Batman villain to be introduced in a videogame rather than via a comic book. The character was created by writer Flint Dille and artist Jim Lee, and DC Comics produced a promotional novel and toys to mark the event. However, Sin Tzu has rarely appeared in the comic series since. Pictured above is the mysterious figure of Arkham Knight, a villain created especially for the upcoming game of the same name. Rocksteady Director Sefton Hill says this new nemesis will "challenge Batman to go head to head with him in lots of different ways".

FIRST 3D REMASTER OF A CONSOLE GAME

In March 2010, less than a year after its original release, *Arkham Asylum* was re-issued and spruced up with additional 3D features. This "Game of the Year" edition supported stereoscopic 3D visuals using TriOviz 3D, which adds visual depth to images for those wearing 3D glasses.

FOR THE WIN

DETECTIVE CODE

In the huge open world of LEGO® Gotham in *LEGO Batman 2: DC Super Heroes* you're going to need help to find all 250 Gold Bricks. Enter the code **MBXW7V** in the Extras menu to become the World's Craftiest Detective. For more on LEGO, see pp.50–51.

MOST VOICEOVERS AS BATMAN

Kevin Conroy (USA) has the honour of donning the verbal cape and cowl more than 123 times across games, films and multiple animated series as of July 2014. Conroy starred as Batman in Rocksteady's *Arkham* trilogy, fighting game *Injustice: Gods Among Us* and *DC Universe Online*. He says: "The way I find the voice is to get into the psychology of the character. I kept getting darker and deeper and deeper in the sound." Kevin clearly has the "dark and broody" tone down to a T.

▶▶FIRST "CROSS-UNIVERSE" *BATMAN* VIDEOGAME

In addition to his numerous solo appearances, Batman has also crossed the rubicon and rubbed shoulders with legends from a different realm. *Mortal Kombat vs DC Universe*, released in 2008 for the Xbox 360 and PS3, was the first game in which Batman and other comic-book heroes fought against characters from outside their own fictional universe.

FASTEST COMPLETION OF *BATMAN: ARKHAM CITY*

Gamer "RoboSparkle" (UK) completed *Batman: Arkham City* in 1 hr 49 min 21 sec on 20 November 2013. This speed-run includes episodes with Catwoman (right), although RoboSparkle notes that "still about a minute can be taken off this time".

The **fastest completion of *Batman: Arkham Asylum*** is 1 hr 57 min 8 sec, achieved by Sean "DarthKnight" Grayson (USA) on 16 August 2012.

Summary: Inspired by 1988's *Wasteland* – with nods to the game throughout the series – Vault-dwelling players carry out quests in a post-apocalyptic America.

Publisher: Interplay/ Bethesda Softworks
Developer: Various
Debut: 1997

MOST POPULAR *FALLOUT: NEW VEGAS* MOD

Project Nevada had 14,289 endorsements as of 27 June 2014 on nexusmods.com. The coders were "snakster", "Kai Hohiro", "delamer", "T3T", "Zealotlee", "Yukichigai", "Gopher", "TheCastle", "x-quake", "Gribbleshnibit8", "Mezmorki" and "Pelinor".

FORD FUSION

The style of *Fallout*'s retro cars was inspired by concepts developed by Ford for nuclear-powered cars at the height of the nuclear age in the 1950s.

FASTEST COMPLETION OF *FALLOUT 2*

"ZombySpootchy" (France), aka Florent, recorded a single-segment completion of *Fallout 2* in 14 min 59 sec on 10 January 2014. A tip for anyone still stuck on their first run through the game is to head over to the Café of Broken Dreams in Junktown. There, a player can be reunited with Dogmeat, a four-legged companion of the main character.

RAREST SEVENTH-GENERATION CONSOLE RPG

In 2008, online retailer Amazon exclusively offered gamers a limited-edition *Fallout 3: Survival Edition*. The jam-packed set bundled the game with goodies that brought the game to life, featuring a version of the in-game stat display Pip-Boy 3000 (rendered as an alarm clock), a toy Vault Boy mascot and a Vault-Tec lunchbox. Alongside these were a *Making of Fallout 3* DVD and an art booklet. It's not known exactly how many units were produced, but by 2014 sealed versions were being snapped up by collectors for upwards of $700 (£400).

MOST LINES OF DIALOGUE IN A SINGLE-PLAYER RPG

Fallout: New Vegas has 65,000 lines of dialogue. Among them is series catchphrase, "War... war never changes," as voiced by game narrator and *Hellboy* actor Ron Perlman.

FASTEST COMPLETION OF *FALLOUT*

Devin Herron (USA) sped through the first *Fallout* in 9 min 19 sec, as verified by speeddemosarchive.com on 22 December 2005.

FASTEST-SELLING MULTI-PLATFORM RPG

Fallout 3 shipped over 4.7 million copies in its first week on sale in 2008.

FASTEST COMPLETION OF *FALLOUT 3*

Gamer "BubblesDelFuego" (USA) achieved an any-percentage completion of *Fallout 3* in 24 min 20 sec on 8 June 2014. Among the many techniques used to speed up the run-through is a subtle time-saving strategy called "slope jumping". Players can save those all-important seconds by timing uphill jumps in order to avoid being slowed down by walking the incline.

187

named locations in *Fallout: New Vegas* (188 with the "Wild Wasteland" trait), from Aerotech Park to Wolfhorn Ranch.

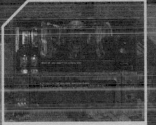

FASTEST SEGMENTED COMPLETION OF *FALLOUT*

Vault-dweller Jakub "Fex" Surma outplayed super mutants, deathclaws and the Master himself to complete *Fallout* in 6 min 54 sec on 22 July 2010. The run was completed in five segments and used exploits, knowledge of the land and luck to spare Vault 13 from doom.

MOST PROLIFIC DEVELOPER OF RPG SEQUELS

Obsidian (USA) has an impressive CV for developing sequels to other company's franchises, with four (*Star Wars: Knights of the Old Republic II – The Sith Lords; Neverwinter Nights 2; Fallout: New Vegas* and *Dungeon Siege III*).

MOST POPULAR *FALLOUT* FAN FILM

Wayside Creations' film *Nuka Break* had been viewed by 2,755,209 people on YouTube as of 1 July 2014, making it the most popular fan-made tribute to the post-apocalyptic series. The 16-minute short follows Vault 10 resident Twig with his companions Scarlett and ghoul Ben (above, Tybee Diskin and Aaron Giles) as they brave the wasteland's weird residents (including merchant Vic Mignogna, top) in search of a bottle of the rare – and refreshing! – Nuka Cola.

INSIDE THE DEVELOPMENT STUDIO

If you could have a dream job at a game developer, what role would it be? And how would you get there? Media Molecule, the studio made famous by *LittleBigPlanet* and *Tearaway*, opens its doors to GWR for an exclusive look behind the scenes. Here, their team share with us the inside secrets of how to break into the gaming industry...

THE COMPANY

Media Molecule was established in 2006 by Mark Healey, Kareem Ettouney, Alex Evans and David Smith. They met while working at Lionhead Studios, and left to create a prototype game they called *CraftWorld*, which was renamed *LittleBigPlanet* for its 2008 release.

"*LittleBigPlanet* will always have a special place in my heart," David Smith says. "I made the first prototype, the first level, the first version of Sackboy."

The team went on to release *LittleBigPlanet 2* in 2011, and a new game called *Tearaway* in 2013.

Media Molecule have won numerous awards, including eight BAFTAs and five Game Developer's Choice Awards.

DESIGNER

Working as a builder in construction is not the most obvious route into building games, but that was the path taken by Media Molecule designer John Beech: "I was very lucky to get my job in the games industry," he admits. "I have no formal qualifications at all. But in my spare time I created levels for *LittleBigPlanet*, which got me noticed." His approach to game design is similarly straightforward. "I think you have to be inspired by everyday things and have the imagination to turn them into something amazing," he says. "The key to it is very simple. When you have made something, ask yourself, 'Is it fun?' If the answer is 'Yes', you are almost there."

It's an attitude to design that has helped to make Media Molecule's deceptively uncomplicated games so inventive and compelling.

JOHN

TEARAWAY™

LittleBIGPlanet™

EVOLUTION OF SACKBOY

LittleBigPlanet was pitched to Sony in 2006. Among the artwork created in the early days were storyboards (top) and demo animations (main screenshot). As the concept was fleshed out, YellowHead turned into Sackboy (inset).

ARTIST

JON

Start-ups such as Media Molecule have always provided inspiration for would-be developers.

Artist Jon Eckersley started off as a fan himself: "I got into games by becoming active in the modding community. That formed the basis of my first portfolio," he says. "To get a role as an artist, you need to show you can deliver great artwork. I'm completely self-taught and I continually paint and draw in various mediums in my spare time, to try to better myself."

industry: "It sounds strange, but the best training for games is to make games!" he says. "Type 'game design' into a search engine: see where it takes you. "The secret is that it takes time and effort – you can't just have a cool idea and expect other people to make it for you. But the results are worth it."

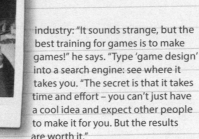

CO-FOUNDER

Dave

David Smith, one of Media Molecule's four founders, is direct about what you need to do to make a career for yourself out of the

NETWORK PROGRAMMER

Under the hood of any great game has to be the code to make social interaction possible. It's a key feature of *LBP* and any successful game in these times of social media.

Amy Phillips works on the network aspects, a role she admits "takes a certain sort of person to enjoy…" Amy is that person, knitting together multiple consoles, helping gamers upload high scores,

AMY

"basically anything involving sending packets over the internet and I'm in!" We've seen the disparate routes that others have taken, and hers is perhaps the most traditional: "I'd recommend a Computer Science course," she says. "Lots of practice coding is always useful, and game jams are great for meeting enthusiastic like-minded people and expanding your portfolio."

THE LITTLE PLANET THAT COULD
For more on the company's breakout hit, *LittleBigPlanet*, turn to pp.54–55.

AUDIO DESIGNER

ED

Any game design team will include one or more designers who focus solely on audio. At Media Molecule, Ed Hargrave is the man who makes the noise. "Most of the time I'm making interesting sound effects," he says, "and making sure they work correctly in the game." You'll never listen to a videogame soundtrack or effect in the same way if you want to do what he does, as you have to develop what he calls your "critical ear" before learning how to master the relevant programs.

"You'll need to learn all about audio production and middleware," advises Ed, "and always keep thinking about how different audio effects are implemented. Once you can make your own interesting sounds, talk to other people who are learning to develop their own games and work with them on a project."

PRODUCER

Michelle Ducker describes her work as "connecting the dots". This is a role for the truly organized, "keeping hold of the bigger picture, pulling together milestones and project goals, recruiting team members". The studio sustains a heavy workload to perfect its games.

MICHELLE

"Even when we have a big deadline, people really pull together and support each other," declares Michelle. "It's a wonderful, magical place full of inspiration, and everyone loves what they do."

COUNTDOWN

30–21

LONGEST MARATHON ON *WORLD OF WARCRAFT*

"Kinumi Cati", aka Hecaterina Kinumi Iglesias Pérez (Spain), played *World of Warcraft* for 29 hr 31 min on 29–30 March 2014, also the **longest marathon on an MMORPG**. She tells GWR: "I always wanted to become a singer and I also love videogames. To raise my profile among young people I thought I'd try to set some records for my gaming. My YouTube channel shows some of my singing performances and also reflects my passion for videogames and Japanese culture in general." For more on Hecaterina's marathon record attempts, turn to p.108.

UNCHARTED

Summary: Keeping up with the Indiana Joneses, Nathan Drake and virtual colleagues such as Lara Croft and Pitfall Harry have kept adventuring and treasure-hunting as ever-popular pastimes.

Publisher: Sony
Developer: Naughty Dog
Debut: 2007

BEST-SELLING PS3-EXCLUSIVE SERIES

Uncharted had sold 17.48 million copies across all three games, according to VGChartz as of 9 July 2014. The best-selling title in the series is *Uncharted 2: Among Thieves*, which has sold 6.39 million copies. *Uncharted 4: A Thief's End* is slated for release as an exclusive PS4 title in 2015.

FIRST PLAYER TO WIN A PLATINUM TROPHY IN *GOLDEN ABYSS*

Gamer "se250tr" lifted the Platinum Trophy in *Uncharted: Golden Abyss* on 20 December 2011, just three days after the game's release. The trophy is awarded to those players who have collected all the other trophies in the game – 55 in total. Only 15.55% have done so.

▶▶FASTEST-SELLING *TOMB RAIDER*

Series reboot *Tomb Raider* registered the franchise's highest week-one sales. Warmly received by critics, the game racked up global sales of 3.4 million during March 2013, making it the biggest new game of the year at that point.

BEST-SELLING PS VITA GAME

With 1.18 million copies sold worldwide, handheld spin-off *Uncharted: Golden Abyss* remains the PS Vita's best-selling game. The prequel to the main series has retained this record since 2012, proving the enduring popularity of Nathan Drake's adventures regardless of platform. On its release – as one of the first Vita titles – *Golden Abyss* was acclaimed as the **most advanced handheld platform game**, capable of displaying 260,000 on-screen polygons.

RAREST PS3 SPECIAL EDITION

All 200 copies of the "Fortune Hunter" edition of *Uncharted 2: Among Thieves* were prizes in a competition involving the multiplayer demo and a PS Home challenge. "Fortune Hunter" included an art book and a replica of the Phurba Dagger (below). Each edition was also signed by the Naughty Dog development team. Copies currently fetch around £2,000 ($3,500).

CROFT ALOFT

Tomb Raider was the series that redefined what action-adventures could be and Lara Croft far eclipses the fame of her *Uncharted* colleague in adventuring. At the height of her popularity in the 1990s, Lara advertised Lucozade on TV in the UK (when it became "Larazade"), featured on the cover of *The Face* and even appeared on stage with rock band U2, via giant video screens.

FIRST PS3 GAME TO OFFER A PLATINUM TROPHY

Sony added trophy support to its PlayStation Network in 2008. For the first time, PS3 gamers could gain virtual recognition of their gaming efforts, as Xbox players did with Achievements. In the summer of 2008, Naughty Dog patched *Drake's Fortune* to offer a platinum trophy – rarest of all – for obtaining all of the bronze, silver and gold trophies in a game. Every subsequent PS3 release has included this feature.

AVID AVI

Will we ever see Nathan Drake on the cinema screen? Avi Arad, producer of the *Spider-Man* films, hopes so. He's been trying to turn *Uncharted* into a blockbuster movie for years – and came close with a script that would have seen Mark Wahlberg playing Drake with Robert De Niro as Sully. That version fell apart and, in 2014, director Seth Gordon was given the directorial reins. In early 2014, Naughty Dog said that a cinematic version of *The Last of Us* (see pp.112–13) is also in the pipeline.

►►FASTEST PERFECT COMPLETION OF *PITFALL!*

Nathan Drake's ancestor is surely Pitfall Harry, the star of Atari's 1982 classic – a game unforgivingly difficult compared with *Uncharted*. That didn't stop Douglas Korekach (USA) from romping to 100% perfect completion on the NTSC version (Mode 1, Difficulty B) with three minutes of the game's 20-minute countdown to spare, on 2 August 2006.

FIRST TV REALITY SHOW WINNER FEATURED IN A VIDEOGAME

America's Next Top Model (USA, 2003–present) motion-captured its hopeful contestants with the help of Naughty Dog. Laura James (USA) won the episode, shown on 28 September 2012, and had her movements incorporated into *Uncharted 3* as the multiplayer taunt for the character of Elena. She also went on to win the entire TV series.

"I got interested in running the series due to a video featuring [the game director] Justin Richmond."

GREG INNES (UK) ON SPEED-RUNNING *UNCHARTED 3*

FASTEST COMPLETION OF *UNCHARTED 3*

On 4 November 2013, Greg "The Thrillness" Innes (UK) completed *Uncharted 3* (main image) in 2 hr 35 min 37 sec. His segmented run was carried out on "Very Easy" mode, since his approach required many fights to be avoided – a tactic that is impossible on higher difficulty settings.

"I got interested in running the series due to a video featuring [the game director] Justin Richmond," said Greg, "who talked about a speed-run by one of their testers in 3 hr 8 min. With *Uncharted 3* being close to its two-year anniversary – and with an advertised time to beat – I decided to run the third game in the series."

Summary: The zombie title that invented the sub-genre of survival horror continues to terrify and titillate in equal measure. Known as *Biohazard* in Japan, *RE* has also spawned eight films.

Publisher: Capcom
Developer: Capcom
Debut: 1996

MOST PROLIFIC SURVIVAL HORROR SERIES

With 30 titles released since its debut, *Resident Evil* just keeps on scaring us. The total includes eight games in the main series, 12 spin-offs and 10 mobile titles. The most recent edition is *Resident Evil 6*, pictured above. A new *Resident Evil* is slated for release in 2015, although a much-anticipated E3 2014 announcement never materialized.

MOST POPULAR FACEBOOK PAGE FOR A SURVIVAL HORROR GAME

Resident Evil's Facebook page hosted 5,873,892 fans, as of 12 June 2014 – the most for any survival horror game property on the social media site. The majority come from the USA, which contributes 25% of its community.

FOR THE WIN

FOLLOW THE HERB

Earn a free herb at the end of each "Raid" mode stage in *Resident Evil: Revelations* by attacking the BSAA emblem with a fully charged melee attack.

FIRST SURVIVAL HORROR GAME

There can be little doubt that *Resident Evil* is the survival horror supremo, largely because it is also its inventor. The term was invented by Capcom to describe the original game upon its release on 22 March 1996. It is common practice in Japan for fans or critics to coin a new genre name for a game, but in this case it was Capcom's own marketing team that came up with it. Luckily for them, it struck a chord with gamers and quickly became an established sub-genre. The first game to draw on horror and suspense in the way that later became associated with survival horror was Atari's *Haunted House* in 1982.

MOST NOVELS IN A GAMING FRANCHISE

Resident Evil has spawned more novelizations than any other videogame. Eighteen books have been published in total, with 13 novels based purely on the games and five based on the movies. Eight authors have penned the books. Pictured here is the novelization of the first *Resident Evil* film, written by Keith R A DeCandido and published in 2004 as a prequel to *Resident Evil: Apocalypse*.

▶▶ FIRST BAFTA AWARD FOR A SURVIVAL HORROR GAME

Undead classic *Left 4 Dead* carved a path for horror videogaming on 8 February 2009 when it became the first survival horror title to scoop a coveted BAFTA gaming award. The co-op zombie title won the award for "Best Multiplayer Game". Its sequel, *Left 4 Dead 2*, won in the same category the following year.

GOING IT ALONE

Fellow action-adventurer *Devil May Cry* began life as *Resident Evil 4* until Capcom deemed it to be too different from the series and more than capable of starting its own.

GREATEST AGGREGATE TIME PLAYING...

Game	Platform	Time	Gamer
Resident Evil 6	PS3	4,050 hr, 49 min	ryocha--n*
Resident Evil 6	PC	2,117 hr, 53 min	Nesbiandcie
Resident Evil 6	X360	3,893 hr, 23 min	Brutaldactyl
Resident Evil: Revelations	PS3	2,017 hr, 4 min	TOYOTACARINA1989
Resident Evil: Revelations	PC	1,246 hr, 31 min	umekichi
Resident Evil: Revelations	X360	2,660 hr, 24 min	NeGo x MaTriX**
Resident Evil: Revelations	Wii U	1,489 hr, 0 min	Sirius

All times correct as of 19 June 2014

* Also the overall record for **greatest aggregate time playing** *Resident Evil 6*
** Also the overall record for **greatest aggregate time playing** *Resident Evil: Revelations*

FASTEST COMPLETION OF *CODE: VERONICA* FOR PS3

Speedrunner "sshplur" charged through the Japanese PS3 version of *Resident Evil – Code: Veronica,* aka *Biohazard – Code: Veronica,* in 1 hr 41 min 14 sec on 19 February 2013.

RISE AND SHINING

The pre-rendered backdrops in the first *Resident Evil*'s mansion setting were inspired by Stanley Kubrick's movie adaptation of Stephen King's novel *The Shining.*

MOST KILLS ON *RESIDENT EVIL: REVELATIONS*

PS3 gamer "yogomesu" set the record for the most recorded kills in *Resident Evil: Revelations* across all platforms, with a mighty grand total of 895,621. This gives yogomesu the *Revelations* record for the **most kills on the PS3**, too. Gamer "NeGo x MaTriX" has the **most kills on *Resident Evil: Revelations* for the Xbox 360**, with 854,316.

BEST-SELLING SURVIVAL HORROR SERIES

Since rising from Capcom's virtual crypt in 1996, the *Resident Evil* series has sold 56.65 million copies across all platforms – including almost every gaming console released in the last two decades. Its most popular chapter, *Resident Evil 5*, is the **best-selling survival horror game** of all time, with 8.39 million units sold.

> "It's never not great fun. It's funny too. The dialogue sounds like it was written by Japanese men that learned their English from repeated viewings of *Commando,* so essentially it's still the best-written game ever"

DANIEL CAIRNS ON *RE4 ULTIMATE HD EDITION*
NOW GAMER

ALIEN GAMES

The 1979 sci-fi horror masterpiece *Alien* (USA/UK), Ridley Scott's "haunted house in space", brought creeping horror into space and thrilled audiences worldwide. The movie and its sequels have gone on to become a massively influential creative force in the world of videogames.

There were 32 titles based on *Alien* between 1982 and 2013, from *Alien* – on the Atari 2600 – all the way up to the infamously disappointing *Aliens: Colonial Marines* (see far right).

Due in late 2014, *Alien: Isolation* is a first-person horror game very much informed by the 1979 movie and is being described as one of the most immersive and terrifying of the big-screen translations.

Over the years, we've seen *PAC-Man* clones, side-scrolling blasters, first-person shooters and even a point-and-click adventure in *Aliens: A Comic Book Adventure* for PC in 1995. Developed by UK-based studio Creative Assembly – known

primarily for their *Total War* strategy games – *Isolation* is a brooding, measured game of cat-and-mouse between the player and the acid-drooling terror that debuted on the *Nostromo* back in 1979 and picked off Ripley's crewmates with merciless efficiency.

Strikingly, there's no gun occupying the lower half of the screen, just the trembling arms of Amanda

BEHIND THE MASK

H R Giger won an Oscar for Best Visual Effects in 1980 as part of the team who worked on *Alien*, particularly for his design of the xenomorph. The artist's signature surrealist style also graced the artwork of album covers and he opened his own museum, but the nightmarish central figure of the Alien has endured as the creation for which Hans Rudolf Giger will always be known.

Ripley, otherwise known as the daughter of the famous xenomorph survivor. She navigates the abandoned *Sevastopol* space station with only a flashlight, a motion tracker and a

painfully sharp awareness of her mortality for company. This is a premise that harnesses the strengths of the original film – the tension, the claustrophobic setting and the feeling of being ill-equipped to take on the perfect predator. But the guns-free approach is surprisingly fresh in the extensive history of games inspired by *Alien*.

SCARY MONSTERS

Most successful takes on the licence centred on attacks by xenomorphs – lots and lots of xenomorphs. These games were action-oriented, andrenaline-charged affairs that featured stylistic elements of the movies more as dressing. The 8-bit sprites found in *Aliens: The*

"WHAT KIND OF THING?"

"I like to combine human beings, creatures and biomechanics," said H R Giger of the art that gave birth to one of the most frightening creatures in cinema and gaming. Fast, merciless and hard to kill, the xenomorph is an awesome enemy for any player, and has found its way into a number of Alien-themed games...

1986

Aliens: The Computer Game: The Activision adventure version of the James Cameron movie tie-in.

1993

Alien 3: The movie is claustrophobic while the game goes for an all-guns-blazing action approach.

1996

Alien Trilogy: A *Doom*-influenced shooter that utilizes elements from the first three *Alien* movies.

the pulse rifles and S.M.A.R.T. guns from the 1986 movie sequel, and there were legions of xenos to use them on. *AvP* ticked all these boxes. It didn't make much of an attempt to spin a cinematic yarn – in fact, it barely had a narrative at all – but it absolutely nailed the atmosphere. Bravely, it let you play as either Predator or Alien and, while it was somewhat uneven playing across the different characters, none of the *Alien* games that came after it did a better job.

SPACE ODDITY

After the disappointment of *Colonial Marines, Alien: Isolation* wisely resisted the allure of pulse-rifle

machismo and departed from the FPS genre. Instead, the latest *Alien* is a game of hide-and-seek stretching over an agonizing, exhilarating single-player game powered by a next-gen engine. In July 2014, Creative Assembly announced two bonus missions set during the time of the original movie, one of which features Sigourney Weaver reprising Ellen Ripley.

Gaming has now reached a level of technical and narrative achievement that means the atmosphere of the big screen – and big-screen aliens – can terrify on consoles and PCs without losing something in translation.

Computer Game followed the narrative beats of James Cameron's bombastic *Aliens* (USA, 1986) movie to the letter and gave way to more impressive 16-bit sprites in *Alien 3* and the fully 3D polygonal beasts lurking in *Aliens Versus Predator* and *Alien: Resurrection.*

LOVING THE ALIEN

In later games, xenomorph graphics began to resemble their cinematic inspiration in detail (in sound, too: *AvP*'s xenos let out blood-curdling shrieks as they clambered walls and ceilings with feline agility) and *Alien* titles formed a recognizable genre of their own. Levels were darkly lit – harking back to the H R Giger movie sets – weapons included

LOST IN SPACE

Gearbox Software's *Aliens: Colonial Marines* scored just 37.91% on GameRankings, as of 28 July 2014, making it the **worst-rated sci-fi shooter** – as low a point for the licence as *Aliens Versus Predator* had been a high. Texas-based Gearbox spent five years creating authentically cinematic immersion, acquiring original sound effects and a musical score as well as the blueprints of movie sets. But bugs, AI problems and poor level design plagued the game.

1999

Aliens Versus Predator: The PC version of the game allows players to be Alien, Predator or Colonial Marine.

2000

Alien: Resurrection: The tie-in with the fourth film in the series, this tense game is let down by a difficult control system.

2013

Aliens: Colonial Marines: The *Alien* story is continued some weeks after the events depicted in *Alien 3*.

2014 (TBC)

Alien: Isolation: Ripley's daughter takes centre stage in this game set in 2137 – with a cameo by her famous mum.

BIOSHOCK

Summary: There are three main titles in this highly acclaimed alternative-history FPS series. *BioShock* takes place in 1960; *BioShock 2* picks up the story in 1968; *BioShock Infinite* jumps back to 1912.

Publisher: 2K Games
Developer: 2K Marin, 2K Boston, Irrational Games
Debut: 2007

ATLAS DUBBED

Rapture founder and *BioShock* antagonist Andrew Ryan's name was inspired by Ayn Rand, author of the 1957 novel *Atlas Shrugged*, which served as inspiration for the *BioShock* series. Both Ryan and Rand were originally from Russia, but moved to the USA to avoid Communism. Just like Rand in her novel, Ryan starts a city to put his beliefs into action.

HIGHEST SCORE IN *CLASH IN THE CLOUDS*

BioShock Infinite's *Clash in the Clouds* DLC challenges players to survive waves of enemies in four game-inspired arenas. As of 15 July 2014, Kenny "klambake7" Jossick (USA) held the highest cumulative score for all four areas, with 1,136,751 points on the PlayStation 3 version. "Emporia Arcade" is the fourth and final arena challenge in *Clash in the Clouds*. As of the same date, Kenny also had the **highest score in Emporia Arcade**, with 908,225 points.

RAREST TROPHY IN *BIOSHOCK INFINITE* FOR PS3

As of 22 April 2014, only 1.8% of *BioShock Infinite* players on the PS3 had been able to collect the "Scavenger Hunt" trophy (pictured above) – the game's gold reward for beating its "1999 Mode" without buying a health kit, salts, lockpick or ammunition magazine from the game's Dollar Bill vending machines.

FASTEST COMPLETION OF *BIOSHOCK*

Jacob "FearfulFerret" Krause (USA) has completed *BioShock* faster than any other gamer. On 5 February 2014, Jacob brought revolution to the underwater city of Rapture in just 48 min 57 sec on the PC version of the game, meaning that he also holds the record for the **fastest completion of *BioShock* on PC**.

631

miles of code floating inside *BioShock Infinite*.

▶▶FIRST GAME TO USE AUDIO LOGS

Before *BioShock*, there was Irrational's *System Shock 2*. Something of a precursor to the *BioShock* games, it was the first title to use audio logs as its main narrative device. These logs were hidden throughout the game and contained important clues as to the Von Braun spaceship's hellish past. Audio logs became a huge component of the *BioShock* games.

SECRET SONG

BioShock Infinite's "The Fraternal Order of the Raven" area contains an ambient soundtrack that, when recorded and sped up to eight times its original speed, reveals a hidden song. Fans are still debating the lyrics, but everyone agrees it's spooky.

MOST POPULAR *BIOSHOCK* FAN ART

The *BioShock* series has proven an inspiration for artists across the globe. On deviantART, the internet's leading fan-art site, Australian artist Patrick Brown's piece "BioShock Infinite" had earned a record 10,764 "favourites" from the online community as of 22 April 2014.

SHOCK ROCK

Keep your ears pricked up in *BioShock Infinite* for old-time versions of songs from the Beach Boys, Soft Cell, Creedence Clearwater Revival, Cyndi Lauper, R.E.M. and Tears for Fears.

▶▶FASTEST COMPLETION OF *SYSTEM SHOCK*

System Shock was one of the first videogames to blend first-person shooting with role-playing mechanics. Dmitry "KhanFusion" K completed the game in just 27 min 31 sec on 23 August 2012.

In 1997, some of the team at developers Looking Glass Studios went on to form Irrational Games. In February 2014, co-founder and creative director Ken Levine announced that Irrational was shutting down and that *BioShock* will be the responsibility of 2K Games.

FOR THE WIN

CODE IT LIKE IT'S 1999

Unlock *BioShock Infinite*'s "1999 Mode" from the start by entering the legendary Konami Code on the main screen: Up, Up, Down, Down, Left, Right, Left, Right (PS3); B / O, A / X (X360). Warning: only experts need apply. The infamous "1999 Mode" is named after the year *System Shock 2* was released.

MOST AUDIO LOGS IN A MULTIPLAYER MODE

In addition to the 129 audio diaries scattered throughout *BioShock 2*'s single-player campaign, the multiplayer mode contains 30 additional audio diaries that can be unlocked and played in the player's apartment as they increase in rank. The logs are the main narrative device of the *BioShock* series, recorded by the citizens of Rapture.

MOST E3 AWARDS

The third title in the series, *BioShock Infinite* won a triumphant 75 editorial awards at E3 2011 in Los Angeles, USA. Among its impressive haul were 39 "Game of the Show" gongs, including the top award of "Game Critics Awards' Best of Show". *Infinite* is set in a dystopian, fictional American city in 1912, where nationalist white supremacists rule with terror. Pictured here are Elizabeth and a Little Sister from *Burial at Sea – Episode 2*, DLC for *Infinite* that was released in March 2014.

Summary: This open-world shooter series has taken players on a tour of the world's most exotic and remote locations and allows them to become a different protagonist each time.

Publisher: Ubisoft
Developer: Crytek/ Ubisoft
Debut: 2004

OPEN WORLD...

Far Cry stands out from other FPS series, with its expansive environments and the opportunities it offers to peel off from the main story to engage in side missions or explore the terrain. While genre-crushers such as *Grand Theft Auto* are very familiar, here we trace the seeds of open-world gaming...

1979: *Adventure* is the **first action-adventure game**. The player character, although only depicted by a simple square cursor, explores a multiscreen landscape.

1981: *Ultima I: The First Age of Darkness* (right and below left) introduces the tiled graphics that would become a staple of the genre. It is widely hailed for its scope and scale.

1984: *Elite* is the **first open-world game**, featuring a wire-frame universe of political systems, trading routes and space stations.

2008: *Far Cry 2* and its Dunia engine create dynamic weather systems in a sprawling 50-km^2 (19-sq-mi) African landscape setting.

2015 (tbc): Indie game *No Man's Sky* is set in an infinite, procedurally generated universe. Planets and solar systems are "built" as you explore and each is different, with flora and fauna that includes space dinosaurs.

MOST PROLIFIC VIDEOGAME FRANCHISE MOVIE DIRECTOR

Including *Far Cry* (Germany, 2008), German director Uwe Boll has directed 10 films based (in many cases loosely) on a videogame, including *House of the Dead* (USA, 2003) and two sets of trilogies (from the *BloodRayne* and *Dungeon Siege* series). Boll's enthusiasm for the games industry, it is fair to note, has not been entirely reciprocated. "Boll seems blind to his own weaknesses as a director," said IGN of *Far Cry*, while *Postal* (Germany, 2007) was nominated for three Golden Raspberry Awards, including Boll himself as Worst Supporting Actor. He won for Worst Director. In 2009, Boll won a Worst Career Achievement from the Razzies, one of only five recipients of the "honour" (including "Bruce" the rubber shark from *Jaws*) since the awards' inception in 1980. The Golden Raspberry citation dubbed Uwe Boll "Germany's answer to Ed Wood".

FOR THE WIN

THE LOST HOLLYWOOD STAR

A live-action web series, *The Far Cry Experience*, was released in 2012 to accompany the games. A nod to it appears as a *Far Cry 3* Easter egg, "The lost Hollywood star", located on a beach in one of the northern islands. Head for coordinates X: 620.6, Y: 557.8 and look for two bodies hanging on a tree. Nearby you will find a man buried in the sand up to his neck. Interacting with the head activates the "Say 'Hi' to the internet" achievement.

FASTEST 100% COMPLETION OF *FAR CRY 3: BLOOD DRAGON*

On 23 August 2013, gamer "ZanderGothSRL" completed *Blood Dragon* in 1 hr 27 min 30 sec. The same player set the **fastest any-percentage completion of *Far Cry 3: Blood Dragon***, with a time of 47 min, on 21 June 2013. A futuristic thriller played at breakneck speed, *Blood Dragon* was a standalone game of 2013 using the same engine and riffing on the title of the previous year's *Far Cry 3* (main picture).

FASTEST DOWNLOADED FREE SDK

Crytek's own CryEngine was used for creating such games as the original *Far Cry* and entries in fellow FPS series *Crysis* (see right). In August 2011, a free version of the CryEngine software development kit (SDK) was made available by the developer and clocked up 108,462 downloads in its first six days online.

10,700,000
copies of the Far Cry series sold as of July 2014.

WORST-RATED WII VIDEOGAME

The astonishing graphics that were such a part of what made the *Far Cry* series a hit on the PC were not to be repeated on Nintendo's Wii. Despite good use of the Wii Remote, *Far Cry: Vengeance* only earned a 37.71% GameRankings score.

Crysis is a first-person shooter set in the year 2020. It was regarded highly enough by *PC Gamer* to be recognized as their Game of the Year and Action Game of the Year in 2008. Speed demon Yuri Zarubin, aka "xsite", raced through the PC version of *Crysis* on its hardest difficulty setting in a 42-min 14-sec segmented speed-run on 10 April 2010.

Yuri also achieved the **fastest completion of *Crysis: Warhead*** by making it through the game's Warhead expansion pack in a mere 26 min 59 sec on 16 August 2010.

FASTEST COMPLETION OF *FAR CRY*

On 20 January 2006, gamer Vladimir "Knu" Semenov finished the first *Far Cry* in the series in a 21-segment run lasting 1 hr 7 min 2 sec. The origins of the game was work on *X-Isle: Dinosaur Island*, created by developer Crytek to demonstrate the capabilities of NVIDIA's GeForce 3 series of graphics processing units (GPU).

"It refreshes the whole ecosystem, so we have different plants and different animals... it just gives us new opportunities that a tropical island didn't."

MARK THOMPSON, FAR CRY 4 NARRATIVE DIRECTOR, ON THE GAME'S "HIMALAYAN" SETTING

MICHAEL MANDO

Far Cry 3 used performance-capture technology for its characters, recording full body, face and vocals simultaneously. Vaas Montenegro, the game's antagonist who captures lead character Jason and his friends, was *Far Cry 3*'s poster character and his "Did I ever tell you the definition of insanity?" monologue won a 2013 Golden Joystick Award for Best Gaming Moment. Michael Mando, who voiced Vaas, initially auditioned for a different character but Ubisoft were so impressed by him that they created Vaas instead and based his likeness on the Canadian actor.

Summary: This PlayStation-exclusive feast of Greek mythology and awesome combat is led by a blade-wielding Spartan called Kratos. There are seven titles in the series.

Publisher: Sony/Capcom
Developer: SCE Santa Monica Studio
Debut: 2005

FIRST HD REMAKE OF A PLATFORM SERIES

In November 2009, Sony re-released the two PS2 *God of War* games for PS3, giving both games a high-def makeover. The success of this release led Sony to continue supporting HD re-releases under the banner "Classics HD". The second series to get the HD treatment was the much-loved *Sly Trilogy* platformer series.

Released on the PS3 in September 2011, the *God of War Collection Volume II* (*God of War Origins Collection* in the USA) included fully remastered versions of Kratos' two PSP adventures, *God of War: Chains of Olympus* and *God of War: Ghost of Sparta*. This made it the **first PSP game remastered in HD with trophy support.**

BEST-SELLING PLAYSTATION-EXCLUSIVE ACTION-ADVENTURE SERIES

The *God of War* series has had sales of 22.76 million since the original hacked-and-slashed on to the PlayStation 2. *God of War III* has been purchased by one in every 15 PS3 owners.

BEST-SELLING PS3 HACK AND SLASH VIDEOGAME

God of War III stands tallest among its hacking and slashing competitors on the PlayStation 3, selling more than 4.67 million copies as of 16 June 2014. The critically acclaimed sequel is the best-selling chapter in the series (see left).

MESSAGE FROM ABOVE

Beat *God of War* on "God Mode" and you'll receive a phone number to a pre-recorded message to hear Kratos praising the gamer's ability and revealing the fate of Ares.

GREATEST AGGREGATE TIME PLAYING *GOD OF WAR: ASCENSION*

Gamer "milliejacqueson" (USA) had played *Ascension* for 1,326 hr 30 min as of 25 March 2014. That equates to just over 55 days of warring. *Ascension* is a prequel to the series, set in an alternative version of ancient Greece.

SCREEN GOD

A *God of War* movie was announced in 2005 with US director Brett Ratner signed up to direct. Ratner has since left the $150-million (£90-million) project, but writers Patrick Melton and Marcus Dunstan still plan to bring Kratos to moviegoers in a suitably epic way.

HIGHEST SCORE ON *GOD OF WAR: ASCENSION*

Gamer "Rudda-Johnny2011" (UK) has earned the most XP in *God of War: Ascension*, with a hefty total of 10,941,690 XP as of 24 March 2014. Rudda also holds the record for the **most multiplayer kills in *Ascension***, with a total of 75,700 victims falling by his blades.

HIGHEST KILL-TO-DEATH RATIO ON *GOD OF WAR: ASCENSION*

Turkish gamer "jackaliso" holds the highest kill-to-death (K/D) ratio in *Ascension*, with a score of 8.8 from 9,448 kills and 1,080 deaths. The K/D ratio represents the average kills achieved per single death.

FASTEST COMPLETION OF *GOD OF WAR*

Philip "ballofsnow" Cornell completed the original *God of War* in 2 hr 16 min 23 sec on 4 April 2006. Philip raised the bar not only by blazing through the game in record time, but also by doing it on "God Mode", the game's most difficult level. The **fastest completion of *God of War II*** was by gamer "shenminiu", aka Li Lihong, in 3 hr 7 mins 25 sec. The record was set over 38 segments on the sequel's notorious "Titan" difficulty mode on 21 December 2007.

DAVID JAFFE
Creator, *God of War*

What was your initial vision?
I wanted our team to make a truly cinematic adventure that made players feel the same way they did as kids watching those epic, high-adventure movies like *Clash of the Titans* or *Raiders of the Lost Ark*. There was a real desire to create a game that tapped into that gut-level, animalistic rage and energy.

How much of Kratos' story did you know going into the first game?
We knew his core story, and we planted seeds for who he was and where he was going. If you go into the first game and look at the art on the walls, you can see how we were planning to explore his confrontation with Zeus, and then later the downfall of other old religions. But at the same time we were very much honed in on making one, awesome stand-alone game.

What makes Kratos such an iconic and lasting character?
He's always been in the hands of really technically talented people. Every time players see him on screen, they know there's going to be a great tour de force of graphics and gameplay technology. On top of that, I believe people generally have an animalistic side, so whenever you see someone really embracing that, and going to town with a devil-may-care attitude, it's very appealing.

What's your favourite boss battle in the series?
I really enjoyed the Hydra. It was the first boss we created and it was the first moment we saw all the pieces come together and really express how badass Kratos can be. I remember watching people test that part. When they realized they could go inside this dead creature's body and retrieve the key, I loved seeing that.

FOE PAS

A trophy for *Ascension* named "Bros before Hos" was renamed "Bros before Foes" in response to criticism. The trophy can be unlocked by dispatching one of the three female Furies in a rather gruesome manner.

Summary: World soccer is packed with fierce rivalry and in videogames the big match is *FIFA* vs *Pro Evo Soccer*. *FIFA* may be winning now, but *PES* and other underdogs have dedicated fanbases.

Publisher: Konami
Developer: Konami
Debut: 1996

MOST WIDELY DISTRIBUTED SOCCER VIDEOGAME SERIES

As of July 2014, the *Pro Evolution Soccer* series had been localized into 19 languages and sold in 62 countries. This compares with 18 languages and 51 countries for its *FIFA* nemesis.

LAST GAME RELEASED FOR THE PLAYSTATION 2

Sony discontinued production of the PS2 in January 2013, after a 12-year run – one of the longest for any console. *PES 2014* was released on 8 November 2013, the 3,870th and final release on the PS2 and a welcome epilogue for those who didn't have access to the latest consoles.

▶▶MOST CONSECUTIVE WEEKS AT NO.1 IN THE PC GAME CHARTS

Gamers who are more happy buying players than running around the pitch won't be surprised that *Football Manager 2014* took the top slot in the PC charts for 18 weeks in the UK. Its run ended on 4 March 2014.

FIRST REFEREE ON A VIDEOGAME COVER

Italian referee Pierluigi Collina was featured in the artwork for *PES 3* and its follow-up, although not in the games themselves. Widely respected, he refereed the World Cup final between Brazil and Germany in 2002.

MOST APPEARANCES ON DIFFERENT SOCCER SERIES FRONT COVERS

The rivalry between *FIFA* and *Pro Evo* extends to their cover stars. Barcelona forward Lionel Messi appeared on the front of *PES 2009*, *PES 2010* and *PES 2011* before EA Sports poached the iconic Argentinian, winner of the Golden Ball as best player of the 2014 World Cup. Messi made his first appearance on *FIFA Street* in 2012 before being featured on the covers of *FIFA 13* and *FIFA 14*.

▶▶LARGEST ONLINE SOCCER MANAGER VIDEOGAME

Soccer has even reached the world of MMOs in the shape of *Hattrick*, in which the player runs a football team via a web browser. The 1997 game has dropped in popularity from its high of 1 million players (the **largest online football manager game ever**) but still retains a base of some 400,000 users.

▶▶MOST TWITTER FOLLOWERS FOR AN ATHLETE

As of 14 July 2014, Cristiano Ronaldo (Portugal, @Cristiano), the face of *PES*, had 27,842,405 followers, putting him top of twitaholic.com. Ronaldo also boasts the **most Champions League goals scored in a calendar year**, with 15 while playing for Real Madrid from 13 February to 10 December 2013, beating Messi's mark of 13.

FIRST VIRTUAL UEFA CHAMPIONS LEAGUE COMPETITION

In February 2014, Konami and UEFA announced a virtual Champions League competition in Europe – the first of its kind. By the end of the season, after a World Finals day for the top *PES* players on 2 July, the best gamers were rewarded from a prize pot totalling €25,000 (£20,585; US$34,620) and memorabilia. The overall winner – Anastasios "apolytosarxon" Pappas representing Greece – took €15,000 (£11,870; US$20,170) and also received Champions League match tickets.

1,000
players recreated with individual animations within *PES 2015*.

►►LARGEST SOCCER GAME DATABASE

While *PES* scores on action, the success of the *Football Manager* series is undoubtedly based on its realism. As of March 2014, the database contained 578,530 entries, 246,437 of which related to players actively contracted to a club. The data is spread across 2,250 soccer clubs, 116 divisions and 51 countries.

►►HIGHEST SCORE ON *FLICK SOCCER! HD*

What tablet footy lacks in sophistication it makes up for in top-scoring satisfaction. Patrick Sinner (Germany) logged on to GWR's Challengers website to record his tally of 8,885,970 points with Full Fat's fun *Flick Soccer! HD* on 23 February 2014.

►►FIRST SOCCER GAME WITH SIDE-ON VIEWPOINT

It's hard to imagine how *PES* would look from above, so established is the "stadium" view. Mattel's *NASL Soccer* on the Atari 2600 was the first to use side-on scrolling in 1979. The **first top-down perspective soccer game** was 1980's *Championship Soccer* aka *Pelé's Soccer*, which featured four-a-side matches on the 2600.

WHO ARE YA?

PES can trace its lineage back to *Goal Storm* in 1996 and perhaps even further – the first *International Superstar Soccer* was released by Konami in 1994 on the SNES. *International Superstar Soccer Pro Evolution 2* was the last before the series took its current name.

LONGEST MARATHON ON A *PRO EVOLUTION SOCCER* VIDEOGAME

Marco Ramos and Efraim Ie (both Portugal) played *PES 2012* for 38 hr 49 min 13 sec at the Aleqro Alfragide shopping centre in Lisbon, Portugal, on 18–20 November 2011. This was later surpassed by the **longest marathon on a sports videogame**, set by Jordan Bloemen and Scott Francis Winder (both Canada) on EA's *FIFA 12*. Their charity attempt lasted for just over two full days – 48 hr 5 min – at the West Edmonton Mall in Alberta, Canada, on 6–8 August 2012.

►►MOST EXPENSIVE SOCCER VIDEOGAME

The major soccer series with their yearly cycles can never hope to become collectors' items. Not so *The Ultimate 11: SNK Football Championship*. The 1996 game was released in arcades and had a limited run on the expensive Neo Geo home console – and there are said to be only 10 known copies of the game in existence. One of those was reported to have been auctioned for $10,000 (£6,370) on eBay.

FOR THE WIN

IMPROVE THE MAP

Are you struggling to see what's happening on the overhead view section of *PES* when the action is taking place on the edge of the pitch? You can select a translucent pitch diagram in the game's settings.

PES 2014 – **the last ever game released for the PS2 console.**

SPORTS ROUND-UP

There are almost as many different kinds of sports videogames as there are real-life equivalents. From the most ultra-realistic depiction of athletic prowess to the button-bashing or remote-waving party games, it's hard not to find something you like. Here, we look at some of the all-time classics across a range of sports.

BEST-SELLING ICE HOCKEY GAME

A 26-year-old game without "NHL" in its name takes top spot in ice hockey. *Ice Hockey* was released by Nintendo in 1988 and had sold 2.42 million copies as of 11 July 2014. It was re-released for Wii in 2006 and Wii U in 2013.

FIRST FEMALE CHARACTER IN A HOCKEY GAME

Lexi Peters (USA) was a young hockey player who wrote to EA in 2011 to complain about the lack of female representation in the franchise. In response EA ended up creating a character around her in *NHL 12*.

LONGEST-RUNNING ICE HOCKEY SERIES

There have been 25 editions of EA's *NHL* series between 1991 and 2013's *NHL 14*. A new entry was due in 2014.

FIRST OFFICIAL OLYMPICS GAME

Olympic Gold for the Mega Drive/Genesis was the game of the 1992 Barcelona Olympics and featured three difficulty levels for seven sports, including swimming, hammer throw, hurdles and archery. Its success prompted publisher US Gold to develop a sequel, the **first official Winter Olympics videogame**, *Winter Olympics: Lillehammer '94*.

BEST-SELLING WINTER OLYMPICS VIDEOGAME

Mario & Sonic at the Olympic Winter Games has sold 7.87 million copies. By comparison, Sega's other 2009 Winter Olympics title – *Vancouver 2010* – struggled to make a dent against the dynamic duo, with sales of just 500,000 copies.

BEST-SELLING VIDEOGAME

With 82.03 million copies sold as of July 2014, *Wii Sports* is a gaming monster. As the best-selling game overall, it's by default also the **best-selling sports game** and the **best-selling Wii game**. But the package of sports, including bowling, above, has always been something of a sales quirk. Although popular, its huge sales largely account from *Wii Sports* being bundled with the 100-million-selling Wii console (see below right).

LONGEST-RUNNING SPORTS VIDEOGAME SERIES

Over 26 years, EA has released 30 *Madden NFL* games. The 2013 edition broke with the chronological titling convention to celebrate its quarter-century with *Madden NFL 25*. More than 40 million people voted for the release's artwork star, the **most votes for a videogame cover**. Former Detroit Lions running-back Barry Sanders (USA) made the grade, with 58% of the vote. The series is set to make a return to its regular naming system with *Madden NFL 15* in 2014 (main picture).

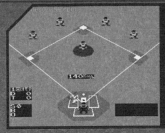

BEST-SELLING BASEBALL GAME

Simple by name and – having been released back in 1983 – simple by comparison with today's advanced sports sims, Nintendo's *Baseball* sold 3.2 million copies, according to VGChartz. In 1985, the game made it from Japan to the USA to form one of the raft of launch titles for the NES. Players could only pitch and bat – all fielding was done by the console.

LAST RETAIL DREAMCAST RELEASE

The Dreamcast remained popular among its fanbase of gaming enthusiasts after it was discontinued in North America in 2001. No surprise, then, that games continued to be made. *NHL 2K2* was released on 14 February 2002 as the last commercial release but non-retail games are still written today.

MOST APPEARANCES ON A VIDEOGAME SERIES COVER

Tiger Woods (USA) featured on 16 game covers, from *Tiger Woods PGA Tour 99* in 1998 through to the final release in the **most prolific golf videogame series**, *Tiger Woods PGA Tour 14*, in 2013. The runner-up is John Madden, who appeared on 14 covers in the *Madden NFL* franchise (see facing page). Woods himself has set the **highest annual earnings for an athlete**, with an estimated $78 m (£51 m) between 2012–13, according to Forbes. Out on the courses, his records include the **most PGA Player of the Year awards won by an individual golfer**, with 11 from 1997 to 2013, and the **youngest winner of the US Masters**, achieved at the age of 21 years 104 days in 1997.

FIRST TENNIS VIDEOGAME

There are basic graphics and then there are oscilloscope displays – normally used only to measure voltage signals. But back in 1958, that's all American physicist William Higinbotham had to render his *Tennis for Two* at the Brookhaven National Laboratory in New York City, USA. Unlikely to give PS4 designers sleepless nights, the game was painstakingly recreated for the laboratory's 50th birthday in 1997, three years after its author's death. The 39 years between versions make for the **longest time between an original game and remake**.

FIRST OFFICIAL MLB PLAYERS ASSOCIATION BASEBALL GAME

The 1990 title *R.B.I. Baseball* hit a home run with its Major League Baseball Players Association (MLBPA) licence. However, it struck out without an MLB licence, meaning that the game had player names but not team nicknames or logos.

LONGEST CAREER AS A BASEBALL GAME DEVELOPER

Don Daglow (USA) wrote an interactive baseball game, *Computer Baseball*, at college in 1971. He was involved in a Kickstarter campaign for a new baseball title in 2012 and remains active in the industry – 43 years after his first title.

BEST-SELLING SPORTS VIDEOGAME (NON-CONSOLE-BUNDLED)

Wii Fit has sold 22.69 million units, putting it in third place overall behind bundled games *Wii Sports* (see opposite) and *Wii Sports Resort* (32.37 million). The top 10 is dominated by Wii titles, which take the first six places.

Summary: If there's something strange in your medieval neighbourhood, the Witchers are on the case, with action-packed quests that have a dedicated fanbase.

Publisher: Atari/Various
Developer: CD Projekt RED
Debut: 2007

FOR THE WIN

ASSASSIN BONUS

Altair from the *Assassin's Creed* series (see pp.152–53) makes a cameo in *The Witcher 2*. You can find him lying face-down in a hay bale at La Valette Castle. Spotting him will net Geralt an "Assassin" bonus, granting 25% more damage when attacking enemies from behind.

MOST CRITICALLY ACCLAIMED GAME BASED ON A BOOK SERIES

The Witcher 2: Assassins of Kings for PC has a GameRankings score of 87.97%, based on 48 reviews. *The Witcher* novels are set within a fantasy world created by Polish author Andrzej Sapkowski (above). There are six saga novels and two anthologies of short stories translated into 15 languages to date.

THE LAST
WISH
INTRODUCING
THE WITCHER
ANDRZEJ SAPKOWSKI

23,000
lines of dialogue in *The Witcher 2*.

HIGHEST SCORE IN *THE WITCHER 2: ENHANCED EDITION* ("ARENA" MODE)

Steam champion "Falleny" had scored 2,147,430,639 points in "Arena" mode as of 25 July 2014. Trailing just one point behind was "Follen [Piero F.]". The Arena was added to *The Witcher 2: Assassins of Kings* after its initial release. The challenge for gamers in the Arena is to prove their might in gladiatorial combat in a Northern Kingdoms town.

MOST DIFFICULT ACHIEVEMENT IN *THE WITCHER 2: ENHANCED EDITION* FOR PC

Only 0.4% of PC players have unlocked the "Madman" achievement in *Assassins of Kings* – and no wonder. The achievement involves beating the game on the "Insane" difficulty level.

MOST DOWNLOADED MOD FOR *THE WITCHER 2: ASSASSINS OF KINGS*

The *"Witcher 2* Full Combat Rebalance" has been downloaded 48,781 times on game-modification site Nexusmods. CD Projekt RED itself created the project to improve everything from the game's visuals, effects and combat balance to its in-game mechanics. Effectively an update to the game, it was released as a mod instead. It's also the **most endorsed mod for *The Witcher 2***, having received the thumbs-up 1,397 times from the Nexusmods community.

> "I confess, I'm not very good at videogames, but I've been told that it is a great example of Poland's place in the new global economy."
>
> **BARACK OBAMA,** US PRESIDENT, ON *THE WITCHER*

GERALT TAKES THE SPOTLIGHT

In 2001, Polish director Marek Brodzki brought Geralt to the big screen in the film *Wiedźmin* (aka *The Hexer* or *The Witcher*), based on *The Witcher* franchise. The movie was a flop, as was the *Hexer* TV series which ran for 13 episodes in 2002 before being cancelled.

MILES TOST

Level Designer, *The Witcher*

With *The Witcher 3: Wild Hunt* on the way, we asked Miles Tost, designer with CD Projekt RED, what to expect in the next epic quest.

Why did you choose the *Witcher* novels as inspiration for a videogame?
The Witcher is an exceptional universe, full of captivating stories and interesting characters. It's also very mature and puts a lot of contemporary problems like racism or the atrocities of war in a totally different perspective. This gives people who experience it a one-of-a-kind feeling of interacting with fantasy that's grown up, and resonates with them on a more personal level.

What will *The Witcher 3* bring to the franchise?
The Witcher 3 (shown left) adds an open world to the already potent mix of superior storytelling and gripping gameplay. We retain the strong story-driven gameplay, we make the narrative even more gripping and marry all this with a vast, open world that just begs to be explored.

Is *The Witcher 3* inspired by any other series?
I think the games we play inspire us and influence how we see the industry and our work in general. As people, we're the sum of our experiences, and in this sense *The Witcher 3* is inspired by every good game we've ever played.

What makes Geralt so appealing as a character?
He's the complete package. He's essentially a monster slayer for hire and a mutated, specially trained mercenary who's not devoid of emotions like other Witchers. At the same time, he has his own codex; a set of rules that makes you respect him. He's the silent badass you fear a bit, but deep down inside you know he'll do the right thing. And he fits the world perfectly.

FASTEST COMPLETION OF *THE WITCHER 2: ASSASSINS OF KINGS* ON "HARD" MODE

Germany's Tobias "Aphox" Baers completed Geralt's quest on "Hard" mode in *Assassins of Kings* in a time of just 2 hr 18 min 17 sec on 2 October 2013.

WORLD OF WARCRAFT

Summary: The MMORPG mainstay celebrated its 10th birthday in November 2014. Millions still enjoy the magical online world that is part of the wider, multi-platform *Warcraft* universe.

Publisher: Blizzard
Developer: Blizzard
Debut: 2004

FIRST PERSON TO COMPLETE *WORLD OF WARCRAFT*

"Little Gray" (Taiwan), who completed all 986 achievements then listed in the Armory (the game's vast searchable database of information taken from the *WoW* servers), became the first person to complete the game on 27 November 2009. Little Gray killed 390,895 creatures, accumulated 7,255,538,878 points of damage, accomplished 5,906

EXPANSION PLANS

The multimedia fantasy *Warcraft* series began in 1994. *WoW*, created 10 years later, is the fourth game set in the gigantic *Warcraft* universe. Its success has been cemented by the five expansion packs, which have combined sales of almost 30 million: *The Burning Crusade* (2007), *Wrath of the Lich King* (2008), *Cataclysm* (2010), *Mists of Pandaria* (2012) and *Warlords of Draenor* (due in late 2014).

FIRST EMMY AWARD FOR A MACHINIMA

"Machinima" is the practice of creating animated films by manipulating game graphics. *South Park* creators Trey Parker and Matt Stone collaborated with Blizzard for the 147th episode of *South Park*, which was named "Make Love, Not Warcraft". The episode first aired in the USA on 4 October 2006 and won the 2007 Primetime Emmy Award for Outstanding Animated Program (For Programming Less Than One Hour) on 8 September 2007.

quests, raided 405 dungeons and hugged 11 players. WOW indeed. Little Gray's achievement was at the height of *WoW*'s fame in the last decade, when it attracted some 12 million subscribers. As of 6 May 2014, it remains the **most popular subscription-based videogame**, with 7.6 million devotees.

MOST EXPENSIVE *WORLD OF WARCRAFT* ACCOUNT

In September 2007, a *World of Warcraft* account for a level-70 night elf rogue called "Zeuzo" was sold for almost £5,000 ($9,500), according to the BBC. The account was able to attract such a high fee because it featured "magical" items such as the twin Warglaives of Azzinoth, owned by only a few *WoW* players. These powerful elements had been rewarded to the character's previous owner for completing some of the game's most difficult challenges. Although the new owner is said to have renamed the character "Shaks" and moved it to another server, it seems that this was all for

LONGEST MMORPG MARATHON

"Kinumi Cati", also known as Hecaterina Kinumi Iglesias Pérez (Spain), played *World of Warcraft* for 29 hr 31 min in Vigo, Spain, on 29–30 March 2014. You can see her in full regalia on pp.88–89.

Hecaterina also holds the record for the **longest JRPG marathon**, achieved after she spent 38 hr 6 min playing *Final Fantasy X* in Barcelona, Spain, from 26 to 28 July 2013. She says her interest in games derives from her passion for all things Japanese.

WORLD OF WARCRAFT WARLORDS OF DRAENOR

FIRST VIDEOGAME PANDEMIC

In September 2005, a deadly virtual plague broke out in *WoW*, affecting thousands of players. Dubbed as the first "world event" in the game, the "corrupted blood" infection meted by Hakkar in the Zul'Gurub dungeon was only supposed to affect players close to his corpse, but transferred to other areas of the game via an in-game virtual pet before spreading from player to player.

LARGEST FINE FOR BREACHING A GAME'S TERMS OF USE

On 16 October 2013, Blizzard won a two-year legal battle against Ceiling Fan Software, developers of the *Pocket Gnome* and *Shadow Bot* bots that enabled players to automate aspects of *WoW*. The writ hit the Fan when a federal court in California awarded Blizzard $7 million (£4.4 million) and issued a permanent injunction against Ceiling Fan to prevent the company from selling, licensing, operating and allowing others to use the bots.

MOST POPULAR RACE IN *WORLD OF WARCRAFT*

As of 17 July 2014, humans were ranked the #1 race for players in EU and US realms, with Goblin ranked as the **least popular.**

nothing. Blizzard reportedly banned the account for the controversial practice of selling in-game accounts and items, which they claimed breached their terms and conditions.

MOST VIEWED VIDEO ON WARCRAFTMOVIES.COM

As of 24 June 2014, the most viewed video on WarcraftMovies was *Tales of the Past III* by Martin Falch, aka Maquan, with 3,848,457 views. The third instalment of a machinima trilogy, it runs for 88 minutes and, according to Falch, took a year and a half to create – at an average of three hours per day.

▶▶FIRST MOVIE BASED ON AN MMO

Dragon Nest is a free2play fantasy MMORPG available in Asia, North America, Russia and Europe. A 3D animated feature film based on the game is scheduled for initial release in China on 31 July 2014. It was produced by Bill Borden, whose credits include the *High School Musical* films.

DRAGON NEST
WARRIORS' DAWN
From the Producer of High School Musical

FOR THE WIN

FINDING THE CHICKEN

You can acquire yourself a chicken companion by following these simple steps:
1. Go to Westfall if you are Alliance or to Brill if you are Horde.
2. Find a group of chickens and repeatedly spam **/chicken**.
3. Eventually one of the chickens will give you a quest, which you should accept.
4. Purchase chicken feed from Farmer Saldean (Westfall)/ William Saldean (Brill).
5. Turn in your quest and you will be rewarded with an egg, which you can take to learn how to summon a chicken.

MMOs

Massively multiplayer online (MMO) games are typically role-playing games (RPGs), and the majority of those are fantasy-based epics. But as this rogues gallery of MMO characters attests, this genre encompasses a range of subjects, from sci-fi and sports to dungeon crawlers and medieval hack and slashers. The records, too, are equally as diverse...

FIRST MMO REALITY SHOW

World of Warcraft inspired *Azeroth Choppers*, the eight-part search for real-world motorbike designs to be used in the game. It debuted on *WoW*'s YouTube channel on 17 April 2014 with 2 million viewers in its first week. Two teams from custom motorcycle workshop Paul Jr Designs (USA) had five weeks to create bikes based on the game's Alliance and Horde factions. Fans voted for the Horde design, which was added as a free playable vehicle. The Alliance chopper **(1)** was later also made available, paid for with in-game currency.

FIRST MMO WITH REAL-WORLD ADVERTS

In February 2005, Funcom's *Anarchy Online* **(2)** began allowing players to sign up for free in exchange for seeing adverts in-game. Non-subscribers passed billboards displaying ads for the US Air Force, Microsoft and road-safety campaigns.

FIRST CONSOLE SPORTS MMO

NHL 09 **(3)** supported the EA Sports Hockey League, which allows players to create and level-up virtual hockey avatars. Gamers can join teams made up of other real-world players and compete with each other in tournaments. The Sports Hockey League will remain supported with 2014's release, *NHL 15*.

LARGEST MMO VOICE CAST

A total of 314 actors recorded lines of dialogue for 2011's *Star Wars: The Old Republic* **(4)**. Among the many famous voices were veteran game voice actors David Hayter, Nolan North and Jennifer Hale, as well as stars of film and TV.

FIRST GRAPHICAL MMO

Using graphics to create its world rather than text, *Neverwinter Nights* was based on the *Dungeons & Dragons* rulebook. The game ran from March 1991 to July 1997 and players paid per hour to play on servers so small that they would queue to join the game. *Neverwinter Nights 2* **(5)** a single-player RPG, followed in 2006.

1

2

3

4

5

FASTEST-SELLING MMO EXPANSION

Cataclysm (6), the third expansion pack for *World of Warcraft*, shifted some 4.7 million copies within a month of its release in December 2010 – 3.3 million of those copies on day one.

FIRST CONSOLE MMO

Phantasy Star Online (7) was released for the Dreamcast in 2000. It was smaller than the likes of *Final Fantasy* would later become, but was a real-time rather than turn-based game.

LONGEST-RUNNING ONLINE GAMING GUILD

First founded in February 1996, The Syndicate had been active for 18 years 162 days as of 11 August 2014. The Syndicate takes part in two games online at any one time and is mostly concerned with *Ultima Online* (8), a game it has been part of since its launch. Its motto is "Long Live The Syndicate", often abbreviated to "LLTS".

FIRST GAMER TO UNLOCK ALL *WORLD OF WARCRAFT* ACHIEVEMENTS

On 19 April 2014, "Хируко" (Russia) unlocked all 2,057 achievements up to and including *Mists of Pandaria* (9).

MOST USERS OF AN MMO

Developer Jagex reports that *RuneScape* (10) has had a total of 220 million user accounts opened on its servers since it was launched in 2001.

6   7   8   9   10

Summary: Ellie and Joel cautiously traverse infection-ravaged America in a game that adds subtlety to the genre, with its nuanced main relationship played out over a finely realized backdrop.

Publisher: Sony
Developer: Naughty Dog
Debut: 2013

FASTEST-SELLING NEW IP FOR PS3

A total of 1.32 million copies of *The Last of Us* were sold in the week of the game's release on 14 June 2013, swiping the title of fastest-selling new IP at the very end of the seventh

FOR THE WIN

SHIVER OF EXCITEMENT

Always keep a shiv in your back pocket. You never know when a locked door will stand between you and a vital stash of ammo and gear or supplements.

MOST CRITICALLY ACCLAIMED CONSOLE DLC

The Last of Us: Left Behind has a GameRankings score of 89.84%. That makes it the **most critically acclaimed action-adventure DLC**, too. A prologue to the original game, it follows Ellie and her BFF Riley (played by Ashley Johnson, above right, and, left, Yaani King) on a journey that pushes their lives and friendship to the brink.

generation. Sony reported sales of 3.4 million units in just three weeks, making it the fastest-selling game overall for PS3 in 2013 and the third-fastest-selling game of the year (behind *Tomb Raider* and *BioShock Infinite*).

HIGHEST-RANKED CLAN PLAYER IN *THE LAST OF US*

A Spanish player known as "zzZyxyHacko2014" rules the clan leaderboards of *The Last of Us*, rising through the ranks over 27 weeks in the game's

400 species of fungi in the real-world genus *Cordyceps*, the brain-destroying endoparasites that destroy humanity in the game.

team-based multiplayer mode to be ranked the No.1 player. (Rank is determined by number of weeks survived.) The multiplayer mode has proved a surprise hit among fans of a game that has such a strong single-player narrative.

MOST CRITICALLY ACCLAIMED PS3 GAME (EXCLUDING SEQUELS)

Sequels dominate the upper reaches of the PS3 chart and

ONE WRONG STEP FOR MANKIND

Naughty Dog creative director Neil Druckmann had first pitched a zombie game when he was at college – to legendary zombie director George A Romero (who passed). *The Last of Us* itself began as *Mankind*, a game in which women were infected and Joel had to deliver Ellie – the only immune woman – to a lab to find a cure. Druckmann rejected the concept as "a misogynistic idea".

> "Everything in survival horror games tries to be creepy on every level, but we wanted to add some colour and natural beauty to that."
>
> **NEIL DRUCKMANN,**
> CREATIVE DIRECTOR,
> NAUGHTY DOG

MOST "GAME OF THE YEAR" AWARDS

The Last of Us earned 249 Game of the Year awards in the year of its release. These comprise 58 fan-voted awards and 191 critic awards, including major wins such as Best Game award at the 2014 BAFTA Awards, at the 14th annual GDC Awards and at the 2014 SXSW Gaming Awards. In second place is *Grand Theft Auto V*, with a total of 158 awards. At the DICE Awards in 2014, *The Last of Us* took a total of 10 awards, cementing a reputation for innovative design that will influence developers for years to come.

FEISTY FUNGUS

The parasitic fungi *Cordyceps*, responsible for the apocalypse in *The Last of Us*, are real. Naughty Dog's Neil Druckmann got the idea for the contagion while watching an ant becoming infected by the fungus in a David Attenborough documentary series called *Planet Earth* (UK, 2006). The parasite takes control of the ant's brain, forcing it to die clinging to a leaf, where the killer fungus spreads its spores.

it's a mark of Naughty Dog's success with new properties that *The Last of Us* is the highest-rated non-sequel game on the PS3. It has a 95.04% average review on gamerankings.com. The developer's own *Uncharted 2: Among Thieves* is No.3 overall on the PS3, with 96.38%.

MOST POPULAR *THE LAST OF US* FAN ART

As of 2 July 2014, Japanese artist Ryo "doubleleaf" Ohara had amassed 6,319 "favourites" from the online community at deviantART for "The Last of Us Collections". The artwork has been viewed 77,432 times.

FIRST FEMALE VOICE ACTOR TO WIN A BAFTA GAME AWARD

Ashley Johnson (USA) won a BAFTA in the Performer category for her portrayal of Ellie (see below left). "Joel and Ellie's relationship ends up becoming a father-daughter bond," said Johnson. "I have a little girl – I try to draw a lot from that and make it as personal as I can and as honest as I can." Troy Baker, who voiced Joel, was also nominated.

70,000,000
Naughty Dog games sold in 30 years. The developer was set up in 1984 by Andrew Gavin and Jason Rubin.

MOST BAFTA AWARD WINS FOR AN ACTION-ADVENTURE GAME

The Last of Us won five awards at the 2014 BAFTA Video Games Awards – for Best Action and Adventure Game, Best Audio Achievement, Best Performer (Ashley Johnson), Best Story and Game of the Year. It also recorded the **most BAFTA award nominations for a game**, with 10, equalling a mark first attained in 2010 by another title from the Naughty Dog stable, *Uncharted 2: Among Thieves*. In 2014, strong BAFTA competition came from *Grand Theft Auto V*, which took three awards.

KINGDOM HEARTS

Summary: The primary colours of Disney and the darker shades of the RPG world painted by Square Enix may seem an unlikely combination, but it's been an imaginative success.

Publisher: Square Enix/Disney
Developer: Square Enix
Debut: 2002

FASTEST SINGLE-SEGMENT COMPLETION OF *KINGDOM HEARTS HD I.5 REMIX*

Gamer "Bizkit047" raced through *Kingdom Hearts HD I.5 ReMIX* in 2 hr 53 min 56 sec on 2 April 2014. The portion of the game played was *Kingdom Hearts Final Mix* on "Beginner" difficulty. "It is the fastest mode in the game," said Bizkit047. "While there's not much of a threat of death until the second half of the run, it can still be intense due to how optimized the category is and how making a single platforming mistake can ruin a run sometimes."

FOR THE WIN

MUSHROOM XIII REMIX

Kingdom Hearts II Final Mix, from 2007, is set to be made available outside Japan as part of *Kingdom Hearts HD II.5 ReMIX*, due in December 2014. One of its hardest challenges is the Mushroom XIII mini-games. Mushroom X is the trickiest – use "pause" frequently to keep track of the fast-moving critters: you need to hit the real one when they stop moving.

FASTEST SINGLE-SEGMENT COMPLETION OF *KINGDOM HEARTS*

Daniel "Sonicshadowsilver2" Tipton (USA) took 5 hr 33 min 35 sec to finish the original Disney/Square adventure on 24 June 2013 on the PS2. A keen *Kingdom Hearts* speed-runner, Daniel has played through other titles in the series, including the 2013 collected versions of the first two games, *Kingdom Hearts HD I.5 ReMIX* (pictured) and the sixth entry in the series, *Kingdom Hearts: Birth by Sleep*.

MOST POPULAR CHARACTER IN *KINGDOM HEARTS*

According to a poll in Japan's *Famitsu* magazine in July 2011, Sora is the favourite series character, with 667 votes. Roxas and Axel, both members of Organization XIII, took second and third place with 495 and 228 votes.

16
Kingdom Hearts games available in Japan including remixes – only 10 had worldwide releases.

ELEVATED IDEAS

Square and Disney used to share an office in Tokyo. The original *Kingdom Hearts* game was the result of a chance meeting in a lift between game producer Shinji Hashimoto and a Disney executive. An initially vague talk about an RPG featuring Mickey Mouse was gradually refined.

BEST-SELLING DISNEY VIDEOGAME

Kingdom Hearts had sold 6.4 million copies according to VGChartz, as of 21 July 2014; other games, such as *LEGO® Star Wars: The Complete Saga*, have sold more but were part of brands bought out, rather than developed, by Disney. Popular characters to have made it into game form include (above from left): the Cheshire Cat, Tarzan, Jiminy Cricket, Alice and Pinocchio. Director Tetsuya Nomura revealed his favourite slice of Disney in the series: "I am particularly fond of the *Nightmare Before Christmas* world [Halloween Town] from the first game."

OLDEST GAME VOICE ACTOR

Christopher Lee (UK, b. 27 May 1922) played Ansem the Wise in *Kingdom Hearts 358/2 Days* aged 87 years 124 days on the game's release in North America (29 September 2009). He broke his own record by playing Saruman in *LEGO: The Hobbit*, aged 91 years 316 days on its 8 April 2014 launch.

FASTEST SINGLE-SEGMENT COMPLETION OF *KINGDOM HEARTS: CHAIN OF MEMORIES*

Chain of Memories was later remixed (as *Kingdom Hearts: Re:Chain of Memories* for the PS2), but the first *Chain of Memories* was originally a GBA exclusive. Keith "The Quiet Man" Skomorowski played as Riku to finish in 1 hr 29 min 5 sec on 2 January 2009.

BEST-SELLING CROSSOVER RPG SERIES

The *Kingdom Hearts* series has recorded sales of 20.95 million copies. Such a devoted fanbase, in addition to enthusiastic reviews from the gaming press, has shown the franchise to be far more than merely a tie-in gimmick with Disney. But *KH* still has a long way to go to catch up with the sales of more than 100 million achieved by that other big Square Enix RPG series – *Final Fantasy* (see pp.136–37).

STRONGEST KEYBLADE IN *KINGDOM HEARTS 3D: DREAM DROP DISTANCE*

"Keyblades" are the main weapons in the universe of *Kingdom Hearts*. In *Kingdom Hearts 3D: Dream Drop Distance*, the Keyblade that does the most damage is Unbound, with a strength rating of 18.

MOST DISNEY FRANCHISES IN A VIDEOGAME

Kingdom Hearts II features 11 Disney franchises, providing playable backdrops as varied as the swashbuckling of *Pirates of the Caribbean* (Disney, 2003) in the shape of the Port Royal world, and the classic fairytale land of *The Little Mermaid* (Disney, 1989) played as Atlantica. Sci-fi fans are catered for in the futuristic land of Space Paranoids, the cool blue landscape from the original *TRON* (Disney, 1982).

BIG IN JAPAN

The home of Nintendo, Sony, Bandai Namco, Sega and countless other gaming heavyweights, Japan has long been seen as a hub of gaming innovation. For almost 40 years, the country has been at the forefront of the industry, with Taito's pioneering *Space Invaders* (1978) and Namco phenomenon *PAC-Man* (1980) dominating arcade halls across the world in the early days of gaming. But while Japan's videogame market has a long history of success, it is currently enduring a period of massive change. Aptly enough, the theme for the 2014 Tokyo Game Show was "Changing Games: The Transformation of Fun".

THE ARCADE EVOLUTION

Japan's biggest gaming export may be the consoles that we play their games on, but back home arcades are still a big deal. Ever since the 1980s, they have been a significant part of urban life in the country. Currently, Japan boasts 9,500 arcades, with more than 445,000 game machines that appeal to kids and adults alike. One of the reasons for arcades' continued success appears to be demographics: much of Japan is heavily urbanized, with capital city Tokyo hosting a population of over 35 million. A large number of those residents commute on Japan's rail and subway network, and the modern arcade scene is dominated by big multi-level arcades located close to major train stations. These are mostly operated by companies with a history of making arcade machines themselves, such as Sega, Namco and Taito.

THE ARCADES

NATIONAL IDENTITY

Among the genres that have attained a sizeable following in Japanese arcades are rhythm games such as *Dance Dance Revolution*, and *danmaku* shooters, in which the aim of the game is not just to destroy the enemy but to successfully navigate the bewildering projectiles aimed at the gamer's avatar.

New game types that surfaced in the mid-2000s include card RTS games such as *Sangokushi Taisen* (below). These titles typically mesh the JRPG and sports genres, and involve players collecting cards representing various characters. Each card contains a radio-frequency tag, enabling it to interact with the arcade machine and create in-game movements. It's a bit like a cross between *Skylanders* and *Magic: The Gathering*.

But there are signs of a shift away from arcades that only offer coin-op cabinets towards venues that are more focused on socializing. These centres charge people according to the amount of time spent there and offer experiences other than just gaming, such as bowling, dining and karaoke. Arcades are adapting and evolving.

GLOBAL APPEAL

Japanese home consoles have dominated the global market for the last 30 years. It all began with Nintendo's Famicom (right), which triumphed in Japan and revived the gloomy North American console market when it was launched there as the NES in 1985. As of July 2014, nine of the 10 best-selling consoles of all time were made by Nintendo or Sony. Yet 2014 saw both corporations post larger than expected losses, partly explained by Sony restructures and Nintendo's Wii U proving to be markedly less popular than the Wii, the **best-selling seventh-generation home console**.

The long-term future for both organizations may be bright, however: Sony's investment in game studios and the early success of the PS4 put it in a strong position, while in 2014 Nintendo announced plans for a brand new console that has created an enormous buzz.

HOME HITS

Japan's unique culture has given rise to a number of gaming genres that, while massively successful in Japan, are less popular in the West. Most prominent among these is the JRPG, typified by the *Dragon Quest* series, whose span of more than 26 years makes it the **longest-running Japanese RPG series**. While RPGs in the West typically offer greater narrative freedom, allowing the player the ability to become the central hero or villain of the game, JRPG titles contain a more linear story that focuses on the main character's relationship with the other members of their group.

Another popular and rapidly growing genre in Japan is dating sims, in

In *Boyfriend Maker* and *LovePlus*, users interact with virtual partners in a bid to impress and woo.

which players attempt to woo virtual guys or girls with nifty dialogue and romantic gestures. According to *Edge* magazine, the genre is booming thanks both to a surge in women using the games, and a host of new dating games on mobile devices. The magazine surmises that, "More so than most Japanese games, romance sims are built on cultural values and social norms that don't translate well outside of the nation's borders…"

Dragon Quest isn't big in Japan – it's huge. Total sales are more than 60 million.

UNLEASH THE BEAST

In the arcade, 2D fighting games – and the *Street Fighter* series (right) in particular – remain among the most popular. Japanese gamers often do very well at the Evolution Championship Series, an annual eSports competition dedicated to fighters. Daigo "The Beast" Umehara (above), a regular at the Shinjuku Taito Station in Tokyo, holds the record for the **most title wins at the Evo Championship Series** with six. For more on fighting games, turn to our *Mortal Kombat* feature on pp.46–47.

If the first 40 years of gaming have taught us anything, it's that whatever the future holds, you can be sure that Japanese gamers and game-makers will still be pioneering, innovating and inventing – both at home and abroad.

KING OF THE SCENE

20–11

BEST-SELLING STEALTH VIDEOGAME SERIES

When it comes to the sub-genre of stealth, one series towers above all others: as of 6 August 2014, the *Metal Gear* series had sold 36.75 million copies worldwide, according to VGChartz. *Metal Gear* has dominated for almost 30 years, from its humble beginnings on the MSX2 home computer right up to the series' eighth-generation debut with *Metal Gear Solid V: Ground Zeroes*. Pictured below with the parachute is Solid Snake in the first game in the series, *Metal Gear* (1987). Near right is Snake in *Metal Gear Solid: Peace Walker* (2010), and the main image is of Venom Snake, hero of *Metal Gear Solid V: The Phantom Pain*, which is set for early 2015 release.

"After each game I begin to think of the story for the next. I didn't have the whole story put together at once when I created the first game. One thing that I try not to do is sacrifice certain things just so I can keep the original story intact. Sometimes I need to accept these inconsistencies."

HIDEO KOJIMA
CREATOR, *METAL GEAR* SERIES

Summary: Although facing ever-more competition, this team-based tactical shooter is still a pillar of the eSports scene. As one of the first commercially released mods, it's also a hero of the modding scene.

Publisher: Valve
Developer: Valve
Debut: 1999

COUNTER-HISTORY

Counter-Strike originally emerged as a mod of Valve's 1998 game *Half-Life* (see pp.72–73). It was developed by Vietnamese-Canadian Minh "Gooseman" Le and American Jess Cliffe. After Le and Cliffe produced their fourth beta, Valve offered them both jobs. In turn, *Counter-Strike* has inspired its own community of keen modders.

 Counter-Strike was banned for over a year in Brazil between 2008 and 2009 after a judge said it could "bring imminent stimulus to the subversion of the social order, attempting against the democratic and rightful state and against the public safety".

HIGHEST-EARNING *COUNTER-STRIKE* PLAYER

Patrik "f0rest" Lindberg (Sweden, right) began playing *Counter-Strike* professionally in 2005. In the following nine years, he personally earned $274,956 (£160,857). Patrik started his eSports career with the Begrip Gaming team in 2005, moving to Fnatic in 2006. Between 2010 and 2012, he played for SK Gaming before joining Ninjas in Pyjamas.

KNIFE-EQUIPPED   FOR THE WIN

Perhaps the most well-known *Counter-Strike* tip is to fire in controlled bursts, or else you'll see your bullets spraying everywhere except on your target. A less obvious tip is to run with your knife equipped rather than your gun. Because it's lighter, you'll run faster, getting you to critical locations earlier and allowing you to play more aggressively. Switching back to your gun is fast, too.

FIRST GAMING CLAN REPRESENTED BY A SPORTS AGENT

For decades agents have represented stars from sports such as soccer and basketball, but it wasn't until 2005 that they stuck their oars into pro gaming. Johan Strömberg (Sweden), who has represented ice hockey and soccer players including former Arsenal FC goalkeeper Rami Shaaban, began representing Swedish *CS* clan Ninjas in Pyjamas (NiP, see below) in January 2005. The team was founded in June 2000, dissolved in 2007, then re-formed in 2012.

FIRST GAME ENGINE OPTIMIZED FOR 64-BIT PROCESSORS

Valve's Source engine, which debuted in October 2004 with *Counter-Strike: Source*, is the first for 64-bit processors. Game engines are the software that designers use to create the core game mechanics. The same engine can be used to develop various different games. *CS: Source* is a remake of the original 1999 game.

91 billion
rounds fired by *Counter-Strike* players in the first year of *Counter-Strike: Global Offensive* (2012--13).

MOST KILLS IN PROFESSIONAL *COUNTER-STRIKE* TOURNAMENTS

As of 21 July 2014, the world's most successful *Counter-Strike: Global Offensive* team was Sweden's Ninjas in Pyjamas, which had amassed 41,436 officially recorded kills in 10,869 tournament matches. NiP's best player is "GeT_RiGhT", who lays claim to 9,749 kills and an average 0.86 kills per round. His average rating, a figure based on various *CS: GO* stats, is 1.32.

LARGEST LAN PARTY

Despite the rise of internet gaming, LAN parties, in which gamers bring their PCs to a venue and play over a LAN (local area network) with reduced lag, are still hugely popular. DreamHack has grown every year since its inception in 1994, and its winter 2013 event, held between 28 November and 1 December in Jönköping, Sweden, attracted 22,810 visitors. A *CS: GO* Championship was one of the main events.

FIRST GAMING CLAN TO LEGALLY BIND ITS PLAYERS

On 1 February 2003, the German clan SK Gaming issued contracts to several Swedish *Counter-Strike* players. SK Gaming has been on the eSports scene since 1997. Originally specializing in *Doom*, the team went on to play *League of Legends*, *World of Warcraft* and *Counter-Strike*. In July 2012, SK Gaming ceased its *CS* division and now concentrates on *LoL* and *SMITE*.

HIGHEST-EARNING COUNTER-STRIKE COUNTRY

The best place to earn a living from *Counter-Strike* is Sweden – perhaps not surprisingly since it's home to the game's highest-earning player (see opposite page). The 285 Scandinavian hot-shot pro players have earned more than $2.67 million (£1.5 million) in gaming prize money.

> "Ten years ago when I invented *Counter-Strike*, it was pretty easy to set yourself apart, but the way the industry has evolved, it's much harder."

MINH "GOOSEMAN" LE
CO-CREATOR,
COUNTER-STRIKE

MOST PLAYED *COUNTER-STRIKE* MAP

Modding is the reason why *Counter-Strike* exists, and player creativity remains fundamental to it. Map-making is the *CS* modder's key battleground. The series' icon is "de_dust" (left), which is its most-played map, and one of the most played multiplayer maps as a whole. "de_dust" was originally designed in 1999 by David Johnston, then still at school. Today, there are many versions for each incarnation of the game, and even an improved sequel, "de_dust2". But they all feature the same Middle Eastern city setting and tightly twisting series of passages and open squares.

The surprising truth behind this definitive piece of multiplayer history is that Johnston was originally trying to copy a map that Valve had shown in just a couple of screenshots for the then-unreleased *Team Fortress 2*.

Nowadays, modders release *CS: GO* maps through the Steam Workshop. As of April 2014, there were 48,606 of them, compared with Valve's 23 official maps.

BEST-SELLING MOD FRANCHISE

According to the game's developer, Valve, *Counter-Strike* has sold well over 25 million units across its various versions and platforms. The original *Counter-Strike* shifted more than 4 million copies. Originally a PC-exclusive, it went on to appear on the Xbox, Mac and Linux, as did *CS: Condition Zero*, while *CS: Source* was only available for Windows, OS X and Linux. *CS: Global Offensive* had the widest release of the series, with ports for the PS3 (USA-exclusive) and Xbox 360 as well as its customary desktop computer versions.

17

SONIC THE HEDGEHOG

Summary: The sassy, spiky supersonic mammal is one of gaming's most enduring and prolific stars, appearing in 21 main series titles since 1991. Two new *Sonic Boom* games are due in late 2014.

Publisher: Sega
Developer: Various
Debut: 1991

BEST-SELLING GAME ON SEGA PLATFORMS

Sega may be predominantly a software developer now, but in the 1980s and early '90s the console wars were largely fought between Sega and Nintendo. In 1991, *Sonic the Hedgehog* became the flag-waver for Sega, and a fine job he did too, racking up sales in excess of 13 million across the Mega Drive/Genesis, Saturn, CD and Dreamcast. No other game on a Sega console sold more copies.

FIRST VIDEOGAME CHARACTER IN MACY'S THANKSGIVING DAY PARADE

Macy's Thanksgiving Day Parade is an American institution. Held every year in New York and famed for its spectacular balloons and floats, the 1993 event heralded the first appearance of a gaming character when the iconic Sonic was featured. His debut did not go well: strong winds blew the giant balloon into a lamp post and punctured it. Pictured above is Sonic's appearance at the 2011 parade.

FASTEST COMPLETION OF *SONIC 2*

The fastest completion of 1992's *Sonic the Hedgehog 2* on the Sega Genesis/Mega Drive is 15 min 18 sec, set on 4 December 2013 by Mike "Mike89" McKenzie. Mike beat his own record by almost a minute. *Sonic 2* saw the series debut of Miles "Tails" Prower, Sonic's loyal fox friend.

BEST-SELLING SONIC GAME

Back in 1991, no one could have predicted that Sonic and Mario would one day join franchise forces and make videogaming history. *Mario & Sonic at the Olympic Games* (below), a tie-in to the Beijing Olympics of 2008, featured eight characters from each franchise competing in a series of Olympic challenges. It had global sales of 12.99 million as of 31 July 2014, which also makes it the **best-selling gaming crossover**. As for the Winter Olympics (above), the **fastest Skeleton Run on *Mario & Sonic at the Olympic Winter Games*** (released for the Vancouver 2010 Games) is a super-speedy 65.05 sec by Shawn Alvarez (USA) on 16 February 2014.

FIRST WII U GAME TO USE CRYENGINE SOFTWARE

Set for late 2014 release, *Sonic Boom: Rise of Lyric* will be the first Wii U title to use the sophisticated CryEngine that was behind titles such as *Far Cry*, *Ryse: Son of Rome*, *Crysis 3* and *Sniper: Ghost Warrior 2*. The game engine, created by Crytek, is renowned for its rendering of lush tropical landscapes and had to be adapted to accommodate *Sonic Boom*'s split-screen gameplay. The *Sonic Boom* titles are set to be a new sub-franchise within the Sonic universe.

SUPERSONIC CG

Sonic Boom was announced as a TV series in October 2013, four months before Sega revealed that two *Boom* games would be released on the Wii U and 3DS in November 2014: *Rise of Lyric* and *Shattered Crystal*. The show will be the first CG-animated *Sonic the Hedgehog* TV series.

HIGHEST-RANKED PLAYER ON *MARIO & SONIC AT THE OLYMPIC GAMES*

As of 16 July 2014, the player with the most game points on *Mario & Sonic at the Olympic Games* was "becky--jay". A score of 1,670 points on the hit Wii sports title placed becky--Jay at the top of the league table at wii records.com.

FIRST SONIC GAME FOR A THIRD-PARTY PLATFORM

Initially exclusive to Sega platforms, Sonic games have gone on to receive a wide release across several consoles and handhelds. *Sonic Adventure 2* was the last title of the series published for Sega when it was released for the Dreamcast in June 2001. It was ported to the Nintendo GameCube and retitled as *Sonic Adventure 2 Battle* in December 2001.

FIRST SONIC/ZELDA CROSSOVER

It wasn't just Mario who battled it out with Sonic in the 1990s. Zelda packed a mighty punch for Nintendo, too. Some 20 years after the console conflict, the hedgehog and princess have united in a brand new Sega-Nintendo tie-in – a Hyrule-themed level for *Sonic: Lost World*, which was made available for the Wii U. The Legend of Zelda Zone was released as free DLC on 27 March 2014 and sees Sonic explore Hyrule's fields and dungeons in Link's trademark green hat and tunic, swapping rings for rupees. For more on the legendary Link and Zelda, turn to pp.156–57.

FASTEST COMPLETION OF *SONIC: LOST WORLD*

On 22 May 2014, gamer "DarkspinesSonic", aka Carlos Johnson, set an any-percentage speed-run record for *Sonic: Lost World* on the Wii U in 1 hr 9 min 34 sec. *Lost World* is the 21st and latest release in the *Sonic* series, as of July 2014. The gameplay sees Sonic, Tails and co try to defeat Doctor Eggman and the Deadly Six. Sales and critical reception for the game, released on the Wii U, DS and 3DS, were disappointing.

BOSS HOG

Sonic the Comic, of which the first edition was printed in 1993, sheds some light on how Sonic came to be. He was an ordinary brown hedgehog until a lab accident involving sneakers gave him blue fur and super speed!

METAL GEAR

Summary: *The Phantom Pain*, insists creator Hideo Kojima, will be "the last one" of the series he works on. But his many fans will take heart from the fact that he has said that before...

Publisher: Konami
Developer: Konami/ Kojima Prod./Platinum
Debut: 1987

BEST-SELLING STEALTH GAME SERIES

As of 6 August 2014, the *Metal Gear* series had sold 36.75 million copies (see pp.118–19). *Metal Gear*, which first appeared on the MSX2 computer, is widely credited for popularizing the stealth action genre. Its nearest competitor is *Tom Clancy's Splinter Cell* franchise, with 16 million sold.

FIRST ONLINE STEALTH GAME

Metal Gear Solid 3: Subsistence was the first game to feature access to *Metal Gear Online*. Sneak missions featured alongside standard multiplayer modes. Further versions of *Metal Gear Online* followed, including a standalone Japanese release in 2008. Online play is said to return in upcoming edition *Metal Gear Solid V: The Phantom Pain*.

BEST-SELLING THIRD-PARTY PS3-EXCLUSIVE GAME

Metal Gear Solid 4: Guns of the Patriots has sold 5.87 million copies and was also the overall **best-selling PS3-exclusive game** until *Gran Turismo 5* was released (see pp.38–39).

FASTEST SINGLE-SEGMENT COMPLETION OF *METAL GEAR SOLID V: GROUND ZEROES*

Gamer "CrumandMimalmo" reported completing *Metal Gear Solid V: Ground Zeroes* in 3 min 54 sec and linked to a YouTube video on 24 June 2014 to prove it. The game was finished at S-Rank, which is only given to the sneakiest of players who avoid killing any guards and remain completely undetected as they rush through the game.

Below: evolution of the Snakes through *Metal Gear* games.

FASTEST COMPLETIONS

• *MGS3: Snake Eater:* Hidenori "Hikari" Kawamoto (Japan), 1 hr 14 min 27 sec, 3 June 2013, "extreme" difficulty.
• *MG* **(single segment):** Marko "Master-88" Vanhanen (Finland), 27 min 57 sec, 15 June 2010.
• *MG* **(single segment, no deaths):** "Master-88", 31 min 55 sec, 14 June 2010.
• *Snake's Revenge* **(single segment, no deaths):** "Master-88", 50 min, 15 April 2010.

►►FIRST FIRST-PERSON STEALTH GAME

Players once relied on the third-person perspective in stealth games to avoid entering the line of sight of opponents. *Thief: The Dark Project* brought a first-person innovation to the genre, placing the emphasis for success on using sound and shadows.

▶▶FASTEST SEGMENTED COMPLETION OF *TOM CLANCY'S SPLINTER CELL*

Gamer "CotySA" polished off the PC version of the first game in the *Splinter Cell* series in a time of 1 hr 12 min 41 sec on the "hard" setting on 13 May 2013. "I would really like to push the main game time under one hour," he said. "If I find some day a better route for one or more missions I will definitely run this game again."

FOR THE WIN

XOF PATCHES

Collecting all the nine XOF patches from the various *MGSV: Ground Zeroes* missions unlocks an extra mission. "Deja vu", formerly a PlayStation exclusive, has Big Boss recreating scenes from the first *Metal Gear Solid*, while "Jamais Vu", which used to be only available on the Xbox 360 and Xbone, offers a mission starring Raiden.

▶▶FASTEST SINGLE-SEGMENT COMPLETION OF *THIEF II*

By the nature of their careful gameplay, stealth titles may not suggest swift completion, but *Thief II: The Metal Age* was run by Joe "SocratesJohnson" Lunde in 1 hr 2 min 9 sec, on 14 November 2013. In Febuary 2014, the fourth game in the series – simply entitled *Thief* and developed by Eidos – was released. It was the first in the franchise since 2004's *Thief: Deadly Shadows*.

SNAKES IN A GAME

Hideo Kojima chose the name "Snake" for the characters in *Metal Gear* as "a being that hides his presence, and sneaks without making any noise". The names Solid and Liquid showed two oppositional states of matter, while Solidus is an indeterminate state between liquid and solid.

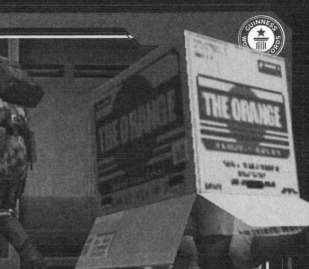

BEST-SELLING STEALTH GAME

Metal Gear Solid 2: Sons of Liberty had sold 6.05 million units as of June 2014. Elsewhere in the franchise, with sales of 1.99 million, *Metal Gear Solid: Peace Walker* for the PSP is the **best-selling stealth game on a handheld console**. The game is also the **fastest-selling handheld stealth game**, with first-week sales of 445,138. Initially a PSP exclusive, *Peace Walker* has since been released for the PS3 and Xbox 360 as part of the *Metal Gear Solid HD Collection*.

MOST PROLIFIC STEALTH VIDEOGAME PRODUCER

Hideo Kojima (Japan) has served as the producer on 23 *Metal Gear* titles and, as of June 2014, his company Kojima Productions was developing *Metal Gear Solid V: The Phantom Pain* (above). Kojima is known for regularly taking inspiration from the movies, and reaction to the trailer for *The Phantom Pain* showed that the cinema world returns his enthusiasm. On the four-minute clip's premiere in 2014, *Pacific Rim* (USA, 2013) director Guillermo del Toro commented, "Kojima-San remains a massive inspiration for me." Director of *Oldboy* (South Korea, 2003), Park Chan-wook said: "*Metal Gear Solid* games are already films, the films of the future."

BORDERLANDS

Summary: The games with more of everything – loot, enemies and, in particular, guns. Bold, funny and flavoured with RPG elements, *Borderlands* swiftly became a popular series.

Publisher: 2K Games
Developer: Gearbox Software
Debut: 2009

FASTEST COMPLETION OF *BORDERLANDS 2*

YouTube speed-runner "Joltzdude139" made it through *Borderlands 2* in the extremely difficult "Ultimate Vault Hunter" mode, with a time of just 1 hr 43 min 22 sec on 28 August 2013. The feat was achieved on the PS3. Joltzdude139 specializes in *Borderlands 2*, hunting out gameplay glitches and providing tutorials to help other players.

MOST ENEMY VARIANTS IN AN FPS

Not only does *Borderlands 2* excel with its range of weaponry, but it has up to 30 enemies and many variants within each class. That means there are at least 300 different opponents facing any player, based around three main classes: creatures, humans and Guardians.

FASTEST COMPLETION OF *BORDERLANDS*

Multiple speed-running record holder William "Youkai" Welch (USA) completed the original *Borderlands* in a time of 2 hr 29 min 2 sec in Oregon, USA, on 24 April 2011. He played the Xbox 360 version of the title and recorded the attempt in 99 segments. It's all the more impressive when you consider that *Borderlands* is a particularly difficult game to speed-run, given its randomly generated weapons and the need to gain experience points.

MOST POP CULTURE REFERENCES IN A VIDEOGAME

There's no shortage of references to other videogames, board games, books, films, TV shows and music lurking in *Borderlands 2*, with 411 of them listed on borderlands.wikia.com. By including Shakespeare, AC/DC, *Wall-E*, *Beowulf*, *My Little Pony*, *Monty Python*, Oprah Winfrey and *Shaun of the Dead*, it's clear that Gearbox spent the majority of game construction with their collective tongues firmly in their cheeks.

516,812,670
enemies killed during *Borderlands 2*'s four-week "$100,000 Loot Hunt".

FOR THE WIN

SANCTUARY IN *BORDERLANDS 2*

Fantastic.

Watch out for the slot machine in Moxxi's bar in the Sanctuary in *Borderlands 2*. If three bandit heads appear when you are playing, run backwards quickly: it's about to drop a grenade in your direction.

LEAST POPULAR CHARACTER IN *BORDERLANDS 2*

Based on statistics taken from a four-week in-game event called the "$100,000 Loot Hunt" that ran from 12 October 2013, the least popular character from *Borderlands 2* is Krieg, who was chosen by just 7% of players. Just above Krieg sat Gaige. To find out who topped the poll, see the opposite page.

> "We imagine what [Borderlands 3] might be and frankly it scares us. It's like, 'That's so crazy and so big that I'm not sure we can succeed.'"

RANDY PITCHFORD, CEO, GEARBOX SOFTWARE
ON *BORDERLANDS 3*

MOST GUNS IN A VIDEOGAME

The first *Borderlands* features some 17,750,000 weapons, a figure more than matched by the second game (above), though Gearbox have not specified a figure for the sequel. They did tell GWR that *Borderlands: The Pre-Sequel!*, due late in 2014, should have even more methods of attack. "We're adding two new variants to the weapons in *Pre-Sequel!*," they said, "laser weapons and cryo-weapons, so GWR should definitely revisit this in the fall when *The Pre-Sequel!* lands..."

A SALT RIFLE

The Veruc is a Dahl assault rifle in *Borderlands 2* and a reference to Roald Dahl's novel *Charlie and the Chocolate Factory*. The card text ("I want that rifle, Daddy") is probably what greedy Veruca Salt would say if she lived on Pandora.

MOST POPULAR CHARACTER IN *BORDERLANDS 2*

The "$100,000 Loot Hunt" that ran in October 2013 established the most popular *Borderlands 2* star as Axton, who took the top spot having been the choice of 29% of all players. Gearbox reported that they received more than a million digital votes and thousands of postcard entries.

MOST VIEWED *BORDERLANDS* VIDEO

As of 11 August 2014, the "*Borderlands 2*: Doomsday Trailer", uploaded to YouTube by "Pixel Enemy", had been watched 3,805,934 times. The clip, uploaded on 22 February 2012, was a preview of gameplay.

BEST-SELLING MULTI-PLATFORM SERIES DEBUT

The *Borderlands* phenomenon broke in October 2009 when the first game sold half a million copies in its first month, and 2 million copies that year. As of August 2014, *Borderlands* had sold more than 5.33 million copies. Its sequel has sold 5.41 million units across all platforms.

LEAGUE OF LEGENDS

Summary: Like *DotA 2*, this PC and Mac MOBA originates in the *Defense of the Ancients* mod for *Warcraft III*. It has quickly grown to become a classic of both home gaming and the eSports scene.

Publisher: Riot Games
Developer: Riot Games
Debut: 2009

LARGEST AUDIENCE FOR AN ESPORTS TOURNAMENT

Videogames have become spectator sports in their own right and none have proved to be as big a draw as *League of Legends*. The Season 3 World Championship, broadcast live over Twitch.tv online on 4 October 2013, was watched by a total of 32 million people, with the number of concurrent viewers peaking at 8.5 million. By comparison, other international live streams of major events have attracted fewer viewers: the British royal wedding in 2011 hit 300,000 concurrent viewers on Livestream.com, and the YouTube stream of the 2012 Olympics reached a peak of 500,000 people.

by Complexity player Robert "ROBERTxLEE" Lee on 12 July 2014. He managed it in the **longest professional *League of Legends* game** in history, clocking in at a time of 1 hr 20 min 34 sec. The five types of minions – Melee, Caster, Siege, Anti-turret cannon and Super – are the foot-soldiers of *LoL*, the automatically generated units that will wade into battle to attack enemy units.

HIGHEST-RANKED *LEAGUE OF LEGENDS* (*LoL*) TEAM

SK Telecom T1 K (South Korea) has a rating of 1,426, putting it comfortably at the top of the GosuGamers table, a full 119 points ahead of the second-placed Edward Gaming. SKT T1 K has an all-time win rate of 78%. The five-strong team had a particularly successful May 2014, winning all seven of their matches. The GosuGamers community, created in 2002, focuses on eSports content around major titles such as *Counter-Strike: Global Offensive*, *DotA 2*, *Hearthstone*, *Heroes of Newerth*, *LoL* and *StarCraft II*.

HIGHEST ATTACK DAMAGE IN *LoL*

The highest basic attack damage stat ever reached in *League of Legends* is 3,019. This value was achieved by the summoner "HD Dubstep" on the champion Hecarim with the assistance of Zilean, Jayce, Orianna and Galio on 23 January 2013. Attack damage increases the physical damage of a unit's autoattack. Numerous things can provide bonus attack damage, including champion abilities, spells, runes, buffs and masteries. The champion's total attack damage is the base damage figure plus the bonus attack damage figure.

MOST ABILITY POWER ACQUIRED IN *LoL*

While the champion Veigar is theoretically able to gain infinite ability power (AP) through use of his Baleful Strikes, the highest amount any human player has managed to amass without the use of bots or scripts is 12,089, achieved by the summoner "Igorath 92" on 25 August 2013. AP is a champion statistic, and it increases the effectiveness of most abilities.

MOST MINION KILLS IN *LoL*

The most minions ever killed in a professional *League of Legends* game is 719, attained

FASTEST 300 MINION KILLS IN *LoL*

A large part of *League of Legends* is the killing of minions to acquire gold. The fastest player to kill 300 minions is "xPeke", aka Enrique Cedeño Martínez (Spain), who managed to do so as Orianna during the Summer Split of the European LCS on 1 July 2014 – against Roccat – in just 21 min 52 sec.

"We're going to disable the public chat rooms until they're useful and accessible. In their current shape they just don't work and can actively create negative experiences for many players."

RIOT GAMES
OFFICIAL STATEMENT ON THE DECISION TO CLOSE *LoL* CHAT ROOMS IN JULY 2014

FASTEST MOVEMENT SPEED IN *LoL*

The fastest movement speed ever reached in *League of Legends* is 14,223, achieved by the summoner known as "Silomare" on the champion Rammus, with the help of Zilean, Galio, Lulu and Nami, on 22 February 2014. Movement speed represents the rate at which a champion travels across a map. One movement speed point equals one game distance unit travelled per second.

LAND THOSE SKILL-SHOTS   FOR THE WIN

If you're having trouble landing skill-shots, line yourself up with a low-health minion between you and your opponent. When the attack that will kill the minion is in the air, fire your skill-shot. The enemy won't be able to react in time to dodge it once the minion dies!

MOST PLAYED ACTION RTS GAME

In January 2014, Riot Games announced that *League of Legends* had 27 million players daily. This titan of the free2play MOBA/action RTS scene is played by 67 million every month and the peak number of concurrent users online is 7.5 million. According to SuperData Research, *LoL*'s 2013 revenue was £378 million ($624 million).

DIE ANOTHER DAY

Regrettably, the *League of Legends* community loves to pick on the little guy. Teemo, the Swift Scout, averages 6.5 million deaths per day, or about 75 deaths per second.

TWITCH.TV

Many of us get our fill of gaming news via magazines or websites. We drool over the in-game shots and lap up the descriptions of new games. Their writers are guides to worlds we want to visit and their opinions spark hot debate. But those fonts of knowledge now face stiff competition from real-time streaming sites like Twitch.tv.

YouTube was the first to change the online gaming community. It grew to feature just about everything filmable – including play-throughs. But Twitch.tv is now the dominant player in game culture, as a site that allows players to broadcast live video of their games. The audience can communicate via chat and may even influence the broadcaster by issuing commands as they talk.

Launched in 2011, by 2013 Twitch had amassed an audience of 45 million unique viewers per month, watching 12 billion minutes of gameplay per month from almost 1 million broadcasters. These figures make Twitch the **largest video site dedicated to videogaming**, with an audience the envy of almost all major TV channels.

And it's only set to grow. Until recently, games broadcasting was the preserve of those who had the money for expensive capture hardware and software and the time to make it all work. Now apps for broadcasting and viewing Twitch are not only built into the PS4 (the **first console with built-in Twitch broadcasting**) alongside rival broadcasting service Ustream, but can also be accessed on the Xbox One, EA's Origin PC gaming service, NVIDIA graphics card firmware and major games such as *EVE Online*.

Riot Games announced that *League of Legends* had 27 million daily gamers in 2013 – a fanbase that helped it become the **most widely broadcast game on Twitch**.

Entering certain keywords into Twitch chat makes *Daylight* even spookier – try typing "feet" to create the sound of footsteps.

Some games can be directly affected by Twitch viewers in chat. In horror FPS *Daylight*, the broadcaster hears effects such as a spooky cat howl when a viewer types "meow".

The most popular channel is "Twitch Plays *Pokémon*", on which viewers can type chat commands to a *Pokémon* game. The first run, in *Pokémon Red*, launched on 12 February 2014 and was finished on 1 March, with 1.16 million people contributing to the **most participants in a single-player online game**. At its peak, the broadcast recorded 121,000 concurrent viewers. The broadcaster, who remained anonymous, said, "I thought most would play around with it for a few minutes and leave, but it's very engrossing to a surprising amount of

ONLINE STARS

SYNDICATE
The **most popular broadcaster on Twitch** is "Syndicate", aka Tom Cassell (UK, below), with 655,716 followers. Tom also boasts 15,929,707 total views of his channel, as of 7 July 2014. While *League of Legends'* Riot Games are top, with 868,583 followers, they are not game streamers.

Tom is also no slouch on YouTube, where "TheSyndicateProject" has 7.6 million followers and his most popular stream has 12.47 million views.

MEN VS GAMES
King of the lighthearted play-through has to be "PewDiePie", aka Felix Arvid Ulf Kjellberg (Sweden), with the **most subscribers on YouTube** – 28.29 million as of 7 July 2014. Back on Twitch, "MANvsGAME", aka Jayson Love (USA), has 199,254 followers and his channel has been viewed some 38 million times.

DAY[9]TV
Voted *PC Gamer*'s "Gamer of the Year" in 2010 and justifying his uplifting tagline of "Be a better gamer", "Day[9]tv", aka Sean Plott (USA), has a knack for explaining high-level play in games such as *StarCraft II*. As of July 2014, he had 162,553 followers on Twitch and over 62 million views.

PHANTOML0RD
"PhantomL0rd", aka James Varga (USA), is a major *League of Legends* figure who – as a result of his fame – was allegedly the target of a denial-of-service attack in December 2013. PhantomL0rd focuses on *LoL* – the **most widely broadcast game on Twitch** – with 663,000 broadcasts between February 2012 and May 2014. At any time, 100,000 people can be watching *LoL* videos and, with over 540,000 followers to his name, James can easily lay claim to many of them.

One of the cornerstones of Twitch is eSports, pitting global gamers head to head in real time. At E3 2014, Twitch hosted several events, including a *Super Smash Bros.* Invitational.

people… I'm glad that it's holding up as well as it is."

The **most concurrent viewers of a gaming livestreaming service** was also on Twitch, on 15 March 2014, when 826,778 watched a weekend of eSports events.

There's more to come for Twitch, particularly with the $970-m (£576-m) buy-out by Amazon (see timeline). Its broadcasters are now personalities and their shows add another dimension to the games they play.

MATTHEW DIPIETRO
VP Marketing, Twitch.tv

Why has streaming become such an important part of gaming culture today?
First, gaming is, at its core, a social experience. Gamers love to play games with each other. Twitch enables that collaborative experience on a global scale in real time… Gamers are connecting with each other. The social video aspect of Twitch cannot be understated.

Also, Twitch is an honest means of deciding what games to buy. In the past, gamers relied on over-produced trailers featuring style over substance. Press conferences and conventions are often sold out and too expensive. Twitch provides a real-time window to these events.

What makes for a game that's great for broadcasting?
Games of all kinds have some presence on Twitch. The game itself is not as important as the quality of the broadcaster and the passion of the community. Broadcasters who entertain and acknowledge their viewers can turn even the most mundane game into a riveting experience. The beauty of Twitch is that you don't have to be a great or competitive gamer to be a star.

TWITCH HISTORY

March 2007: Emmett Shear (left) co-founds Justin.tv, a 24-hour reality website that streams co-founder Justin Kan's entire life to the internet via a webcam.

May 2007: Justin.tv opens up the service to a second livestreamer and soon new channels are being added at a rate of two a day, with popular subjects including entertainment, pets and, at the top of the list, gaming. Avid *StarCraft II* (left) viewer Shear decides to focus on gaming.

March 2011: Job adverts go live for a new Justin.tv site that has the intention of becoming "the world's best live eSports site".

June 2011: Shear and Kan (left) launch Twitch, initially attracting 3 million visitors every month.

May 2012: Twitch wins a People's Choice Webby Award in the gaming category.

November 2013: The PS4 launches, the **first console to feature built-in Twitch broadcasting**. By early December it contributes 10% of all Twitch activity.

February 2014: Twitch becomes the fourth-largest source of web traffic at peak times in the USA.

March 2014: Direct broadcasting to Twitch from the Xbox One begins.

August 2014: Amazon signs a deal to purchase Twitch for a reported $970 million (£576 m) in cash. It may be that the retail giant will sell directly to gamers, as well as provide Twitch an unrivalled network and perhaps sponsor eSport celebrities.

Summary: The madcap karting series shows no signs of putting on the brakes – indeed, it continues to innovate with features such as anti-gravity, ATVs and Mario Kart TV.

Publisher: Nintendo
Developer: Nintendo/various
Debut: 1992

FIRST CROSSOVER CHARACTERS IN A KART VIDEOGAME

Crossover characters are becoming increasingly popular in various genres, but 2005 title *Mario Kart Arcade GP* was the first kart game to put PAC-Man, Ms. PAC-Man and Blinky the red ghost into karts as playable characters. The second version of this arcade game also included Mametchi from *Tamagotchi*.

The ever-innovative karting series also turned karting on its head. *Mario Kart 7* on the 3DS featured the **first flying karts** – when a racer gets big air, wings sprout from their kart to help it glide over a track shortcut – and also the **first underwater karts** – when karting into water, propellers pop out, helping racers to cruise along the sea floor.

MOST HEATS IN A KART VIDEOGAME COMPETITION

Held between 5 and 12 April 2008, the largest kart game tournament in the UK was a *Mario Kart Wii* preview event called the "Grand Wii". Organized by retailer GAME, it featured 30 regional heats held in stores across the UK. Each winner went on to the final on 12 April, where they battled it out for the top prize: a very cool Mario-themed VW Beetle.

BEST-SELLING KART GAME

Mario Kart Wii had sold 34.53 million copies worldwide as of 8 July 2014, making it not just the biggest karting game but also the single **biggest-selling racing game** of all time, powering ahead of *Mario Kart DS* in second place and *Gran Turismo 3: A-spec* on the PS2 in third (for more on *GT*, see pp.38–39).

FASTEST SINGLE-SEGMENT SPEED-RUN ON *MARIO KART WII*

Quick laps are impressive, but a single-sitting run – an uninterrupted play-through of an entire game – requires a different skill set altogether. Proving he has the stamina and the skill, Jose Karica (Panama) completed *Mario Kart Wii* (2008) on "Hard" difficulty in an exceptional 1 hr 7 min 9 sec on 3 February 2009.

FASTEST COMPLETION OF *SUPER MARIO KART* CIRCUIT 1

Sami Çetin (UK) completed Circuit 1 in the PAL version of *Super Mario Kart* (1992) on the SNES in a lightning-quick 57.90 sec on 25 December 2013. Çetin is also the record holder for the NTSC version, completing the same circuit in an even speedier 56.19 sec.

FASTEST COMPLETION OF MAKA WUHU IN *MARIO KART 7* (3DS)

The fastest completion of Maka Wuhu (aka the Wuhu Mountain Loop) on the 3DS is 1 min 6.51 sec by Jacob Adams Queen (USA) in Fort Mill, South Carolina, on 3 August 2013.

▶▶MOST REAL-LIFE DRIVERS IN A KART GAME

F1 Race Stars (Codemasters Birmingham, 2012) features 24 real-world F1 drivers such as Lewis Hamilton, Sebastian Vettel and Fernando Alonso.

If you factor in fictional drivers, the **most playable characters in a kart-racing game** is 33 (including DLC and drivers exclusive to certain gaming platforms) in *Sonic & All-Stars Racing Transformed* (Sumo Digital, 2012).

LONGEST-RUNNING KART-RACING SERIES

With 21 years 275 days between the launches of *Mario Kart* (1992) and *Mario Kart 8* (2014), the series is the most durable kart-racing franchise. The latest edition debuted in Japan on 29 May (and in Europe and North America on 30 May) and sold 1.2 million copies just two days. Not only does this make *Mario Kart 8* the **fastest-selling kart game (opening weekend)**, but it also propelled the series past the 100-million mark (**best-selling kart-racing series**).

MOST TIME-TRIAL WORLD RECORDS HELD ON *SUPER MARIO KART* ON THE SNES*

Name	Records	Ties
Guillaume Leviach	27	4
Karel van Duijven-boden	14	7
Sami Çetin	14	1
Florent Lecoanet	6	1
Oliver Segarra Gonzalez	5	3
Pierre L'Hoest	3	1
Shingo Fukushima	1	–
Guilherme Arantes	1	–
Tyler Worley	1	–

All times correct as of 30 March 2014
*PAL and NTSC records combined

NO TO MARIO

The original intention was *not* for Mario to feature in Nintendo's kart-racing game at all, says developer and director Hideki Konno. At first, the game involved a normal human in overalls with an oil can and banana for weapons. The idea to use Mario and co came later.

FIRST HIGH-DEF *MARIO KART* GAME

Taking advantage of the HD capabilities of the Wii U, *Mario Kart 8* is the first *Mario Kart* videogame to benefit from high-definition graphics. "The visuals aren't just crisp and 60-frames-per-second smooth," reported *High-Def Digest*, "they're absolutely voluptuous in imagination and colour. This is Nintendo's most glorious realization of the Mushroom Kingdom yet, absolutely exploding and dense with charm, bright-eyed fantasy and impeccable precision."

4

control schemes that *Mario Kart 8* can use: the Wii U GamePad, Wii U Pro Controller, Wii Wheel and Wii Remote and Nunchuk.

Summary: Street racing, pro racing, police chases, tuners, exotic cars, muscle cars – this series has it all. Mixing real-world locations with fictional ones, the old stalwart is still very much speeding along.

Publisher: EA
Developer: Various
Debut: 1994

MOST PROLIFIC RACING GAME SERIES

With 25 titles released between 1994 and 2013, the *Need for Speed* series contains more games than any other racing franchise. It has appeared on multiple platforms from Android to Zeebo, and has crossed genres with MMOs in *Need for Speed: Motor City Online* and the free2play *Need for Speed: World*. *Rivals*, released in 2013, is the series' 25th title.

MOST DRIVERS SPONSORED BY A VIDEOGAME PUBLISHER

EA has sponsored seven drivers across the Formula Drift, Time Attack and FIA GT3 motor-racing disciplines under the banner of *Team Need for Speed*. EA has also sponsored drivers in endurance races such as the 24 Hours of Le Mans and the Nürburgring 24-hour race, in which Team Need for Speed came fourth in 2010. Although the team is no longer active, EA retains the record as no other publisher has been so supportive of pro racing.

FOR THE WIN

SAVE YOUR SPEEDPOINTS

When you gain SpeedPoints in *Need for Speed: Rivals* as a Rider, it makes sense to save them regularly at Hideouts. If you are caught by the police, they'll snatch any unbanked points off you.

BEST-SELLING DRIVING VIDEOGAME SERIES

The *Need for Speed* series has sold an almighty 93.14 million copies, according to VGChartz. Driving games such as *Forza Motorsport*, *Gran Turismo* (see pp.38–39) and *Need for Speed* come under the racing umbrella but primarily use real-world cars and tracks, unlike some karting titles or futuristic racers. The **best-selling *Need for Speed* game** is *Need for Speed: Underground 2*, which has sold 10.94 million copies.

HIGHEST SCORE ON *NEED FOR SPEED: WORLD*

Finnish gamer "GIGAXER0" had accumulated 1,019,863 points on *Need for Speed: World* as of 7 July 2014. GIGAXER0 used a total of 107 cars in achieving this feat. *Need for Speed: World* was previously known as *Need for Speed: World Online*.

MOST STUDIOS TO WORK ON ONE RACING GAME SERIES

The Need for Speed was the very first game in the enduring series, and it was developed by the now-defunct Pioneer Productions. Since then, some 24 developers have worked on various games in the franchise, including EA Black Box and Criterion Games, producers of the *Burnout* racing series. Ghost Games and Criterion collaborated on the latest release in the series, *Need for Speed: Rivals*.

HIGHEST-GROSSING FILM BASED ON A RACING GAME

The Hollywood movie *Need for Speed* was released on 14 March 2014. As of 19 July 2014, it had grossed $203,277,636 (£120,770,708) worldwide, making it one of the most lucrative videogame movies of all time. It fared especially well in China, where car ownership has become more commonplace over the past 20 years. The **highest-grossing videogame spin-off film** overall is 2010's *Prince of Persia: The Sands of Time* (USA), which grossed $335,154,643 (£208,897,000).

HIT THE BREAK

No *Need for Speed* title was released in 2014 – but a new game is in the works. Ghost Games boss Marcus Nilsson explained that EA had given them an extra year to produce a new title. He said: "We are already deep in development on our next game. We're excited and ready."

HIGHEST SCORE ON *NEED FOR SPEED: RIVALS*

Brazilian PC gamer "jhowkNx" is at the top of the *Rivals* leaderboards, with a score of 173,811. This is the highest score across all platforms – the PC, PS3, PS4, Xbox 360 and Xbox One. Appropriately enough, jhowkNx's licence plate is "KING".

MOST PLATFORMS FOR A RACING GAME SERIES

As of July 2014, *Need for Speed* games had appeared on 21 different gaming platforms: Sony's PlayStation, PS2, PS3, PSP, PS Vita and PS4; the 3DO; Nintendo's Game Boy Advance, GameCube, DS, Wii, 3DS and WII U; Microsoft's Xbox, Xbox 360 and Xbox One; Sega's Saturn and Dreamcast; and iOS, Android and Windows Phone mobile platforms.

FASTEST COMPLETION OF "MAIN STREET" CIRCUIT IN *NEED FOR SPEED: WORLD*

Gamer "MESK94" (France) completed the "Main Street" track in a time of just 1 min 8.569 sec. The McLaren F1 Elite is the vehicle of choice for the fastest drivers around the 3-km Main Street, including MESK94.

The **fastest completion of the "Hastings" circuit** in the same game is by Ukrainian "OSECOSE", who crossed the

MOST CRITICALLY ACCLAIMED *NEED FOR SPEED* GAME

You have to stick it in reverse and ride all the way back to 2010 to find the *Need for Speed* game critics rated higher than any other. According to reviews aggregator gamerankings.com, *Need for Speed: Hot Pursuit* on the PS3 is the cream of the crop with a score of 88.86%. The GamesRadar review said, "Quite simply, there is no better, more accessible racing game out there."

finishing line in 6 min 2.097 sec. Sounds sluggish? It isn't – Hastings is an epic 15.06 km (9.3 mi) in length. As with Main Street, the McLaren F1 Elite comes up trumps. With a top need of 330 km/h (205 mph), it's easy to see why.

20

games in the mainline *Need for Speed* series, as well as the number of years that the franchise had been in existence by 2014.

LONGEST MARATHON ON A *NEED FOR SPEED* GAME

Kenny Drews and Florian Fleissner (both Germany) played *Need for Speed: Most Wanted* (2012) for an impressive 33 hr exactly at City Center Langenhagen in Hannover, Germany, from 31 May to 1 June 2013. The 19th title in the racing series, *Most Wanted* made use of Kinect on the Xbox 360, allowing players to use voice commands such as "engine start". The **longest marathon on any racing game** lasted 36 hours and was achieved by Simon Platt and Ralph Cooper (both UK), who played *Grid 2* from 30 May to 31 May 2013.

Summary: The veteran RPG has spawned offshoots that include movies, a radio station and even an eatery, in the shape of Tokyo's Eorzea Cafe in Japan. Perhaps Chocobo is on the menu…

Publisher: Square/ Square Enix
Developer: Square/ Square Enix
Debut: 1987

MOST SOUNDTRACKS RELEASED FOR A VIDEOGAME SERIES

Squareenixmusic.com calculated that 173 *Final Fantasy* soundtracks have been released. The figure includes the main series up to 2010, but not the Chocobo spin-off titles.

Some *Final Fantasy* albums have managed impressive sales figures, such as *Final Fantasy VIII Original Soundtrack*, released in 1999 and selling over 300,000 copies in Japan alone that year.

FOR THE WIN

FINAL FANTASY XII QUICKENING

It's well worth learning to use Quickenings (combos) – especially against bosses or hard enemies. They are particularly useful in pack attacks. If you switch out one character each time you do a chain of Quickenings, you can have big hitters that are enough to kill a lot of bosses. Just remember to be careful, as unleashing the chain even a little too early may be fatal.

FIRST RADIO STATION DEDICATED TO A VIDEOGAME

On 17 November 2003, Square Enix and AOL Radio launched a radio station that featured

MOST PROLIFIC FINAL FANTASY CHARACTER

A powerful fighter, Gilgamesh (above) first appeared in *Final Fantasy V* and his total game count stands at 13 in various guises. Initially he was an enemy but later became a friend to the player's parties. Moving down the evolutionary chain, the Chocobo is the nearest thing the series has to a mascot and is the **most prolific** *Final Fantasy* **creature**, having appeared in a total of 57 games.

200 tracks from the *Final Fantasy* series. Available until April 2004, it made a return in July 2006 owing to popular demand. A group of fans then picked up the musical baton and still operate Final Fantasy Radio at finalfantasyradio.co/ listeners-lounge.

MOST WIDELY RELEASED FINAL FANTASY GAME

The original *Final Fantasy* is available on at least 10 different platforms, including iOS, Android and Windows Mobile.

BEST-SELLING FINAL FANTASY GAME

Final Fantasy VII has sold 9.72 million copies on the PlayStation. It's in second place on the platform overall behind *Gran Turismo*, the **best-selling PlayStation game**. As a series, *Final Fantasy* has sold more than 105 million copies.

FIRST FINAL FANTASY TO USE VOICE ACTORS

The English version of *Final Fantasy X* was the first in the series to use spoken dialogue, and featured James Arnold Taylor (above) as Tidus. Taylor has voiced Ratchet from *Ratchet & Clank*, Obi-Wan Kenobi in *Star Wars: The Clone Wars* (USA, 2008) and the title character in TV's *Johnny Test* (Canada/ USA, 2005–present). Other actors included John DiMaggio (Jake in *Adventure Time*) voicing Wakka and Kimahri.

SEMI-FINAL FANTASY

Final Fantasy XIV: A Realm Reborn was a hasty reworking of the critically panned *Final Fantasy XIV*. It features a new engine and story as well as revamped gameplay and interface. Following PS3 and PC editions, a PS4 version (above) came out in April 2014, the eighth-generation debut of a series that has been around since the NES back in the third generation of consoles.

LONGEST MARATHON ON A JAPANESE ROLE-PLAYING GAME (JRPG)

"Kinumi Cati", aka Hecaterina Kinumi Iglesias Pérez, played *Final Fantasy X* for 38 hr 6 min on 26–28 July 2013. Although her elaborate game costumes often make people think she is Japanese, Hecaterina is from Spain. You can read more about her feats on p.88 and p.108.

There's no doubt that she's keen to break records. Kinumi even liked GWR's strict conditions for keeping her attempts open for public viewing: "This is kind of cool because you never know who's going to come and watch," she said. "Last time, a TV reporter and a camera crew came to make a surprise interview while I was trying to have a little nap before the record."

100,000,000
hours of *Final Fantasy XIV* played online, as of February 2014.

MOST PROLIFIC RPG SERIES

Final Fantasy runs to 61 incredibly diverse titles, from the numbered entries to their associated games and the army of spin-offs (but not games outside of the RPG genre). Shown here is *Final Fantasy XIV: A Realm Reborn*, while the wait for what was first called *Final Fantasy Versus XIII* continues. In what is the **longest development period for a JRPG**, *FF Versus XIII* was begun in May 2006 and then retitled *Final Fantasy XV* in 2013 – but was completely absent from E3 in 2014. The game will not appear until 2015 at the very earliest.

ANGRY BIRDS

Summary: The avian and porcine puzzler took over the world but is not done yet: "OK, we have two billion downloads... and it's a good start," says developer CEO Peter Vesterbacka.

Publisher: Rovio
Developer: Rovio
Debut: 2009

HIGHEST SCORE ON *ANGRY BIRDS* FOR IOS

The gamer "to mock a mockingbird" sat perched atop the *Angry Birds* iOS leaderboards on the AngryBirdsNest website, with a total score of 53,618,360 as of 19 June 2014. This tally includes top scores in all eight original episodes of *Angry Birds*.

HIGHEST SCORE ON *ANGRY BIRDS STAR WARS II*

Gamer "Wicket182" (USA) used plenty of Force to rack up 27,666,200 points by 23 June 2014. The same player achieved an equally impressive score of 26,868,020 on the debut, the **highest score on *Angry Birds Star Wars***.

HIGHEST-RANKING *STAR WARS* IOS APP

LEGO®'s outing takes the record for the **biggest-selling *Star Wars* game** (see pp.50–51), but *Angry Birds Star Wars II* ranks 48th overall as the most downloaded app in Apple's iTunes app marketplace.

MOST VIEWED FAN FILM BASED ON A PUZZLE GAME

FunVideoTV's "ANGRY BIRDS dance GANGNAM STYLE" clip is an homage to PSY's monster hit of 2012. Uploaded to YouTube on 29 November 2012, the animation has gone on to attract 46,066,896 views.

HIGHEST SCORE ON *ANGRY BIRDS FRIENDS*

With a score of 48,908,920, player "bambenio" was top of the pecking order in *Angry Birds Friends* – originally called *Angry Birds Facebook*. Over in the tie-in game with movie *Rio* (USA, 2011), "Manu Malin" recorded the **highest score on *Angry Birds Rio***, with 45,204,750.

FIRST THEME PARK BASED ON A PUZZLE GAME

Angry Birds are roosting all over the real world. The first official theme park is in the Särkänniemi Adventure Park in Finland. Elsewhere, in the country's capital of Helsinki, is the **first official videogame merchandise shop** selling from a single franchise. Overall, the Birds have the **most theme parks based on a game**, with the other two in Malaysia and in Thorpe Park in the UK. In addition, the Angry Birds Activity Park opened on 25 May 2013 at Lightwater Valley also in the UK, following Angry Birds Space Encounter opening at the Kennedy Space Centre in Florida, USA, in March 2013.

MOST VIEWED *ANGRY BIRDS* YOUTUBE VIDEO

Rovio created the 1-min 45-sec *Angry Birds & The Mighty Eagle* to promote the optional bird of prey paid-for character. The clip has been viewed 105,828,487 times.

MOST DOWNLOADED MOBILE GAME SERIES

With 2 billion downloads and counting as of May 2014, those furious fowl in all their incarnations are the most downloaded of all mobile games, facing off the likes of *Candy Crush Saga* (with 500 million downloads in its first year to November 2013). When Apple released its list of the all-time best-selling iOS games in July 2013, the original *Angry Birds* had flapped to the top position in both the paid-for iPhone and iPad apps chart, although the company did not release actual download figures.

▶▶LARGEST ARCHITECTURAL GAME DISPLAY

Angry Birds doesn't have the puzzle game roost all to itself. *Tetris* remains a big title, particularly in the version made on 5 April 2014 (above) by Frank Lee (USA). It took up 11,111.2 m² (119,600 sq ft) of the Cira Centre in Pennsylvania, USA, with 1,400 LEDs. The **largest game of Tetris** (inset) measured 105.7 m² (1,138.7 sq ft) on 15 September 2010, and was made by *The Gadget Show* (UK, North One).

$100,000

invested by then unknown Rovio in developing their 52nd game – *Angry Birds*.

FASTEST ROVIO GAME TO RANK NO.1

Bad Piggies hit the top of the App Store in just over three hours on 27 September 2012. It was helped by a global launch promotion that included images of piggies on balloons, trucks and electronic displays.

MOST PEOPLE IN A MOBILE PHONE GAME RELAY

Nokia organized a marathon *Angry Birds* session on 11 June 2011, when 2,030 people played the game in Kuala Lumpur, Malaysia. Each participant was challenged to clear or fail one level of the game over the course of 10 hours.

CATAPULT TO SUCCESS

When *Angry Birds* was released, it sold just 30,000 to 40,000 copies in three months. But this was enough for it to hit No.1 in the Finnish, Swedish, Danish, Greek and Czech Republic App Stores. From there, it caught the attention of the all-important UK and US markets.

LARGEST GAME OF *ANGRY BIRDS*

US talk show host Conan O'Brien presented a live-action version of the game in his studio in 2011. Firing giant inflatable birds from an oversized catapult, O'Brien played on the rivalry between Rovio's Iceland and Nordic neighbour Sweden by aiming at inflatable green pigs under IKEA furniture.

MOST EXPENSIVE KART

Rovio's foray into kart racing with *Angry Birds Go!* wasn't without controversy. While it faced up to inevitable comparisons with Mario's racing behemoth, the free-to-play's in-app purchases came in for criticism. Most expensive was the Big Bang Special Edition kart, which could be unlocked in the game for a hefty £34.99 ($49.99) on its launch in December 2013. Rovio's line of physical toys – the Telepods made by Hasbro – include *Go!* cars that can also be bought separately and used in the game.

KILLER APPS

The blockbusting apps on Android, iOS and Facebook are the titles that transcend all boundaries: games such as *Hay Day* and *Candy Crush Saga* are instantly accessible and easily playable, which at least partly explains their enormous appeal to a broad demographic. What's more, up-and-coming designers and entrepreneurs can develop killer apps speedily and cheaply at home – and for the lucky ones who strike gold, they are entering a social gaming market worth $8 billion (£4.8 billion) in 2014.

SUPERSTAR SUPERCELL

A new star on the social gaming scene, Finnish developers Supercell made waves in 2013 with the success of *Clash of Clans* and *Hay Day*, both available on iOS and Android. Those two games alone earned the company $892 million (£541 million) in revenue in 2013. *Boom Beach* was released in 2014, and the company is looking to expand through TV "app-vertising", a relatively new approach for social developers such as Supercell, who want to promote their games to a mass audience. The *Clash of Clans* TV spot was first broadcast on 23 December 2013, and its YouTube upload had been viewed 21,700,151 times as of 20 August 2014, making it the **most viewed YouTube video for a gaming app TV commercial.**

FISH AND FOWL

At the height of its popularity, *Flappy Bird* (left) was the No.1-ranked app on both Android and iOS with around 50 million downloads, earning £30,000 ($50,000) a day from in-app advertising. Then, quite unexpectedly, Vietnamese developer Dong Nguyen announced that he would be removing the game from sale over concerns that it was too addictive. A spate of clones rapidly followed. In one 24-hour period covering 26–27 February 2014, it was reported that one-third of new iOS games released were *Flappy Bird*-inspired. The most successful of those was *Splashy Fish* (right), which attracted 5 to 10 million daily users playing 250 million games per day, according to *Business Insider*.

THE CURIOUS CUBE

As of 18 June 2014, the **most expensive in-app purchase** was the Diamond Chisel in Peter Molyneux's experimental game *Curiosity – What's Inside the Cube?* It was priced at 3 billion in-game coins, an eye-watering £47,000 ($75,000) in real-world money. The game invited players to chip away at a big block, each layer unveiling something new. The Diamond Chisel increased tapping power by a factor of 100,000.

After seven months and 69 billion individual blocks, the gamer who chipped away the final layer was Bryan Henderson from Edinburgh, Scotland, UK (right); his prize will be to star in 22Cans' next game *Godus*.

KIM'S SIM

Celebrities are taking a slice of the app game pie, too. Released on 25 June 2014, freemium celebrity-sim *Kim Kardashian: Hollywood* was a smash hit, earning $1.6 million (£962,000) in its first five days according to developer Glu Mobile, and analysts predict it will earn $200 million (£120 million) in in-app purchases.

DRAGONS' DEN

Candy Crush Saga and *Clash of Clans* may be more familiar to Western gamers, but neither can lay claim to being the **first mobile game to earn $1 billion**. That honour goes to *Puzzle & Dragons*, an iOS and Android game that has been a sensation in Japan. Tokyo-based developer GungHo revealed that 91% of its $1.5-billion (£910-million) revenues in 2013 were from its triumphant mobile title. By May of that year, *Puzzle & Dragons* had been downloaded by more than 13 million mobile gamers. *P&D*'s achievement differs from *FarmVille*'s record (see left) because it is exclusively a mobile app, whereas the farming sim was a Facebook-based app.

STUD FARM

At its peak, Facebook phenomenon *FarmVille* had 83.8 million players a month, and by February 2013 it had earned more than $1 billion (£661 million) in in-game player purchases – the **first gaming app to earn $1 billion**. The game's popularity declined as quickly as the fortunes of its developer, Zynga, which has been eclipsed by King. Sequel *FarmVille 2* was the 16th most popular Facebook app globally as of 20 August 2014.

CRUSHING THE (A)PPOSITION

King's *Candy Crush Saga* continues to sit happily at the top of Facebook's app chart, ahead of *Farm Heroes Saga* and Spotify, according to AppData, making i: the **most popular Facebook app**. The sugary puzzle game is nothing short of a casual-gaming phenomenon, played as it is by millions of people of all ages, many of whom do not consider themselves gamers. There were an estimated 7.7 million daily average users as of August 2014, raking in around $1 million (£600,000) every day in revenues for the imperious King.

www.guinnessworldrecords.com/gamers

POKÉMON

Summary: With 3DS remakes of 2002's *Ruby* and *Sapphire* editions due in late 2014 to include "Mega"-revamps of gameplay, the popularity of the RPG series remains high.

Publisher: Nintendo
Developer: Game Freak/ Creatures Inc
Debut: 1996

FASTEST POKÉMON

Deoxys (Speed Form), a Pokémon introduced in *Pokémon Emerald*, has a base speed stat of 180 points. Designed by Ken Sugimori, its name is a play on deoxyribonucleic acid, or DNA. The world of science returned the favour in calling a newly discovered protein (used in transmitting visual information to the brain) "pikachurin" after Pikachu, making it the **first protein named after a videogame character**.

LARGEST BESTIARY IN A VIDEOGAME

Pokémon X and *Y* has 719 different Pokémon, including all six generations of Pokémon from the Kanto, Johto, Hoenn, Sinnoh, Unova and Kalos regions.

BEST-SELLING 3DS GAME

The two variants of the 2013 *Pokémon* release, *X* and *Y*, form the best-selling 3DS game, with 11.45 million sales according to vgchartz.com as of 8 August 2014. They are the **first games to sell over 10 million units on the 3DS** (*Mario Kart 7*, with 9.69 million sales, is racing up behind). *Pokémon* began life on a handheld, the Game Boy, and with the later N64 *Pokémon Stadium*, became the **first console game to transfer data from a handheld**. Character info from the Game Boy titles *Red* and *Blue* could be transferred to the N64.

FASTEST SINGLE-SEGMENT COMPLETION OF *POKÉMON Y*

Speed-runner and swimming lifeguard "iMAX1UP" (Guatemala) finished *Pokémon Y* in 3 hr 52 min 45 sec on 28 February 2014. Not bad for a game that would take the average player well over 30 hours to complete.

FOR THE WIN

POKÉMON AMIE

It may seem like Nintendo's answer to Tamagotchi, but the new Amie feature in *X* and *Y* – interacting with and feeding a Pokémon – can be used for the practical purposes of increasing experience bonus, helping to avoid attacks and landing critical hits.

FIRST *POKÉMON* CHARACTER

Pikachu may be the one on all the lunchboxes, but Rhydon (above) was the first Pokémon ever designed. Mew (left) was the **first Pokémon to be trademarked**.

MOST VIEWED FAN FILM BASED ON AN RPG

The first part of the four-part video "POKÉMON IN REAL LIFE!" (Smosh, 2011) has been viewed 40,709,244 times since being uploaded to YouTube on 22 April 2011. Putting Pokémon battles in everyday life were a cast including the co-founder of the series' production company Smosh – Anthony Padilla as Ash Ketchum (above) – and Brian Rife playing Pikachu (above right).

MOST WINS OF THE POKÉMON TRADING CARD GAME WORLD CHAMPIONSHIPS

The Pokémon TCG World Championships are held annually, and Jason Klaczynski (USA) won in 2006, 2008 and 2013. He studies biochemistry and is also a professional poker player. "Cards encompass my life," he said.

FIRST FISH TO "PLAY" A VIDEOGAME

US college students Catherine Moresco and Patrick Facheris programmed a hack of the original *Pokémon* to respond to the movements of their dorm-room fish. As of 31 August 2014, a total of 3,422,540 Twitch users had watched the live stream of Grayson playing the game.

20,000,000,000+
Pokémon trading cards printed and circulated since 1999.

BEST-SELLING RPG SERIES

With sales of the main series tipping 204.24 million worldwide, *Pokémon* is by far the best-selling RPG series ever created – although much of its success comes from Nintendo's habit of selling multiple versions of the game, from *X* and *Y* all the way back to the debut of *Pokémon Red Version* and *Pokémon Green Version*. Speaking of which… originally released in Japan as *Pocket Monsters Red* and *Pocket Monsters Green*, the Game Boy classics have together sold a (pocket) monstrous 31.37 million copies, making them the **best-selling *Pokémon* game**. Sequel releases *Gold* and *Silver* have second place with a very respectable 23.10 million units sold.

LONGEST-RUNNING TV SPIN-OFF FROM A VIDEOGAME

The *Pokémon* TV series made its Japanese TV debut on 1 April 1997. Its 840th episode, "The Wriggling Forest of Ohrot!", aired in Japan on 7 August 2014 in its 17th season.

TOYS-TO-LIFE

From Pinocchio to Buzz Lightyear, the idea of toys coming to life has always been a hit with kids. Toy manufacturers have come a long way in creating a sense of realism by using technology to combine toys with games in ever-more advanced ways...

Once upon a time, interactivity meant Teddy Ruxpin, a cuddly bear from 1985 whose mouth and eyes moved as he "read" stories recorded on cassette tapes placed inside him. His equivalents today, like the *Skylanders* range, don't so much tell stories as become them by making an appearance in their owners' videogames.

The *Skylanders* concept is simple. Place a physical toy on a special "portal" connected

to a console and the character leaps into fully animated life on screen. Each figure is then both a toy in its own right and a hero in a fully playable game. Players can even swap components to make entirely new characters in *Skylanders: Swap Force*. It all makes Teddy Ruxpin seem a bit, well, threadbare.

USE THE (NEAR FIELD) FORCE
The clever tech behind Activision's *Skylanders* is Near Field Communication (NFC). Devices fitted with NFC that are close to each other – or touching – can transmit data. The system is used on some travel networks: as passengers board a bus or enter a station, they take out a credit card-style pass and touch it on a pad to register their journey. *Skylanders* works the same way, the passive figures communicating wirelessly with receivers in the powered portals to exchange information. *Spyro's Adventure* was the **first game to use NFC** on its release in 2011.

"We had a lot of crazy ideas, but the one that stuck was toys," Alex Ness, chief of staff for *Skylanders* developer Toys for Bob, told GWR. "The Wii, with its controller, was a new way to play games that hadn't

been done before but, instead of trying to leverage off that, we said, 'Well, let's find another new way to play games.' Toys are these perfect whimsical things that we all had as kids, and we all thought about playing with them in games. Luckily, Activision was crazy enough to say, 'OK'."

Skylanders is already one of the most successful game series of all time, if its toy sales are included. By 2014 it had outpaced *Star Wars*, *Transformers* and *WWE* in the USA. The series generated more revenue than Activision's *Call of Duty: Ghosts*, and by July 2014 almost 13 million views were recorded on YouTube for the

"Tall Tales" trailer for *Skylanders: Giants*, the **most viewed *Skylanders* video**. Serious collectors have got in on the act and the **rarest *Skylanders* figures** (600 promotional Spyro, Gill Grunt and Trigger Happy toys, given away at E3 2011) sell for over $1,700 (£1,000) on eBay.

MONSTERS UNIVERSITY
James P Sullivan on the Infinity Base (along with Mike) and in the *Disney Infinity* campaign.

SKYLANDERS
The phenomenally successful series makes its characters the heroes of their own, family-friendly videogames.

SPIDER-MAN PLAY SET
Marvel is set to join *Disney Infinity* in 2014 with, clockwise around Spidey: Nova, Venom, Iron Fist and Nick Fury.

Not all toys have had such happy careers in the world of electronic showbiz, though. Anyone remember Wappy Dog? If not, you won't be alone. This robotic pooch, also created by Activision, hit the shops shortly after Spyro and his *Skylanders* pals but seemed very much like a novelty add-on to the Nintendo DS-exclusive game so didn't enjoy the same success.

TO INFINITY AND BEYOND
In August 2013, Disney embraced the playable toy craze with *Disney Infinity*. Players control characters from Disney movies and TV shows such as *Toy Story* (USA, 1995), *Frozen* (USA, 2013) and *Phineas and Ferb* (USA, 2007–present). As well as movie-specific levels, players can mix and match any number of characters, with a 2014 sequel set to add Marvel superheroes to the line-up.

Infinity extends into Disney's Orlando theme park in Florida, USA, where entry is by radio-frequency wristband. Not many people know it, but gamers can put one of these wristbands on the *Infinity* portal to unlock in-game dragon toys and props!

AMIIBO, AMIGO
Nintendo is a late arrival to the scene, but it has two advantages. Gamers don't

need to buy a portal as the Wii U gamepad has an NFC connector built in, and Nintendo's amiibo range of figures, first released in 2014, are based around familiar characters from the Nintendo universe. Rather than buy a figure for a standalone game, fans will be able to drop a Mario or a Peach into a range of titles, starting with *Super Smash Bros.* for the Wii U, due late 2014, with *Mario Kart 8* to follow. A reader will connect to the 3DS version. Nintendo's entry underlines the success of a genre which, despite the odd hiccup, has taken toys to a new dimension.

BEST-SELLING INTERACTIVE GAMING TOYS
As of July 2014, more than 175 million *Skylanders* figures and play sets had been sold. Since the launch of *Skylanders: Spyro's Adventure* in 2011, characters such as *Swap Force*'s Magna Charge (left) have helped bring in over $2 bn (£1.2 bn) for publisher Activision.

AMIIBO
Mario to the rescue! The launch of Nintendo's range of toys for games may provide a much-needed boost for the ailing Wii U console.

TRAP TEAM
Toys for Bob are to return in late 2014 with a new *Skylanders* game and characters.

HIGHEST MARGIN OF VICTORY AGAINST THE COMPUTER ON *2014 FIFA WORLD CUP BRAZIL*

All in all, 2014 was an excellent year for German gamer Patrick Hadler. Not only did his nation win the World Cup for a fourth time, but on 28 May he also won a match 321–0 in the official videogame of said World Cup. Patrick played as Germany against the Cook Islands.

In addition, Patrick has set records for the **highest margin of victory against the computer on** *FIFA 14* (322 goals) and the **highest margin of victory against the computer on** *FIFA 13* (307 goals). Of his victories, Patrick says: "I deliberately chose a weak opponent and sometimes the goalkeeper dives completely the wrong way, which keeps things amusing."

7" GOAL
11 M. KLOSE

SAMSUNG

GUINNESS WORLD RECORDS

CERTIFICATE

The highest margin of victory against computer on 2014 FIFA World Cup Brazil is 321 goals and was achieved by Patrick Hadler (Germany), in Rethem, Germany, on 28 May 2014

OFFICIALLY AMAZING

RECORD HOLDER

PLAYSTATION

Summary: The fantasy open-world series turned 20 in 2014, and entered the realm of MMORPGs with ZeniMax Online Studios' *The Elder Scrolls Online* (*ESO*) – the 19th entry in the franchise.

Publisher: Bethesda
Developer: Bethesda
Debut: 1994

LARGEST OFFICIAL GAME GUIDE BOOK

The Legendary Collector's Edition of the official guide book for *The Elder Scrolls V: Skyrim* contains 1,120 pages, 785,000 words and 4,025 screenshots, profiling over 350 quests, 500 monsters and 2,000 items.

FIRST PLAYER CROWNED EMPEROR IN *THE ELDER SCROLLS ONLINE*

"Morkulth" holds the distinction of being the first to be crowned Emperor. This was achieved on 30 March 2014 on the Dawnbreaker campaign during the game's early access period. "Morkulth" was aided by his guild, Entropy Rising, in conjunction with another guild, PRX. He said: "My determination to be the best at anything and everything always keeps my mind focused on what I want."

MOST READABLE BOOKS IN A VIDEOGAME

The Elder Scrolls Online contains 2,235 readable books of in-game lore and legend. If you take the time to read them all, you'll have digested about 480,000 words.

ESO also boasts the **most unique non-player characters (NPCs) in a videogame**, with an impressive figure of 10,202. In total, there are 61 million different items in the game. As of 14 July 2014, it was exclusive to Windows and Mac, but PS4 and Xbox One versions are due by early 2015.

40,656,000 weapon variations in *The Elder Scrolls Online*.

SWORDS LORE

Vijay Lakshman, Lead Designer on the original 1994 *Elder Scrolls* game, is responsible for much of the series lore: he was inspired to create the name Khajiit by the Japanese term for swordsmanship, Kenjutsu.

MOST CRITICALLY ACCLAIMED FIRST-PERSON RPG

It's *The Elder Scrolls V: Skyrim* that rules the critics' charts for first-person role-playing titles. The Xbox 360 version of the game has a towering GameRankings score of 95.15%. In *Skyrim*, the aim of the game is to defeat Alduin, the ferocious dragon, while developing skills in combat, magic and stealth.

FIRST MULTIPLAYER *ELDER SCROLLS* GAME

An Elder Scrolls Legend: Battlespire, released for PC in 1997, was the first game in the series to offer both a co-operative story mode and team-based competitive multiplayer modes. The player takes on the role of The Apprentice, who must locate and defeat the devilish Mehrunes Dagon.

FASTEST SINGLE-SEGMENT COMPLETION OF *SKYRIM*

Finnish speed-runner "MrWalrus3451" completed *Skyrim* in just 45 min 38 sec on 19 July 2014. He used various exploits – including a trick that lets you pass obstacles by pushing an object through them. This record also omits load times.

FOR THE WIN

MULTIPLES CHOICE

Unlike the choice between Alliance and Horde factions in Blizzard's timeless *World of Warcraft*, *The Elder Scrolls Online* gives you a three-way choice between the First Aldmeri Dominion, the Daggerfall Covenant and the Ebonheart Pact. This is a decision you cannot go back on, so choose wisely.

Creature attacks!

1 ⚔ 3 ◆ 5 📖 7 ❓

FIRST *ELDER SCROLLS* MOBILE GAME

Released in August 2003, *The Elder Scrolls Travels: Stormhold* was developed for the Nokia N-Gage and other Java-based phones (rather than for PC or consoles). It required players to escape from Stormhold prison by trading items and battling enemies in randomly generated dungeons.

MOST COMPLETED STEAM ACHIEVEMENT IN *THE ELDER SCROLLS V: SKYRIM*

An impressive 89.6% of those who played *Skyrim* via the Steam platform on PC earned the Unbound achievement, making it the most completed achievement in the game. It is unlocked by finishing the game's introductory section. This means that 10.4% of players didn't even get as far as completing the opening before giving up.

FIRST NON-JAPANESE GAME WITH A PERFECT *FAMITSU* SCORE

Shukan Famitsu is Japan's most respected gaming magazine, selling around half a million copies every week. It is one of a range of five gaming mags under the *Famitsu* title. Since its creation in 1986, only 22 games have been given a perfect score of 40. *Skyrim* was the first non-Japanese game to receive this honour.

BEST-SELLING RPG FOR XBOX

The 2002 release *The Elder Scrolls III: Morrowind* is the best-selling role-player on the original Xbox, with 2.86 million global sales according to vgchartz.com. It sold 200,000 more than the original *Fable*, the second best-selling RPG on Microsoft's first gaming console. By comparison, sequel *The Elder Scrolls IV: Oblivion* sold 4.17 million on the Xbox 360.

BEST-SELLING WESTERN RPG

The Elder Scrolls V: Skyrim has sold an impressive 17.06 million copies across all platforms. As well as near-universal critical praise and a host of awards, it also spawned three DLCs, all of which were released in 2012.

The **best-selling Japanese RPG** is *Final Fantasy VII* (see pp.136–37) from 1997, which has shifted 9.72 million units, while the **best-selling RPG** overall is *Pokémon Red*, *Green* and *Blue* (see pp.142–43), with remarkable sales of more than 31 million.

BATTLEFIELD

Summary: *Battlefield* has made its reputation as a multiplayer shooting fest. The 2014 standalone entry in the extensive series, *Hardline*, is the first not to be developed by DICE.

Publisher: EA
Developer: DICE/Visceral Games
Debut: 2002

MOST KILLS IN *BATTLEFIELD 3*

Crack-shots gamer "fiLthyyYyYyyyy" (USA) had made 611,558 kills as of 30 April 2014.

MOST JET KILLS IN *BATTLEFIELD 3*

Jet kills involve attacking the enemy using a jet plane. "GrieferKiller" had finished off 171,561 opponents this way, as of 24 June 2014.

MOST MELEE KILLS IN *BATTLEFIELD 4*

As of 30 April 2014, "MT-RISE" had registered 44,984 stabbings on battlelog.battlefield.com. This player's five favourite weapons are all cutting implements.

LARGEST LIVING "EASTER EGG"

The *Naval Strike* DLC features a megalodon shark measuring 18 m (59 ft) in length. This extinct species of shark (*Carcharodon megalodon*), believed to have lived 50–4.5 million years ago, can be seen on the "Nansha Strike" map. To make it appear, position 10 players around the buoy situated between flag A and B on the large Conquest configuration. The shark kills the players around the buoy.

CHINA SYNDROME

DLC *China Rising* features a battle for superiority on the Chinese mainland. It's fair to say that this didn't go down well in China, where *Battlefield 4* was banned in December 2013. Calling the game a threat to national security, the Chinese government added its translated name, *ZhanDi4*, to a list of officially censored words.

MOST PROLIFIC FPS SERIES

Battlefield has 26 editions to its name, including two *Battlefield 4* expansion packs. DLC *Dragon's Teeth* and *Final Stand* are due for release in 2014, as is standalone *Battlefield: Hardline*. The most critically acclaimed of the series is 2005's *Battlefield 2*, with a GameRankings score of 90.07%. Although the game was one of those for which server support was withdrawn in June 2014, diehard fans in the PC community looked set to try to keep it online themselves.

BEST-SELLING TACTICAL SHOOTER

Battlefield 3 had global sales of 16.64 million by June 2014, according to VGChartz.

HIGHEST-RANKED CO-OP TEAM IN *BATTLEFIELD 3*'S "OPERATION EXODUS"

"AFK_Assassin007" and "NewAccountName1" had scored 1,979,399,936 points in "Operation Exodus" on the "hard" setting as of 24 June 2014. "Exodus" involves a group of marines defending a weakened POW camp.

1,126,387,717 vehicles destroyed in *Battlefield 4* as of 9 April 2014.

MOST SIMULTANEOUS PLAYERS IN AN XBOX ONE GAME

A maximum of 64 players can join in with a *Battlefield 4* campaign online. The game runs at 60 fps, with its immense scale similar to that achievable on PC architecture. Something had to give to get to such a level, and in this case the action is depicted in under 1080p to allow support for the number of players. The latest console generation is the first to deliver the same large server experience as a PC game.

MOST MELEE KILLS IN *BATTLEFIELD 3*

Gamer "Acula-3" (Ukraine) logged 312,661 melee kills by 23 June 2014.

FASTEST COMPLETION OF *BAD COMPANY 2*

"-KFC-", aka Szymon Kiendyś (Poland) completed a segmented speed-run of *Battlefield: Bad Company 2* in 1 hr 16 min 3 sec between 30 July and 15 August 2010.

LARGEST FPS MULTIPLAYER MAP

"Bandar Desert" is a map in the third DLC instalment of *Battlefield 3: Armored Kill*, released in 2012. Although the area was not revealed by EA, the map is 2,400 m (7,874 ft) long. Designer Inge Jøran Holberg says that the inspiration was "Atacama Desert" from *Battlefield: Bad Company 2*.

LONGEST HEADSHOT IN *BATTLEFIELD 4*

Headshots are trickier to accomplish than body shots. So hats – and the rest of the head – off to "undertaker080119", who killed at 5,231.7 m (17,164 ft 4 in), as recorded on the bf4stats.com site on 6 March 2014. This feat can only be achieved by firing from a helicopter in one corner of the map, at an angle, against a target in the opposite corner.

> "I want to be a cop who doesn't play by the rules... I want to use the word 'perp!'"
>
> **IAN MILHAM,**
> **VISCERAL GAMES**
> ON *BATTLEFIELD: HARDLINE*

MOST REAL-WORLD FIREARMS IN A VIDEOGAME

As of 23 June 2014, the 98 guns in *Battlefield 4* included assault rifles such as the AK-U12 and SCAR-H; shotguns such as the 870 MCS and SPAS-12; and sniper rifles such as the AWS, added in the *Naval Strike* expansion pack in 2014.

Take away the necessity to have real-world weapons and you have *Borderlands* by Gearbox. The game's procedural system was capable of creating over 17.75 million guns by modifying factors such as ammo type and manufacturers. Realistic it might not be, but it meant *Borderlands* took the record for the **most guns in a videogame**.

TAKING THE HARDLINE

It was cops and robbers time for the *Battlefield* franchise as EA unveiled *Battlefield: Hardline* at E3. The autumn 2014 game shares the Frostbite engine and has much of the gameplay feel of its predecessor. The radical departure is the setting, with an urban crime theme implemented by Visceral Games. The cityscape includes new gadgets such as ziplines and grappling hooks, and applies trademark *Battlefield* realism to police vehicles.

FOR THE WIN

SPOTTING

In multiplayer games, be sure to spot an opponent or enemy vehicle so that your whole team will be able to see them. It's good practice to do so – *Battlefield 4* is all about playing as a team, first and foremost, and you'll get bonus points for every kill you help facilitate. For example, if you only have short-range weapons and the enemy is at a distance, let your mate with a sniper rifle take them out.

Summary: The most anticipated element of *Assassin's Creed: Unity*, due in late 2014, is the 2–4-player co-op mode, ideal for stealthy killers to work revolutionary Paris in packs.

Publisher: Ubisoft
Developer: Ubisoft
Debut: 2007

SHORTEST DEVELOPMENT TIME FOR A TRIPLE-A STEALTH GAME SEQUEL

AC III was released on 30 October 2012, just 350 days after *AC: Revelations*. Almost a full year (364 days in total) separated that game from the 2013 entry *AC IV: Black Flag*.

FASTEST COMPLETION OF *ASSASSIN'S CREED: REVELATIONS*

François "Fed981" Federspiel (France) completed *Revelations* in 2 hr 48 min 41 sec on 3 October 2010. François' primary weapon choice was the speedy Hookblade. He also made use of "The Lost Archive" – a downloadable expansion that enables players to increase the capacity of the hidden gun's ammo pouch to 12 bullets.

FASTEST 100% COMPLETION OF *ASSASSIN'S CREED II*

François "Fed981" Federspiel (see box above) holds multiple records for other *Assassin's Creed* games too. On 8 April 2014, he finished a 100% run of *AC II* in 7 hr 9 min 51 sec and 157 segments and previously set the overall **fastest completion of *Assassin's Creed II***, with a time of 5 hr 42 min 16 sec on 26 March 2011. Speedy François also achieved the **fastest completion of *Assassin's Creed: Brotherhood***, stopping the clock after a brisk session lasting 2 hr 23 min 41 sec, on 3 March 2013.

HIGHEST SCORE IN *ASSASSIN'S CREED IV: BLACK FLAG* DEATHMATCH

As of April 2014, gamer "Hakuya13" had scored 22,250 points in the free-for-all Deathmatch after 357 sessions on the PS4 version of the game. Deathmatch is played without the aid of the compass to locate targets, although the map is smaller than those of other multiplayer modes.

MOST WATCHED E3 GAME TRAILER

As of 24 July 2014, Ubisoft's trailer for *Assassin's Creed III* had been watched 18,171,196 times since the clip, set in the years around the American Revolution, was uploaded to YouTube on 4 June 2012. Ubisoft kept second place in the family, with 2010's *Assassin's Creed: Brotherhood* trailer notching up 16,449,050 views.

MOST USER-CREATED BOMBS IN A STEALTH VIDEOGAME

Players could make up to 300 different bombs in *Assassin's Creed: Revelations* by combining various types of casing and gunpowder strength. The results could be lethal, tactical or, as with Stink Bombs, diversionary – as well as very smelly.

ASSASSIN'S CREED IV: BLACK FLAG BY NUMBERS

Time played: 451 centuries 62 years 131 days 19 hr

Animus fragments collected: 964,721,963,817

Ships destroyed: 5,372,737,156

Animals killed: 911,939,185,646

Sea creatures harpooned: 1,295,005,143,470

Treasure chests found: 980,305,303,180

In-game currency earned: 17,067,733,199,799

Figures correct as of 22 May 2014

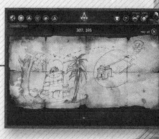

▶▶ BEST-SELLING NEW GAME IP AT LAUNCH

Ubisoft's *Watch_Dogs* shares some stealth elements with *Assassin's Creed* and characters have crossed over between the two games, although they do not share universes. Hotly anticipated by fans, *Watch_Dogs'* story of hacker Aiden Pearce (above) recorded sales of 4 million by the end of its first week on 3 June 2014. The figures are all the more impressive for a new franchise that doesn't rely on the recognition of fans enjoyed by established series.

MOST ANIMALS KILLED IN *ASSASSIN'S CREED*

As of 22 May 2014, a total of 2,206,944,329,116 creatures had been killed for crafting and upgrades in *Assassin's Creed IV: Black Flag*. This total includes sea creatures harpooned – a big draw with the game's focus on all things piratical and seafaring – as well as animals killed on land. The spoils of the hunt can be used to make anything from health upgrades to nifty accessories such as ammunition pouches.

WHALE OF A TIME

When the whaling element of *Black Flag* was revealed, animal charity PETA – who had previously complained about Mario's Tanooki suit legitimizing the wearing of fur from the *tanuki* (Japanese raccoon dog) – labelled the hunting of whales in the game as "disgraceful". Ubisoft were ninja-fast with a riposte: "History is our playground in *Assassin's Creed. Assassin's Creed IV: Black Flag* is a work of fiction that depicts the real events during the golden era of pirates. We do not condone illegal whaling, just as we don't condone a pirate lifestyle of poor hygiene, plundering, hijacking ships and over-the-legal-limit drunken debauchery."

FOR THE WIN

ACCESS THE "ARRR MATEY" CHEAT

Finish 20 of the optional Abstergo Challenges to be found in *Black Flag* and you'll have the ability to turn on the "Arrr matey" cheat. While you won't be able to save the game in this mode, you will be able to hear Edward's best pirate impressions as he barks old favourites such as "Yo-ho-ho and a bottle of rum" and "Shiver me timbers".

LONGEST MARATHON ON AN *ASSASSIN'S CREED* GAME

Tony Desmet, Jesse Rebmann and Jeffrey Gamon (all Belgium) played *Assassin's Creed: Brotherhood* on the Xbox 360 for 109 hr exactly – more than 4.5 days – at the Belgian digital channel GUNK's World Record Gaming Evenement in Antwerp, Belgium, from 18 to 22 December 2010. The winning team scooped 3,000 euros (£2,542; $3,943) for being the last three of 20 entrants left gaming. The same attempt also set an overall record for the **longest marathon on an action-adventure game**.

189,481,818
overall kills in *Black Flag*'s multiplayer as of 30 April 2014.

HIGHEST SCORE ON *ASSASSIN'S CREED IV: BLACK FLAG* WOLFPACK

Players can hunt together strategically in Wolfpack mode to take out targets. "Foniasophobia" is at the top of the PS4 *Black Flag* leaderboards, scoring 82,070 points solo and 326,205 as part of a team, as of 29 April 2014. Above is *Black Flag* multiplayer character The Puppeteer.

GREATEST AGGREGATE TIME PLAYING *ASSASSIN'S CREED*

As of 22 May 2014, a staggering combined-platform total of 451 centuries 62 years 131 days 19 hr had been clocked up globally on *Black Flag*. Gamers could take a well-deserved few minutes off, secure in the knowledge that they'd beaten even *Assassin's Creed III*'s impressive total by at least 100 centuries. The earlier title was played for a collective total of 321 centuries 92 years 39 days 11 hr.

07 FIFA

Summary: The choice of game modes, fluid play and the comprehensive licence deals struck by EA continue to ensure that *FIFA* is one of the most successful franchises in gaming.

Publisher: EA
Developer: Various
Debut: 1993

MOST GOALS SCORED FROM THE 18-YARD LINE IN *FIFA 14* IN ONE MINUTE

Patrick Sinner (Germany) scored 10 goals in a minute on 30 March 2014, while Shawn Alvarez (USA) set the **most goals scored from the 18-yard line in *FIFA 13* in one minute**, with 10 on 5 October 2013. Sinner equalled the record on 13 October 2013.

FIRST SOCCER GAME TO ACCURATELY REPLICATE KITS

Although goalkeepers wore generic kits, the rest of the squads in *World Cup 98* faithfully replicated the kits of the national teams taking part in that year's tournament. Kit manufacturer logos were included as well.

MOST ACTIVE USERS OF A SOCCER VIDEOGAME

FIFA 09 introduced Ultimate Team, allowing players to create and manage their own club, signing and trading players. The series had, as of March 2014, attracted 21,849,017 unique team players.

TOP SPOT

EA Sports signed a deal with FIFA to keep their franchise going until 2022. By the time the current deal ends, FIFA will have run for 29 years – making it the longest licence deal for a soccer game by quite some distance. Not bad for a game that, in 1993, EA believed might only sell 300,000 copies in Europe.

264,000
FIFA matches played every day in Ultimate Team mode.

FIRST FIFA-BRANDED SOCCER GAME

The footy world of the early 1990s was dominated by *Sensible Soccer* and *Kick Off*. In 1993, EA broke into the field with their first FIFA licence, *International Soccer*, developed by Extended Play Productions. It did much to popularize the isometric view of the pitch, rendering the players in a 3D perspective even while the game itself was in 2D.

MOST TEAMS IN A WORLD CUP GAME

With the World Cup an increasingly distant memory, soccer fans can experience the highs and lows all over again in *2014 FIFA World Cup Brazil*, playing through all the qualification stages in a game that features 203 national teams.

MOST APPEARANCES ON A GAME COVER BY A SOCCER PLAYER

Manchester United and England forward Wayne Rooney (UK) has appeared on the covers of all seven *FIFA* games from *FIFA 06* to *FIFA 12*. In total, Rooney has been the main artwork star for more than a quarter of all the main series of *FIFA* games.

Overall, the **most appearances on a game cover** was set by golf's Tiger Woods at 16 (for more on Woods, see p.105).

MOST PROLIFIC SOCCER FRANCHISE ON ONE PLATFORM

With 19 games in total, more *FIFA* titles were released on the PS2 than on any

FIF 5 ULTIMATE TEAM · FOOTBALL FO HO · ORTS FIFA · @EA TSFIFA · EA SFOOTBALL · GO other console. *FIFA* games were released on an annual basis for 13 years on the PS2, from *FIFA 2001* to *FIFA 14*. In addition, there were the 2002 and 2006 World Cup tie-ins, two editions of *FIFA Street* and the Japan-only *FIFA Soccer World Championship*. Rival *Pro Evolution Soccer* (see pp.102–103) had 13 entries on the PS2.

(see pp.102–103)

FOR THE WIN

PENALTY SHOOT-OUTS

The tensest part of any World Cup match – in videogaming as well as in the real thing – is the penalty shoot-out (as fans of six teams attested in 2014). Make the best of it in *FIFA* if you're playing the goalkeeper. Put off the opposing player by moving around or, if you can, time it so that you make your save in the split second after the ball has been kicked.

MOST SUPPORTED SOCCER CLUB IN A VIDEOGAME

With 717,000 fans within *FIFA 14*, Real Madrid (Spain) is the most supported club. They sit comfortably ahead of Barcelona with 643,000 fans and, just behind, Manchester United with 631,000 cheering them on.

BEST-SELLING SOCCER VIDEOGAME

FIFA 14 had sold 14.51 million copies as of 25 July 2014, according to vgchartz.com, beating its predecessor *FIFA 13* by 100,000 sales. The PS3 version of *FIFA 14* sold 5.95 million units alone with Xbox 360 accounting for 4.01 million sales.

FASTEST-SELLING SPORTS VIDEOGAME

FIFA 13 sold 4.5 million units in less than a week in September 2012, a feat that even its successor couldn't match, despite being available in eight formats. Commentators suggested gamers had either spent all they wanted on the previous week's *Grand Theft Auto V* launch or were waiting for the next-generation console versions before committing to a soccer game.

MOST EXPENSIVE VIDEOGAME CASE

A DVD box for *FIFA World Cup 2006* was made of sterling silver and 18-carat gold by jewellery company Theo Fennell. Originally given away in a competition, it was later sold by the winner for £4,800 ($9,500) at Bonhams, London, UK, on 4 June 2007. The case was hand-engraved and set with 0.96-carat brilliant cut diamonds in the EA logo.

FIFA FEE

The original FIFA licence was relatively cheap. EA discovered this was because it included no player names, likenesses or logos... All of that would come much later on.

MOST WORLD CUP-LICENSED VIDEOGAMES BY ONE PUBLISHER

EA has published seven World Cup games since acquiring the licence in 1998. These include *FIFA: Road to World Cup 98* and *FIFA 06: Road to FIFA World Cup*, which were published to complement the World Cup games themselves. The runner-up is publisher U.S. Gold, which issued three tie-in games between 1986 and 1994.

MOST WINS OF FIFA INTERACTIVE WORLD CUPS

Only two players have won the FIWC title twice since its 2004 inception. Bruce Grannec (France) won in 2009 and 2013, equalling the mark of Alfonso Ramos (Spain), who won in 2008 and again in 2012.

BEST-SELLING SOCCER VIDEOGAME FRANCHISE

The *FIFA* series has sold 125.82 million copies, according to VGChartz as of 25 July 2014. With global sales totalling £3.6 bn ($6 bn), it can also boast the **highest revenue for a soccer videogame franchise**. The juggernaut of a series is set for another boost with the launch of *FIFA 15* in September 2014. Shown here is *FIFA 15*'s Clint Dempsey (right), a former Premier League player who has been with the Seattle Sounders since 2013. In 2012, he was the first American player to score a hat-trick in the Premier League.

Summary: Link's tireless rescue missions to save Princess Zelda continue apace, with 2014 crossover *Hyrule Warriors* and a new game in development for the Wii U set to land in 2015.

Publisher: Nintendo
Developer: Nintendo
Debut: 1986

BEST-SELLING *LEGEND OF ZELDA* GAME (MULTI-PLATFORM)

With total sales of 8.56 million, *The Legend of Zelda: Twilight Princess* is the series best-seller, according to VGChartz. The game was released on the GameCube and Wii in 2006. The **best-selling *Legend of Zelda* game (single platform)** is 1998's *The Legend of Zelda: Ocarina of Time*, which was available on the N64 and has sold 7.6 million copies.

RAREST *LEGEND OF ZELDA* GAME

In August 2013, gaming memorabilia collector Tom Curtin (USA) sold a rare copy of the original *Legend of Zelda* on eBay for $55,000 (£35,900). The cartridge contained a playable pre-release prototype that is thought to be unique.

FASTEST-SELLING *ZELDA* GAME

Nintendo of America president Reggie Fils-Aimé revealed that Wii title *The Legend of Zelda: Skyward Sword* sold 535,000 copies during its first week at retail in North America from 20 November 2011. The series has always enjoyed its largest share of sales in the USA. As of 8 August 2014, *Skyward Sword* had sold 3.77 million units worldwide. The 2011 title is a prequel, set before all other *Zelda* games.

BIG BOSS MAN

The Legend of Zelda: Ocarina of Time 3D was the first game in the series to allow players to fight each of the bosses one after the other. This "Boss Challenge" mode was not in the original N64 release of 1998, but it was one of several new features added to the updated version for the 3DS in 2011.

FIRST VIDEOGAME EASTER EGG APPEARANCE AWARDED AS A PRIZE

In 1990, *Nintendo Power* magazine in the USA ran a contest in which the winner would feature in NES title *The Legend of Zelda: A Link to the Past*. For his prize, winner Chris Houlihan was awarded an in-game room containing 45 blue rupees and a plaque reading "My name is Chris Houlihan. This is my top secret room. Keep it between us, OK?" It proved so elusive that its existence was largely unknown until years after the game's initial release in 1991.

MOST VIEWED FAN FILM BASED ON *ZELDA*

The YouTube video "*THE LEGEND OF ZELDA* RAP [MUSIC VIDEO]", produced by Smosh, had racked up 49,719,846 views as of 8 August 2014. The **most viewed fan film based on an action-adventure videogame** overall is "*ULTIMATE ASSASSIN'S CREED 3* SONG [Music Video]", a video produced by the same team and based on Ubisoft's stellar series, which has accumulated a total of 53,554,080 views.

FIRST HOSPITALIZATION FROM A *LEGEND OF ZELDA* INJURY

On 2 March 2014, Local 2 news in Houston, Texas, USA, reported on an incident involving a replica of the Master Sword from the *Zelda* series. Cosplayer Eugene Thompson (pictured) was caught up in an altercation with his girlfriend's estranged husband when he grabbed Thompson's replica Master Sword. In the ensuing scuffle, the husband was injured in the chest and leg while Thompson was hit over the head with a flower pot. Both men were taken to hospital.

NEW THIS MORNING
Man Stabbed With Sword Over Ex-Wife
WEST HARRIS COUNTY

FIRST FIRST-PERSON *LEGEND OF ZELDA* PORT

On 5 February 2014, Randy "Ubiquitron" Bennett released a beta version of *The Legend of Zelda* as a first-person 3D game for the Oculus Rift virtual-reality headgear. Bennett used the same retro graphics and textures as featured in the iconic NES title. For more on the Oculus Rift and Project Morpheus VR sets, turn to pp.194–95.

74,800,000
total copies of *Zelda* games sold worldwide as of 8 August 2014.

MOST CRITICALLY ACCLAIMED ACTION-ADVENTURE GAME ON WII U

The Legend of Zelda: The Wind Waker HD, the 2013 remake of the GameCube title, has a 91.08% average score on GameRankings. Eurogamer awarded the game 10/10, saying, *"The Wind Waker* is crisp and energetic, spirited and soulful, just a little bit wayward – and it hasn't aged a day." *Zelda* also lays claim to the **most critically acclaimed action-adventure game** overall, with the original *The Legend of Zelda: Ocarina of Time* averaging a towering rating of 97.54%.

FASTEST COMPLETION OF *OCARINA OF TIME*

Regular speed-runner Cosmo Wright set the any-percentage record for *The Legend of Zelda: Ocarina of Time* (non-tool assisted) by completing it in 18 min 32 sec on 26 April 2014.

The **fastest completion of *The Legend of Zelda: Skyward Sword*** was achieved by "Paraxade" in 5 hr 39 min on 28 April 2012, using a save glitch to increase his speed.

Gamer "Kryssstal" (USA) clocked the **fastest completion of *The Legend of Zelda: A Link to the Past*** in 1 hr 24 min 31 sec on 13 August 2013.

Speed-running the original *Zelda* game is always a hot contest. The **fastest completion of *The Legend of Zelda*** was by "Darkwing Duck" (USA) in 31 min 7 sec on 20 May 2014.

BEST-SELLING HANDHELD NARRATIVE-ADVENTURE GAME

The most successful portable entry in the *Zelda* series to date is 1993's *The Legend of Zelda: Link's Awakening*, which has sold 6.05 million copies worldwide. The game was originally released for the Game Boy, and subsequently re-released for the Game Boy Color as *The Legend of Zelda: Link's Awakening DX.*

The Legend of Zelda: Ocarina of Time, a seminal N64 title, is the **best-selling action-adventure game on a Nintendo platform** with sales of 7.6 million. The updated and revised version, an exclusive for the 3DS, has sold 3.38 million copies.

FIRST GAME FRANCHISE TO BE AWARDED A SPIKE VIDEO GAME HALL OF FAME AWARD

In 2011, the Spike Video Game Awards (now known simply as VGX) introduced a Hall of Fame gong, and the *Zelda* series became the first franchise to be honoured with it. This annual award show has been lauding the best in gaming since 2003. Pictured here is Link from the 18th instalment in the series, *The Legend of Zelda* (working title), scheduled for the Wii U in 2015.

WOMEN IN GAMES

More women are playing games than ever before. In fact, according to the Entertainment Software Association, nearly half of all gamers are female. But what about those who make the games? Videogaming's female figureheads share their tips of how to get on in a famously male-dominated field.

The videogame industry is changing and there are now more opportunities than ever for women. It's welcome news for Dr Jo Twist (pictured right), who represents UK games companies as the first female CEO at Ukie.

"It's incredibly important that we get more girls coding and being creative at a young age," she says, "so that they consider working in the industry to create games of the future." Her advice for getting into gaming is simple: "Follow your passion and don't worry if you don't know where you'll end up. Sometimes your passion can take you in unexpected directions."

"Love creativity, be honest, be giving, listen, have integrity and be proud of your industry."

DR JO TWIST
CEO, UKIE, ON HOW TO SUCCEED IN GAMING

THE SCRIPTWRITER

Rhianna Pratchett is a writer and story designer. She has penned the scripts for games such as *Heavenly Sword* and 2013's *Tomb Raider*, and in 2008 she won the Writers' Guild of Great Britain Best Videogame Script award for *Overlord*.

Where do you find your inspiration?
I love the work of Joss Whedon and Terry Gilliam. The 1980s was a great decade for fantasy movies and strong action heroines, particularly Ellen Ripley in *Alien* (USA, 1979) and Sarah Connor in *Terminator* (USA, 1984).

What are the most rewarding parts of your job?
Receiving feedback from players who have enjoyed the games I've worked on and getting to work with hugely talented and creative individuals.

What advice would you give to someone hoping to do your job?
Play lots of different games and look at how they use narrative. Always keep working on your writing skills and make industry contacts through forums and industry events like GDC [Game Developers Conference] and GameHorizon.

LEADING LADIES

Among the early recognizable female characters was Nintendo's Princess Peach (left). Today, the characters played by gamers are likely to be less the helpless damsel in distress and more likely to be nuanced, realistic figures such as Ellie (right). Even Lara Croft (opposite page) has evolved into a grittier proposition as a character.

START CODING

The **first female games programmer and designer** was Carol Shaw (USA). She began her career at Atari in 1978 and later joined Activision, where she designed *River Raid* and *Happy Trails*.

Her trailblazing was followed by Dona Bailey (USA), who became the **first woman to design an arcade game**, in 1981. She was interested in non-violent games and the only idea that Atari suggested which appealed was the one that became the iconic *Centipede*.

On the other side of the fence are gaming journalists. Among them is Ellie Gibson, who writes for the Eurogamer website (and can also boast to be the only writer to have contributed to every *Gamer's Edition*!). Her advice for budding journalists is to "read… not just games websites but books, magazines, newspapers. The best way to improve your writing is to read what's already out there."

CHARACTER BUILDING

The evolution of female characters, alongside their real-life equivalents, has been encouraging, if patchy at times. Nintendo's *Princess Peach* made her debut in 1985's *Super Mario*

Bros. and, despite Mario creator Shigeru Miyamoto saying he wanted her to be "stubborn but cute", she has left damsel-in-distress-hood behind to become a playable character in her own right and to have her own game, *Super Princess Peach*. In a role reversal, it was up to Peach to rescue Mario and Luigi from the clutches of Bowser.

A TOMB OF ONE'S OWN

Lara Croft was always the star from the start of the first *Tomb Raider* in 1996, even if dodgy love interests and an obsession with her physical attributes have threatened to overshadow her achievements at times. We had to wait until 2013 and *The Last of Us*'s Ellie to see a real turning point: a normal girl who displays impressive courage and resilience. As women's voices become louder in the industry, here's hoping for more like her.

THE INDIE DEVELOPER

Dr Emily Thomforde is a games designer based in Edinburgh, Scotland. Together with her husband, James Montgomerie, she produced *Coolson's Artisanal Chocolate Alphabet*, which won the 2013 Scottish BAFTA award for Best Videogame.

What does your job involve?

As an indie developer, I do everything! I sketch the prototypes, program the game, compose the music and sound effects, draw the graphics and do the marketing, but most of my actual hours are spent testing and refining the game until it's the most fun it can possibly be.

Any words of wisdom for aspiring indie developers?

Cultivate interests in lots of different things, be proud of having your own point of view and put all of your love into everything you make.

> "Most of all, work on developing your own voice. Be honest in your writing and let your personality shine through."

ELLIE GIBSON
JOURNALIST, EUROGAMER.NET, ON BREAKING INTO GAMES JOURNALISM

THE YOUTUBE STAR

Jane Douglas is the co-editor of YouTube channel Outside Xbox. Jane helps to write, edit and present videos, some of which have received upwards of 3.5 million views.

What do you like most about your job?

Our community is full of kind and clever and basically delightful people, in full contradiction to toxic nastiness elsewhere on the internet. They're a reward every day.

What inspires you?

I am full of admiration and envy for people who make the games I love and for people who are funny about videogames. Women in particular, on both counts.

COUNTDOWN

05–01

FIRST VIDEOGAME TO SELL 2 MILLION COPIES ON PS4

According to vgchartz.com, in the week ending 22 March 2014 *Call of Duty: Ghosts* reached the 2-million-sales mark on the PS4. Among the new faces is a furry one, Riley, a playable dog character (below), and new maps include a Scottish castle.

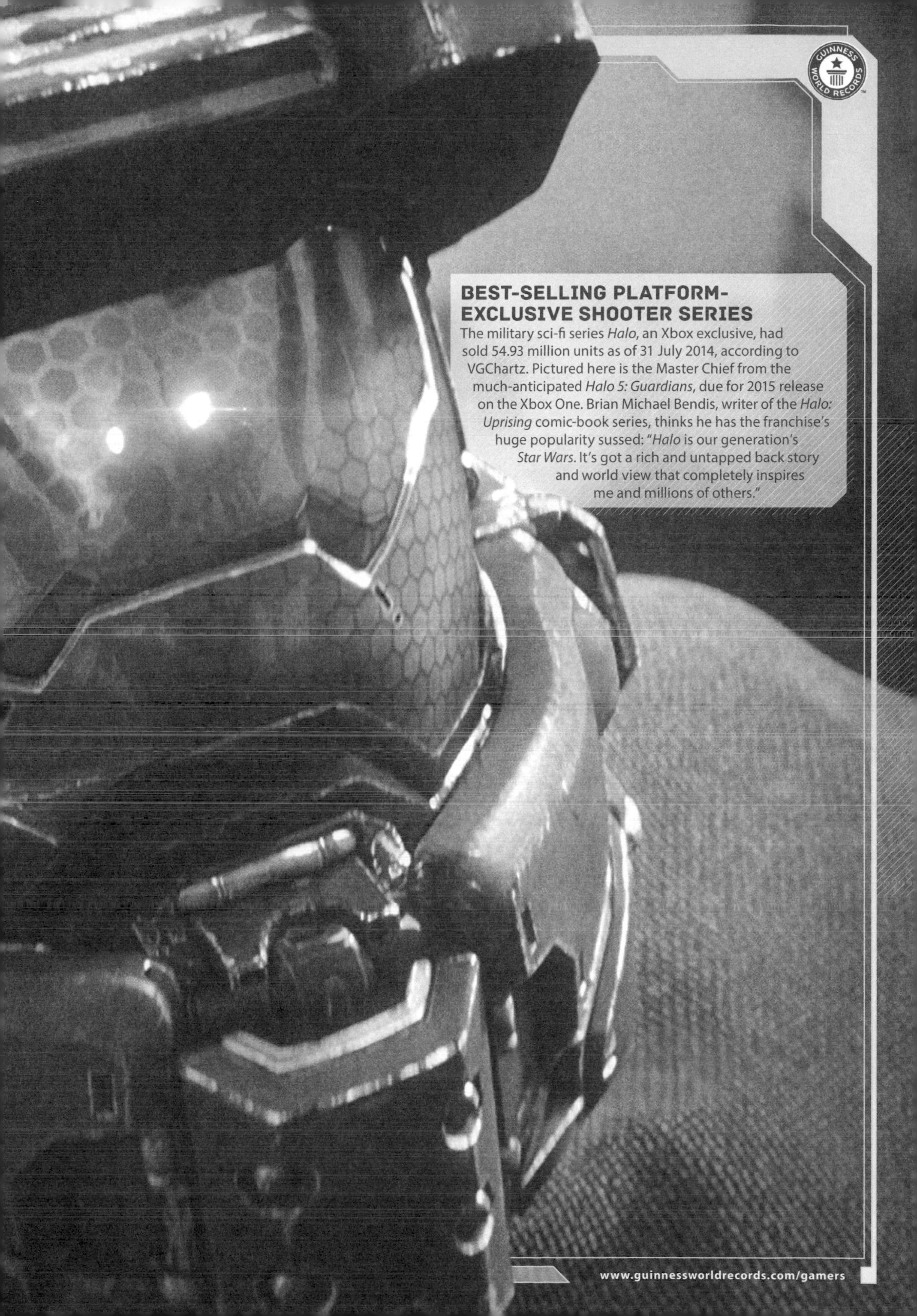

BEST-SELLING PLATFORM-EXCLUSIVE SHOOTER SERIES

The military sci-fi series *Halo*, an Xbox exclusive, had sold 54.93 million units as of 31 July 2014, according to VGChartz. Pictured here is the Master Chief from the much-anticipated *Halo 5: Guardians*, due for 2015 release on the Xbox One. Brian Michael Bendis, writer of the *Halo: Uprising* comic-book series, thinks he has the franchise's huge popularity sussed: "*Halo* is our generation's *Star Wars*. It's got a rich and untapped back story and world view that completely inspires me and millions of others."

05 HALO

Summary: The iconic, hugely popular Xbox-exclusive sci-fi shooter series is set to take centre-stage once more in 2015, with new release *Halo 5: Guardians* and a Spielberg-produced TV tie-in.

Publisher: Microsoft Studios
Developer: Bungie/ 343 Industries
Debut: 2001

FASTEST SINGLE-SEGMENT COMPLETION OF *HALO 4* ON "LEGENDARY" DIFFICULTY

Proficient speed-runner Jonathan "ProAceJOKER" Carroll (USA) completed *Halo 4* in "Legendary" mode in just 1 hr 36 min 51 sec on 2 August 2014.

LONGEST SPACESHIP IN THE UNSC FLEET

The UNSC *Infinity* has a length of 5,694.2 m (18,681 ft 9 in), which is longer than 51 American football pitches. The ship made its first appearance in *Halo 4* and is the first *Infinity*-class warship commissioned into the UNSC Navy following the conclusion of the Human-Covenant War in 2553.

HIGHEST-EARNING *HALO* PLAYER

Aaron "Ace" Elam (above right) has accumulated career earnings of $237,575 (£148,625) since he started playing *Halo* professionally in 2009. He also set the record for the **highest individual earnings in a *Halo* tournament** after winning the *Halo 4* Global Championship (above), organized by 343 Industries in Seattle, Washington, USA, on 1 September 2013. Aaron beat fellow American "iGotUrPistola" in a one-on-one *Halo 4* death-match to scoop $200,000 (£128,900).

BEST-SELLING SCI-FI SHOOTER

With worldwide sales of 11.92 million as of 4 August 2014, *Halo 3* is the most successful sci-fi shooter of all time. The game sees Master Chief team up with The Arbiter in another epic battle with the Covenant. Along with *Combat Evolved Anniversary*, *Halo 2* and *Halo 4*, the third instalment in the series has been given a remastering for *The Master Chief Collection*, due for the Xbox One in late 2014. *Reach* and *Halo 3: ODST* do not feature.

RAMPANT STATES

In the *Halo* universe, AIs have an average life span of seven years before they go through the three stages of Rampancy – Melancholia, Anger and Jealousy. Cortana, however, is one of two AIs who may have achieved a theoretical fourth state – Metastability – prior to her death.

MOST ACTIVE *HALO 4* PLAYER

The *Halo 4* enthusiast "SHOOTemUUp325" is by far the most active *Halo 4* player, with an extraordinary 40,452 online games played as of 4 August 2014. With a kill-death ratio of 1.90, SHOOTemUUp325 is more of a team player than an MVP, but it's safe to assume that this gamer knows the layout of the *Halo 4* maps like the back of their hand. They have achieved a 73% win rate and an average of 30.31 medals per game, too. Second-placed gamer "Soeiv 17" lags behind with "only" 21,095 games played and a win rate of 34%.

HALO TV

You wait 13 years for a *Halo* TV series, and then two come along at once. First up is *Nightfall*, executive-produced by legendary British film director Ridley Scott (*Alien*, *Blade Runner*, *Gladiator*), which is a live-action, five-episode web series due on the Xbox One, Xbox 360 and other Microsoft devices in late 2014. *Nightfall* will bridge the stories of *Halo 4* and *Halo 5: Guardians*. *Halo: The TV Series*, meanwhile, is due to air in late 2015 on the Xbox One and US cable channel Showtime, with Steven Spielberg producing. See pp.26–29 for more on the show and TV/gaming crossovers.

FIRST FPS TO SELL 10 MILLION COPIES

On 8 August 2009, *Halo 3* became the first FPS to cross the 10-million-sales threshold. It remains both the best-selling *Halo* game and the only *Halo* title to sell over 10 million.

▶▶ MOST POPULAR CONSOLE VIDEOGAME BETA FOR A NEW IP

One of the most anticipated titles of late 2014 is Bungie's brand new FPS *Destiny*, set for PS3, PS4, Xbox 360 and Xbox One. With 4,638,937 players, *Destiny* became the most popular console beta for a new intellectual property. The *Destiny* beta began on 17 July 2014 for the PlayStation 3 and PlayStation 4. It was then opened up for the Xbox 360 and Xbox One on 22 July 2014 and concluded on 27 July 2014.

1,116,882
gamers who completed Halo 4's "Campaign" mode within five days of its release.

HIGHEST-GROSSING SCI-FI SHOOTER (24 HOURS)

Halo 4 grossed a stunning $220 million (£137.6 million) in its first 24 hours on 6 November 2012, with total first-day sales reaching 3.1 million. Its day-one total also means that *Halo 4* takes the records for the **highest-grossing first-day sales for a single-platform shooter** as well as the **highest-grossing first-day sales for an Xbox 360 exclusive**. It went on to sell 9.08 million copies. *Halo 4* is set in 2557, four years after *Halo 3*, and it sees Master Chief and Cortana sparring with the Covenant once again, and also with the Warrior-Servant Prometheans.

FOR THE WIN

PINK DEATH MACHINE

The Needler has been a staple of the *Halo* series since its debut in 2001. In *Halo 4* multiplayer, you can acquire the pink death machine in an Ordnance drop, and it takes just seven needles to instantly kill an enemy Spartan with a supercombine explosion.

GRAND THEFT AUTO

FASTEST ENTERTAINMENT PROPERTY TO GROSS $1 BILLION

Grand Theft Auto V grossed $1 bn (£625 m) in the three days following its worldwide release on 17 September 2013. That's a billion dollars grossed faster than any movie, as well as any other game. Developers Rockstar claimed that $800 million (£500 m) was made in just one day alone. By August 2014, *GTA V* was close to hitting a total of $2 bn (£1.17 bn) in sales.

"We're definitely in that realm of excitement and misery at the same time. It's not supposed to be easy. Each time, we push everything to its limit."

SAM HOUSER
ROCKSTAR CO-FOUNDER, ON CREATING *GTA V*

Summary: The series' fifth main entry broke seven records in three days. *GTA Online* launched in October 2013. "We don't know what *GTA 6* will be," says Rockstar, "but we've got some ideas."

Publisher: Rockstar/BMG Interactive
Developer: Rockstar/DMA
Debut: 1997

FIRST CONSOLE EXPANSION PACK

Released in 1999 as an add-on for the first *Grand Theft Auto*, *GTA: London, 1969*, an *Austin Powers*-inspired game, took players to England's capital at its "swinging" height. It had 32 missions and 30 era-specific vehicles, including a Union Jack sports car. Groovy, baby!

FASTEST 100% *GTA III* COMPLETION

Beating any *GTA* game with 100% completion is no easy task, but John "Silmaranza" Breedon finished every mission in *GTA III* in a segmented PC run of 6 hr 32 min on 10 April 2011. That impressive time took him almost a year to get right. On 13 January 2014, prolific *GTA* speed-runner "Eidgod" set the **fastest single-segment completion of *GTA III*** with an any-percentage time of 1 hr 11 min 57 sec.

HIGHEST REVENUE FROM AN ENTERTAINMENT PRODUCT IN 24 HOURS

Grand Theft Auto V was released on 17 September 2013 and, within a day, had made $815.7 m (£511.8 m), according to VGChartz. That made it the **best-selling game in 24 hours**, as well as the **best-selling action-adventure game in 24 hours** and also the **fastest entertainment property to gross $1 bn** (£625 m), a feat accomplished in three days. Not bad going at all!

GRAND THEFT REDEMPTION

When Michael moves into his new house in the hills in *GTA V*, study his bookshelves carefully. You'll see a book called *Red Dead*, written by J Marston. That's a reference to Rockstar's *Red Dead Redemption* (see pp.44–45), which concludes with Jack Marston promising to write a book about his outlaw father, John.

MOST POPULAR USER-CREATED JOB IN *GTA V*

GTA V players can design their own challenges – or "jobs" – and share them. Desert-highway race course "Jumps Jumps Jumps", uploaded by Dylan "iTzPressure" Collins in December 2013, had 8.3 million downloads and 4.2 million likes from other players as of 12 August 2014.

FOR THE WIN

MAKING A KILLING IN *GTA V*

If you want to make a stack of cash early in *Grand Theft Auto V*, pay close attention when you start getting assassination missions from Lester. Every character he asks you to kill works for a company and each company has a rival on the game's stock exchange. Using your insider knowledge, invest all your cash in the rival outfit, complete the mission and sell the stock afterwards. You'll make a fortune.

FIRST VIDEOGAME COMPANY TO RECEIVE THE BAFTA FELLOWSHIP

On 12 March 2014, Rockstar Games received a lifetime achievement at the British Academy Games Awards. The Fellowship is usually given to individuals – including Gabe Newell and Peter Molyneux – and Rockstar is the second company to receive it, after film producers Merchant Ivory in 2002. Above, from left, are Rockstar's Aaron Garbut, Sam Houser, Dan Houser and Leslie Benzies.

FASTEST-SELLING GAME BOOK GUIDE

The *GTA V Signature Series Guide* sold 21,530 copies in its first week in the UK, according to figures from Nielsen BookScan. Published on 17 September 2013, it beat the record set by the *GTA IV Signature Series Guide* (18,200 copies in its first week in 2008).

THE TRUTH IS OUT THERE

There are references to aliens and UFOs sprinkled throughout *Grand Theft Auto V*. During the prologue you can find an alien frozen in the ice under a bridge, and there's a sunken UFO at the top of the map. Complete the game to 100%, however, and you'll get even more alien visitors in the skies over San Andreas. One hovers over Sandy Shores, another is above Fort Zancudo, but the most impressive flies above Mount Chiliad in the early hours of the morning during storms.

MOST SUCCESSFUL *GTA ONLINE* MULTIPLAYER CREW

The five-man Violent Pacification has 1,171 wins and no losses in the PS3 edition of the game. Violent Pacification's leader "tb4u01" has spent more than 1,108 hours in the game, killed 7,930 other players and earned $17.9 bn of in-game currency. Who says crime doesn't pay?

MOST SUCCESSFUL *GTA ONLINE* PLAYER

"iSuccessfuls-" plays on the Xbox 360 and has 63 wins and five losses for a 92.65% victory ratio on the Major League Gaming leaderboard.

18

original songs on the *GTA V* soundtrack. They were played at a concert during the New York Film Festival in September 2013.

LARGEST BUDGET FOR AN ACTION-ADVENTURE VIDEOGAME

With an estimated budget of $137.5 m (£87.4 m) – not including marketing – *GTA V* is the most expensive action-adventure console game, although Rockstar did not disclose full details of the game's budget. By May 2014, *GTA V* had generated approximately $2 bn (£1.1 bn), according to Forbes, more than recouping the expense. By August 2014, with sales of 35.94 million copies, *GTA V* was the **best-selling action-adventure game**.

BEST-SELLING ACTION-ADVENTURE SERIES

Grand Theft Auto has sold 141.66 million copies in all its incarnations and platforms to date. Take-Two Interactive, who own Rockstar, reported that 185 million units of *GTA* games had shipped worldwide as of 27 May 2014. *GTA IV* is the **most critically acclaimed seventh-generation action-adventure game**, with a GameRankings average score of 96.85% across its PS3 and Xbox 360 versions. The score is not quite enough to worry *Super Mario Galaxy*, whose 97.64% makes it the **highest-rated console game**.

MINECRAFT

LONGEST MARATHON ON A STRATEGY GAME

Austrian gamer Martin Fornleitner played strategy and open-world game *Minecraft* for a blockbusting 24 hr 10 min in Vienna, Austria, on 19–20 August 2011. Martin played the game on a Sony Xperia Play handset. His achievement also set the record for the **longest marathon on *Minecraft***.

ls.com/gamers

MINECRAFT

Summary: The blocky juggernaut that is *Minecraft* rolls on, with sales of the PC/Mac edition averaging 16,000 every single day. The game arrived on the Xbox One and PS4 in August 2014.

Publisher: Mojang/Microsoft/Sony
Developer: Mojang/4J Studios
Debut: 2011

LARGEST INDIE GAME CONVENTION

Some 7,500 people attended MineCon 2013 at the Orange County Convention Center in Orlando, Florida, USA, on 2–3 November 2013. MineCon has been an annual fixture for diehard *Minecraft* aficionados since its inception in 2010. The first event, more of an informal get-together, attracted around 50 fans. In 2011, the number jumped to 4,500.

A NOTCH ABOVE THE REST

Although originally created for PC by one man, Markus "Notch" Persson (pictured above in avatar form), the desktop and Pocket Editions of *Minecraft* were developed by eight people, including Jens "Jeb" Bergensten, at Mojang's studio in Stockholm, Sweden. The Xbox 360, PS3, Xbox One, PS4 and PS Vita editions, meanwhile, were created by a team of 24 developers at 4J Studios in Scotland.

MOST CONCURRENT PLAYERS IN ONE *MINECRAFT* WORLD

Minecraft isn't designed to support hundreds of players in a world at once, so when the YouTube channel Yogscast (which specializes in *Minecraft*) squeezed together 2,622 players on 1 August 2011, it was hardly playable. But they were all together nonetheless.

MOST DOWNLOADED *MINECRAFT* PROJECT

The user-created project The Dropper, by "Bigre" (Belgium), had been downloaded 1,145,546 times as of 7 August 2014. In The Dropper, players must fall through a series of structures and shapes, aiming to reach the bottom without hitting an obstruction first.

***Minecraft* Copenhagen and, inset, the real Copenhagen.**

FIRST COUNTRY MODELLED AT FULL SCALE IN A VIDEOGAME

In April 2014, the Danish Geodata Agency launched a 1:1-scale recreation of Denmark in *Minecraft*, featuring every building and feature of the 43,000-km² (16,602-mi²) country for players to explore. The project was designed to promote the agency as well as to teach urban planning and geography in schools. The number of blocks used is around 4 billion.

STRONGEST *MINECRAFT* BLOCK

In a game all about blocks, it's pretty useful to identify the hardiest of them all. The strongest block, Bedrock, is easily found by mining straight down. Also known as Adminium, it is unbreakable in normal game mode, preventing players digging too deeply and falling into The Void below.

LOCATING EMERALD ORE

Emerald Ore is the rarest mineral block and is exceedingly precious, since you use the gems to trade with villagers. You'll only find them in Extreme Hills biomes, where you'll see epic mountains, cliffs, waterfalls and lots of cave systems. So you'll need to do some trekking, and even then you'll tend only to find them one at a time, rather than in seams like iron. There's one trick, though – they only appear between layers 4 and 32, so that narrows your options a little.

ARCADE

MOST-PLAYED XBOX LIVE GAME

As of May 2014, players of *Minecraft: Xbox 360 Edition* had spent a total of 1.75 billion hours – or 199,772 years – playing the game, making it the most played title in the history of Xbox Live Arcade. According to Microsoft, *Minecraft* had sold 12.4 million copies as of April 2014, making it the **best-selling XBLA game**.

MOST POPULAR GAME BETA

Over 10 million gamers signed up to play *Minecraft* during its beta period, which ran between 20 December 2010 and 18 November 2011, the day of the game's official release on PC/Mac.

LONGEST *MINECRAFT* TUNNEL

The longest tunnel in *Minecraft* is 10,502 blocks (equating to 10,502 m; 34,455 ft) and was achieved by Lachlan Etherton (Australia) at the EB Games store in Greenwith, Australia, on 3 August 2013. The digging and mining took around 50 minutes to complete, the lighting of the tunnel took 20 minutes and the full walkthrough of the tunnel to complete the record attempt lasted 10 minutes.

MOST VIEWED FAN FILM BASED ON A VIDEOGAME

The overall most popular fan film based on a videogame of any genre is called "'Revenge' – A *Minecraft* Parody of Usher's DJ Got Us Fallin' in Love – Crafted Using Noteblocks". Based on *Minecraft*, the video was uploaded to YouTube by user "CaptainSparklez" in August 2011 and had been viewed 139,888,399 times as of 7 August 2014.

LONGEST JOURNEY IN *MINECRAFT*

In March 2011, Kurt J Mac (USA) began an epic journey to the edge of *Minecraft*'s vast world – the fabled "Far Lands" – in "Survival" mode, recording his travels on his YouTube channel "Far Lands or Bust!". He uses his annual checks of how far he's walked to raise money for charity. On 6 March 2014, three years into the trek, he discovered he'd walked 1,479,940 blocks (1,479,940 m; 919,592 mi) from his original spawn. The "Far Lands" are about 12,550 km (7,800 mi) from the original spawn point.

MOST *MINECRAFT* SNOW GOLEMS BUILT IN ONE MINUTE

Snow golems comprise two snow blocks stacked on top of one another with a single pumpkin or jack-o'-lantern for a head. Using a specially created channel, gamer Nachtigall Vaz (Brazil) was able to create an army of 70 snow golems in 60 seconds on 7 January 2013.

225,000,000 *Minecraft* worlds created on the Xbox 360 since its launch on 9 May 2012. That's an average of 314,685 worlds made every day, as of 15 April 2014.

LARGEST REAL-WORLD PLACE CREATED IN *MINECRAFT*

Using its geographical data for the UK, the Ordnance Survey created a map of Britain and its islands in *Minecraft*. It uses 22 billion blocks to represent 224,000 km² (86,500 mi²) of mainland Great Britain's 229,848 km² (88,743 mi²). Each block represents a ground area of 50 m² (538 ft²). Shown here is prehistoric monument Stonehenge in Wiltshire.

BEST-SELLING INDIE GAME

Although its console versions are published by the big studios, the original *Minecraft*, published by Mojang, is a true indie hit. As of 7 August 2014, the official site for the game listed total PC and Mac sales at 16,176,201, a number slightly greater than the entire population of Ecuador. Mojang remains an independent outfit with just 40 employees. For more on the explosion in independent gaming, turn to our feature over the page.

Independent developers have always been making games. In the 1980s, they tinkered with early home computers such as the ZX Spectrum or Apple II. In the 1990s, it was all about PCs, highlighted by the runaway success of Id Software's *Doom*. PCs then became home to a vibrant modding culture, where players would build new levels and designs for already-released games.

Today, the indie development scene is massive, releasing hundreds of games a year and spanning huge hits like *Minecraft* and progressive, innovative designs such as *Papers, Please* (inset right).

Many indie games look back with fondness to 8-bit and 16-bit classics with pixelated graphics, platforming and chiptune music, but they add modern twists – randomly generated elements or RPG-like customization. Others are highly expressive, using stylized or hyper-real graphics to heighten the player's experience, as in *NaissanceE* and *Dear Esther*. Then there are open-worlders that allow gamers to play freely, such as *Kerbal Space Program* and *Sir, You Are Being Hunted* (main image above). Indie gaming is all about variety.

Working for themselves, indie developers tend to be a lot more creative than the big studios, trying out new ideas, reacting to what their fans like and using games to express themselves. If you want to play games at the cutting edge of game design, look first to the indies.

Key to the rise of the indie

INDIE KID

We talk to **Sean Murray** (right), the founder of Hello Games, developer of the *Joe Danger* series (left) and *No Man's Sky*, a forthcoming sci-fi exploration game.

Why are you an indie developer?
It's about the freedom to make what we want to make. It's not like I didn't get to make some cool things when I worked for big studios, but now, if we come up with an amazing idea for an iPad game, we can just go make it. We don't need to prove that it's a good idea to anyone but ourselves. I don't think we could be making *No Man's Sky* if we worked for a big developer. The thought of convincing bosses that it will make money and be possible to finish just makes me feel a bit ill. But we knew in our hearts it was exactly what we should be doing; that it would be amazing and people would want it. So we just went ahead.

What is the future for indie titles?
For me, indie games are so important to videogaming that it's time we upped our ambitions and really started to challenge the mainstream industry with huge experiences that people can get lost in. It's started with *Minecraft*

and *DayZ*, and we can do much more, too – we began making *No Man's Sky*, which is set in an infinite, procedurally generated universe, with just four people. Just think what else indie developers can make.

scene is the internet. Using Skype to communicate, many developers can work from home, often thousands of miles from their collaborators. They can also use crowdfunding sites and social media to help finance development, and then distribute their games through Xbox Live, Steam on PC, the Play Store or iOS App Store.

So many games are coming out today that the main challenge for indies is raising awareness. An indie developer doesn't only have to be good at design and programming and have a good eye for art, but also has to be an able marketeer, aware of how to publicize their games at consumer and trade shows as well as online.

Without the huge advertising budgets of major studios, the harsh truth is that most indie titles never gain fame. For many, indie developing can seem overwhelming, but for others, this kind of control and meticulous involvement is precisely what attracts them to the liberating, exciting and unpredictable world of independent games.

GAME MAKERS

Many indie developers are now taking advantage of the proliferation of cheap and even free development tools and engines to turn their dreams into reality: GameMaker is great for 2D games, while Unity can produce rich 3D titles. Designed so that you can start making games with surprisingly little knowledge and experience, they're supported by helpful communities – the indie scene being well-known for its friendliness and inclusivity.

STARS OF INDIE

Highlights from the front line of the indie revolution...

Hyper Light Drifter (2014)
A beautiful action RPG characterized by brightly stylized pixel graphics. Its Kickstarter campaign aimed to raise $27,000 (£16,100), but ended up with an incredible $645,158 (£385,400).

Spelunky (2009)
Randomly generated levels and plenty of secrets make this incredibly demanding platformer almost endlessly playable, with a combination of great knowledge and fine motor skills a must to reach the endgame.

Ridiculous Fishing (2013)
Catch as many fish as you can, throw them high and shoot them out of the air. This curio was originally made for browsers, before developers Vlambeer produced an iOS version. It scooped an Apple Design Award in 2013.

Limbo (2010)
An object lesson in building atmosphere with simple graphics and no language, this horror adventure platformer has enjoyed both critical acclaim and strong sales, and has been released on most gaming platforms from smartphones to Linux.

Braid (2008)
With painterly 2D graphics, smart and imaginative design and a subtle storyline about obsession and destruction, Jonathan Blow's puzzle platformer was one of the first indie games to hit seventh-generation consoles.

BEST-SELLING VIDEOGAME SERIES

Starring in more than 180 games, Mario had accumulated in excess of 528.99 million global sales (including core platformers, fighting games and dance spin-offs) as of 29 July 2014, making Mario's the best-selling videogame franchise of all time. The original *Super Mario Bros.* turns 30 in 2015 while the man himself – first conceived as a character called Jumpman – made his Wii U debut in 2013 with all-new platform action in *Super Mario 3D World*.

SUPER MARIO 3D WÖRLD™

SUPER MARIO BROS.

Summary: Gaming legend, symbol of Nintendo's superpower status, mascot of many a console and arch-enemy of Bowser: to many, Mario remains *the* icon of the videogames industry.

Publisher: Nintendo
Developer: Nintendo
Debut: 1983

FIRST PLATFORM VIDEOGAME

Although not the title star, the diminutive plumber with the impossibly bushy moustache

caught the eye when he featured in the 1981 Nintendo arcade game *Donkey Kong*, the very first platformer. But back then Mario was known as Jumpman. *Donkey Kong* was the first game created by legendary Japanese designer Shigeru Miyamoto.

BEST-SELLING DS GAME

As of 12 August 2014, *New Super Mario Bros.* had sold 29.48 million copies since its launch in 2006, according to VGChartz. The highly acclaimed side-scrolling platformer marked a significant moment in gaming history, as it was the first new 2D platform game starring Mario since *Super Mario Land 2: 6 Golden Coins* for the Game Boy in 1992. Direct sequel *New Super Mario Bros. 2* was released on the 3DS in 2012.

LONGEST-RUNNING VIDEOGAME CHARACTER

Mario just keeps on giving. Including his first appearance in *Donkey Kong* (1981), the plumber has featured in a total of 388 games across all ports and platforms (although not always as a playable character). His image owes a lot to early tech limitations: on the low-res hardware of the early 1980s, it was easier to animate a moustache than a mouth.

BEST-SELLING MARIO GAME

Super Mario Bros. has sold 40.24 million copies, owing largely to it being bundled with the NES (Famicom in Japan) upon the console's release in 1985. Its sales also make it the **best-selling platformer**. The first Mario title to be set in the Mushroom Kingdom, it also heralded the debut appearances of the characters Bowser, Princess Toadstool (known later as Princess Peach) and Toad.

MEET YOUR MAKER

One of Nintendo's major announcements at E3 2014 was a new title for the Wii U in which gamers can create 2D Mario levels using the GamePad controller. *Mario Maker*, due for release in early 2015, allows players to adopt the graphics of the original NES *Super Mario Bros.* or the more modern HD variety.

BEST-SELLING THIRD-GENERATION CONSOLE VIDEOGAME

Mario's colossal impact on Nintendo's early success cannot be overstated. *Super Mario Bros.* became the best-selling game on third-generation platforms with its sales of 40.24 million, while *Super Mario World* on the SNES, which sold 20.61 million, holds the record for the **best-selling game for fourth-generation consoles**.

The hat-trick of success for Mario and Nintendo was completed when 1996's *Super Mario 64*, for the N64, sold 11.89 million and became the **best-selling game for fifth-generation consoles**. Although *Super Mario* sales remain decent going into the eighth generation, the Wii U's struggles have affected Mario's popularity: the latest game, *Super Mario 3D World*, was released in 2013 and has sold a modest 2.19 million copies.

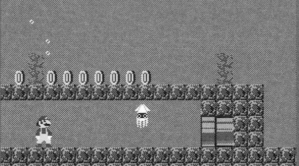

FIRST USE OF A PLATFORMER IN A BRAIN STUDY

A 2013 study carried out by the Max Planck Institute for Human Development and Charité University Medicine, St Hedwig-Krankenhaus in Berlin, Germany, concluded that playing videogames can increase brain size. Scientists ran an experiment whereby 23 adults played *Super Mario 64* on a Nintendo XXL for 30 minutes each day for two months. Test results outlined "increases in the brain regions responsible for spatial orientation, memory formation and strategic planning as well as fine motor skills".

FIRST *SUPER MARIO* GAME FOR A NON-NINTENDO SYSTEM

The first direct sequel to *Super Mario Bros.* was not even released on a Nintendo console. *Super Mario Bros. Special* in 1986 was the first Nintendo-licensed follow-up to the NES hit and was released on the NEC PC-8801 and Sharp X1 series of Japanese PCs two years before *Super Mario Bros. 2.*

FASTEST 120-STAR COMPLETION OF *SUPER MARIO 64*

On 22 May 2014, speed-runner "Puncayshun" completed *Super Mario 64* and collected all 120 stars in just 1 hr 43 min 42 sec. Speed wizard "Blubber", meanwhile, achieved the **fastest completion of *Super Mario Bros.*** in a lightning-fast time of 4 min 57.69 sec on 27 June 2014. The **fastest completion of *Super Mario Galaxy 2*** was achieved in 4 hr 20 min 37 sec by gamer "snowymountain" (Sweden) on 15 July 2013.

FIRST MOVIE BASED ON A VIDEOGAME

Sûpâ Mario burazâzu: Pîchi-hime kyushutsu dai sakusen!, or *Super Mario Bros.: The Great Mission to Rescue Princess Peach!* (near right), was a 60-minute anime film released exclusively in Japan in 1986, directed by Masami Hata. A VHS release followed, but the film never made it to DVD or Blu-ray.

The **first live-action movie based on a videogame** was *Super Mario Bros.* (USA, 1993), starring Bob Hoskins, Samantha Mathis and John Leguizamo.

FASTEST-SELLING SINGLE-PLATFORM VIDEOGAME

New Super Mario Bros. Wii was released in November 2009 and within eight weeks had clocked up worldwide sales of more than 10 million, making it the fastest-selling videogame on just one gaming platform. It is the first Mario main-series title since the original *Mario Bros.* in 1983 to feature simultaneous multiplayer gameplay. *New Super Mario Bros. Wii* has gone on to sell 27.5 million copies.

CALL OF DUTY

BEST-SELLING FPS SERIES

Call of Duty: Advanced Warfare, due late 2014, is the first game in the Advanced Warfare arc and takes the action into the mid-21st century. As of 25 July 2014, the series had sold 188.9 million copies across all platforms. The 2013 *Ghosts* edition sold more than 20 million copies, so will *Advanced Warfare* take the franchise over the 200 million mark?

"This has the scale and the scope of the equivalent of four Hollywood movies in it. It has hundreds of hours of multiplayer gameplay. It has full cooperative mode. It takes an army of industry vets to create this kind of content."

MICHAEL CONDREY
CO-FOUNDER, SLEDGEHAMMER GAMES

gamers

01 CALL OF DUTY

Summary: Despite being overshadowed by *GTA V*, *Ghosts* (2013) still sold 20 million units. The futuristic *Advanced Warfare*, set for late 2014, is Sledgehammer Games' first solo *CoD* title.

Publisher: Activision
Developer: Infinity Ward/Treyarch/Sledgehammer
Debut: 2003

FOR THE WIN

THE CHAIN SAW

One of the more unusual firearms in *Call of Duty: Ghosts* is the Chain SAW. It's classed as a Light Machine Gun but you can only fire it from the hip. Stick a Muzzle Break and Rapid Fire on this bullet hose and it's like having a toned-down mini-gun.

FIRST MILLION-SELLING VIDEOGAME FOR XBOX 360

Call of Duty 2, a launch title for the Xbox 360, was the first game for the Microsoft system to sell 1 million copies, reaching a total of 1.91 million, of which 1.73 million were sales within the USA. The PS2 version sold a total of 2.67 million copies worldwide.

BEST-SELLING SHOOTER GAME

Call of Duty: Modern Warfare 3 had sold 29.75 million units across all gaming platforms as of 11 August 2014, according to VGChartz. *CoD* is also comfortably the **best-selling shooter series on the Wii**, with total sales of 7.66 million for *CoD 3*, *CoD: World at War*, *CoD: Modern Warfare: Reflex Edition*, *CoD: Black Ops* and *CoD: Modern Warfare 3*. As for the Wii's successor, the **best-selling shooter game for Wii U** is *Call of Duty:*

Black Ops II, with worldwide sales of 240,000. This may sound disappointing next to the mammoth sales on other platforms, but sales of the Wii U have underwhelmed and *CoD* is traditionally more popular on Sony and Microsoft platforms. This is evidenced by the series holding records for the **best-selling shooter series for PlayStation 3**, with total sales of 67.95 million units across all titles released for the console, and the **best-selling shooter series for Xbox 360**, with collective sales of 83.83 million.

FASTEST SUBMACHINE GUN IN *CALL OF DUTY*

With a maximum rounds-per-minute rating of 1,888, the Skorpion EVO is the speediest *CoD* submachine gun. It achieves the record in *Black Ops II* with the Rapid Fire attachment, taking its standard 1,250-RPM

rating to a barely controllable 1,888 RPM. So much for short, controlled bursts…

FASTEST TIME TO CAPTURE THE FLAG IN *CALL OF DUTY: BLACK OPS II* (BLINDFOLDED, TEAM OF TWO)

Brothers and regular record-breakers Tristen Geren and Taylor Geren (both USA) clubbed together to capture the flag in *CoD: Black Ops II*, while blindfolded, in just 38.40 seconds in Fredericksburg, Texas, USA, on 16 September 2013.

HOUSE OF CoDs

Hollywood star Kevin Spacey brings a shot of star quality to proceedings with his role in *Call of Duty: Advanced Warfare*. The Oscar-winner takes on the role of arch villain Jonathan Irons, the head of Atlas. But the *House of Cards* and *American Beauty* star says he is not a gamer.

MOST FOLLOWED VIRTUAL DOG

It turns out that Riley, the playable German Shepherd from *Call of Duty: Ghosts*, is a dab hand at social media. As of 11 August 2014, the terrorist-tackling pooch had attracted 28,305 followers on his unofficial parody Twitter account @CollarDuty.

▶▶FIRST *TITANFALL* PLAYER TO REACH GENERATION 10

The two developers behind *Call of Duty*, Jason West and Vince Zampella, set up Respawn Entertainment in 2010. Their first game was the highly anticipated FPS *Titanfall*, released in 2014.

Gamer "DownTuClown" reached *Titanfall*'s Generation 10 – the highest experience level in the game – after just 3 days 9 hr 5 min playing the mech-battling shooter.

HIGHEST-EARNING *CALL OF DUTY* PLAYER

As of 11 August 2014, Damon "Karma" Barlow (Canada) is the most successful professional *Call of Duty* player, making a total of $229,628 (£136,842) in his career, according to e-Sports Earnings.

Barlow won the *Call of Duty* Championship in 2013 as a member of team "Impact" and again in 2014 as a member of team "compLexity". "Impact" – consisting of "Karma", Adam "Killa" Sloss, Marcus "MiRx" Carter and team captain Christopher "Parasite" Duarte – became the **first winner of the CoD Championship** with victory on 7 April 2013 and prize money of $1,000,000 (£651,687).

25 billion

hours of *CoD* games played since the release of *CoD 4: Modern Warfare* in 2007 – that's 2.8 million years in total!

MOST-VIEWED FAN-MADE LEGO FILM BASED ON A VIDEOGAME

"Lego Black Ops", a parody of *CoD* using LEGO™ figures, had amassed 20,424,239 views on YouTube as of 11 August 2014. Created by veteran LEGO film-maker "Keshen8", the 1-min 37-sec clip was made with LEGO weapons crafted by custom toy-maker BrickArms.

BEST-SELLING SHOOTER GAME PUBLISHER

As of 11 August 2014, publisher Activision had sold a phenomenal 213,960,000 videogames in the shooter genre. The *Call of Duty* franchise is responsible for 188,060,000 of those units sold. Activision was founded in 1979 by four former Atari programmers, becoming the **first third-party videogame console developer**. Starting out with games for the Atari 2600, they went on to develop and publish shooters including *Doom 3* (2004), *Predator* (1987) and the *Asteroids* port for the PlayStation (1998).

YOUR NEW FAVOURITE GAMES

Will 2015 herald a new golden age of gaming? A huge and varied roster of new titles for the eighth-generation consoles suggests that it might just be a vintage year. Here are a handful of brand new games that you may struggle to turn off…

EVOLVE

Scheduled release: Q1 2015
Platforms: Xbox One, PS4, PC

Four gamers controlling humans vs a fifth gamer controlling an alien beastie: *Evolve* has all the makings of a modern classic. Originally scheduled for release in October 2014, the sci-fi co-op FPS is now due in February 2015. The buzz surrounding Turtle Rock's new IP is enormous, and little wonder following its Best of Show gong at E3. The Xbox One-only beta is due to start in January 2015.

THE ORDER: 1886

Scheduled release: Q1 2015
Platform: PS4

First announced at E3 2013, *The Order* is an action-adventure title set, appropriately enough, in 1886. The plot centres on an alternative-history version of London, UK, where bloodsucking monsters cause unbridled carnage. Enter an order of knights to save civilization. Gameplay footage looks sumptuous, cinematic and very bloody.

NO MAN'S SKY

Scheduled release: 2015
Platforms: PS4, PC

Set in a procedurally generated universe which promises to be far larger than any other open world, each player starts on their own planet before venturing into space to explore. The universe is said to be so large that just seeing another player could be a special occasion. *No Man's Sky* has been talked about as the beginning of a new gaming genre.

DYING LIGHT

Scheduled release: Q1 2015
Platforms: PC, PS3, PS4, Xbox 360, Xbox One

The team that brought you *Dead Island* offers up more gruesome zombies, open-world style. This survival-horror melee battler will feature online multiplayer co-op mode for up to four players. But the twist here is that the virus that has infected the hordes has infected you, too…

EVERYBODY'S GONE TO THE RAPTURE

Scheduled release: 2015
Platform: PS4

The Chinese Room, who developed the experimental *Dear Esther*, returns with this 1980s open-worlder set in a remote part of Shropshire, UK, during an apocalypse. In the words of the dev team, it is "a story about people and how they live with each other. But it's also about the end of the world."

DESTINY

Scheduled release: September 2014
Platforms: PS3, PS4, Xbox 360, Xbox One

An open-world, online multiplayer sci-fi shooter from the makers of *Halo* – *Destiny* has all the ingredients and word-of-mouth excitement needed to make it a monster hit and an eighth-generation blockbuster. Set in a post-apocalyptic universe 700 years from now, *Destiny*'s player characters, the Guardians, are tasked with defending the last city on Earth from brutal extraterrestrial species.

STAR WARS: BATTLEFRONT

Scheduled release: 2015
Platforms: Xbox One, PC, PS4

In May 2013, Disney handed development of the *Star Wars* games over to EA, and the team is visiting original film locations for inspiration. The 2015 edition will be the third in the *Battlefront* series and the first since 2005. Although EA is yet to reveal a great deal, trailer footage shows that the planet Hoth and forest moon of Endor will feature.

INSIDE

Scheduled release: 2015
Platform: Xbox One

Playdead, the developers behind the innovative indie hit *Limbo*, are back with more creepy minimalism. Unveiled at E3 2014, details about *Inside* remain sketchy, but the platformer is as stunning as *Limbo*, and every bit as dark.

YOSHI'S WOOLLY WORLD

Scheduled release: Q1/Q2 2015
Platform: Wii U

This side-scrolling platformer starring Mario's loyal dino is the first Yoshi console game since 1998's *Yoshi's Story* on the N64. Super-cutesy and super-fluffy, all the characters and environments in the game are made of yarn, felt, cloth and cotton. Instead of eggs, Yoshi hurls balls of yarn at enemies.

HARDWARE

BEST-SELLING EIGHTH-GENERATION CONSOLE

Sony's PlayStation 4 was released in the USA on 15 November 2013, in Europe on 29 November 2013, and on 22 February 2014 in Japan. By August 2014, Sony reported that PS4 had sold 10 million units worldwide, beating the Xbox One by at least 3 million. However, the new consoles are still babies in generational terms and there is still everything to play for.

Best-selling first-generation console
Magnavox Odyssey (1972): 330,000 units

Best-selling second-generation console
Atari 2600 (1977): 27.64 million

Best-selling third-generation console
Nintendo Entertainment System (NES, 1983): 61.91 million

Best-selling fourth-generation console
Super Nintendo Entertainment System
(SNES, 1990):
49.1 million

Best-selling fifth-generation console
Sony PlayStation (1994):
104.25 million

Best-selling sixth-generation console
Sony PlayStation 2 (2000):
157.68 million

Best-selling seventh-generation console
Nintendo Wii (2006):
101.04 million

Best-selling eighth-generation console
Sony PlayStation 4 (2013):
10 million

PS 4

Ever since it arrived on 15 November 2013, Sony's PlayStation 4 has gone from strength to strength, fast becoming the **best-selling eighth-generation console** (see pp.186–87) in the battle against Microsoft's Xbox One. With constant updates gradually ticking off its announcement promises, the PS4 can now stream directly to YouTube, as well as letting you edit gameplay videos, use the PlayStation Camera for speech recognition and even pre-load games to avoid slow download times on launch days.

228,000,000 presses of the DualShock 4's Share button since the PlayStation 4's release.

MULTIPLAYER MADNESS

In an exciting step forward for consoles, the PS4 version of *Far Cry 4* (due for release in November 2014) allows two-player co-op online with only one person having to own a copy of the game. Downloading an app on to the PS4 allows you to join up with a friend for some explosive, elephant-riding action in the Himalayas.

WAYS TO PLAY

Via PlayStation Live, over 150 million spectator sessions were logged by June 2014 on Twitch.tv and Ustream. As more people watch, developers are experimenting with different ways for viewers to dictate play. Games reported to have made use of PS4's interactive streaming so far are *Tomb Raider: Definitive Edition* (above) and *Dynasty Warriors 8*.

Plastic casing with EMI shield

WHITE OUT

Sony is due to introduce an exclusive Glacier White PS4 to celebrate the release of *Destiny* in September 2014. An Urban Camouflage-printed DualShock 4 will also hit the stores, adding to the ever-growing line-up of colours.

WIRELESS AUDIO   FOR THE WIN

Want to use a headset without having annoying wires stretched out across the living room? Plug your headphones into the DualShock 4, hold down the PS button and select "Adjust devices". From there, hit "Output to headphones" and then "All audio" and you'll have your game in your ears – and no trip hazards!

Motor driver IC

Optical drive board

UNCHARTED TERRITORY

With developers now escaping the shackles of last-gen performance limitations, games are beginning to make the most of the PlayStation 4's extra processing power. Naughty Dog's *Uncharted 4: A Thief's End*, scheduled for release in 2015, will be Nathan Drake's first outing on the new console, and in-game footage is staggeringly detailed. From the directors of *The Last of Us*, which was given a PS4 reboot in 2014, *Uncharted 4* will be a Sony-exclusive title as an older Drake takes on a new, dangerous quest to hunt out pirate treasure – all with a higher pixel count than ever.

FULL STREAM AHEAD!

For those of us with favourite games still only playable on the PS3, the beta of PlayStation Now, which launched on 31 July 2014, felt like a godsend. With over 100 titles available, such as *Saints Row IV* (inset) and *God of War: Ascension*, PlayStation Now uses the Gaikai cloud service to stream old games directly to the new console. It is also set to work with the PS Vita and compatible Sony BRAVIA TVs.

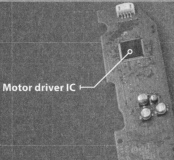

Heat sink

Motherboard

Power supply

Hard disk drive

Cooling fan

Optical drive

PLAYSTATION TV

Sony's microconsole was released outside Japan for the first time in 2014. Running the same software and chipset as the PlayStation Vita, it allows you to play a vast selection of Vita titles as well as PS classics such as *Crash Bandicoot* and *Spyro the Dragon* on the big screen via HDMI.

Plus, with the addition of PlayStation Now, Sony's online game-streaming service (see "Full Stream Ahead!" opposite), there are plenty of PS3 titles to choose from too. Handily, PlayStation TV can also serve as a Remote Play device if you don't fancy lugging your PS4 upstairs to your bedroom.

INTO THE MATRIX

While Project Morpheus looks like it might send you straight into a cyberpunk movie, this virtual-reality headset is Sony's answer to Oculus Rift for the PS4. It's currently still a prototype, but with a 1080p display, 3D audio, an accelerometer and gyroscope all built in – not to mention full PS Move compatibility – this is already an impressive way to get your head into a game.

Sony has revealed that the unique light bar installed on the PS4's DualShock controller was designed specifically with the Morpheus headset in mind, for seamless motion-tracking using the PlayStation Camera. Compatible games to date include racing simulator *Project CARS* by Slightly Mad Studios (inset) and the upcoming Kickstarter project *Loading Human*, a sci-fi-adventure title slated for 2015 release.

XBOX ONE

Out of the starting gate a week later than the PS4, on 22 November 2013, the Xbox One endured a slower start than its Sony rival, but still sold a solid 3 million by the end of 2013. After a rocky announcement event, a strong emphasis on their television services and the departure of executive Don Mattrick in 2013, Microsoft is now focusing firmly on the gaming side of the machine. With Halo 5: Guardians on the way in 2015, and a renewed focus on indie developers, Xbox is trying to show gamers where its allegiances now lie.

XPERT ADVICE

Get multitasking with the Snapping feature by speedily double-tapping the Xbox button on the controller to swap quickly between windows. If you don't want to use a thumb, then saying "Xbox, switch" will let Kinect do the job for you.

Motherboard

Casing

SATA II hard drive

XBOX FITNESS

For people who want to get in shape but don't fancy the gym, the *Xbox Fitness* app offers an interactive home workout with famous trainers such as Jillian Michaels, Tony Horton and Shaun T. Using the Kinect to track heart rate, energy and muscle exertion, *Xbox Fitness* could have you working up a sweat in no time.

ID@XBOX

With no charge for development kits and publishing support, Microsoft's self-publishing program, ID@Xbox, makes it even easier for indie developers to get their game on to the Xbox Store. Games can be updated for free, too. Microsoft promise that it will eventually be possible to develop titles from the Xbox One itself. For now, highlights include the new game from *Limbo* devs Playdead, *Inside*, and the early animation-styled side-scroller *Cuphead*, with Double Fine, Vlambeer and Crytek also participating.

Blu-ray/DVD drive

Speaker

GAMESCOM

With Xbox One sales figures at around 5 million, half those of the PS4, Microsoft used Gamescom in August 2014 to announce a slew of alluring new games, including the beta of *Evolve* and an Xbox-exclusive priority period for its DLC, a plethora of indie titles such as *Goat Simulator*, *Smite* and *No Time to Explain*, and the roller-coaster title *Screamride*.

GREAT SCOTT!

Produced by British film director Ridley Scott, the first episode of the *Halo* live-action series *Nightfall* (inset) is set to be included with *The Master Chief Collection* in late 2014. The plot centres on a previously unknown character, Agent Locke, who will become central to *Halo 5: Guardians* (left), set for 2015. Microsoft and 343 Industries have also announced the Halo Channel, which will broadcast live Twitch-enabled gameplay and original content based around *Halo*.

With every main game in the series collected on one Blu-ray, as well as additional never-seen-before cinematics, *The Master Chief Collection* allows players to revisit more than 100 multiplayer maps in full 1080p at 60fps.

KINECT GETS A KICKING

In May 2014, Microsoft removed the compulsory Kinect 2 from the Xbox One bundle, taking the price into direct competition with the PS4. Despite the Kinect 2's technical prowess – advanced motion tracking with Real Motion Technology – very few games were making the most of its capabilities.

Fan

Heat sink

Wi-fi board

RF module board

BRIGHT SPARK

A free2play Xbox exclusive with endless potential, *Project Spark* (above left) is a customizable game creator that lets your invent whatever games you want before sharing them online. From shooters to side-scrollers and dungeon crawlers to MOBAs, everything can be created then personalized with up to four other players.

Microsoft's SmartGlass technology can be utilized in *Project Spark* to create touch-based games that wouldn't previously have been possible with just the Xbox One (game stats screen above right). "Our goal is to open players' imaginations and give them the tools they need to create anything they can dream up," says Sax Persson, director at *Spark* developers Team Dakota. "Combining SmartGlass with Xbox One lets us deliver on that promise."

X-CLUSIVES

Xbox One isn't short on exclusive games. The monster-packed *Scalebound* (above), announced at E3 2014, is helmed by *Devil May Cry* director Hideki Kamiya and is something of a coup for Microsoft. *Sunset Overdrive* (inset) is a gleefully over-the-top TPS high on demonic energy drink, while *Forza Horizon 2* puts you in the driving seat of more than 200 of the world's most spectacular cars. *Rise of the Tomb Raider* will also be a timed exclusive on Xbox One.

HANDHELDS

There's no denying the pull of mobile gaming. We're still StreetPassing on the 3DS and now streaming PS4 games on the go with the PS Vita. In 2014, new versions of existing handhelds arrived, alongside revamped classic games and plenty of exciting new titles too.

SONY PLAYSTATION

The second-generation PlayStation Vita was released in May 2014 with an upgraded battery, design tweaks and a 5-in (12.7-cm) IPS LCD display with a backlight. With 1 GB of internal storage, gamers can get started without a memory card.

Minecraft appeared on the slimmed-down Vita in 2014 without dropping any features. It also allowed game saves to be transferred between the PS3 version and the Vita.

Games could also be streamed from the PlayStation 4, making the Vita ideal for *Assassin's Creed: Unity* at bathtime and *Alien: Isolation* at bedtime.

It was time to say goodbye to the PlayStation Portable in 2014, as production stopped in Japan. Gamers bade a fond farewell to the **first handheld videogame console with an optical disc**, which underwent five redesigns over its nine-year life, including the diminutive PSP go.

NINTENDO

The glasses-free 3DS got quirky life sim *Tomodachi Life* in 2014. *Super Smash Bros.* is also set to make its highly anticipated portable debut in 2014 for the 3DS, allowing players to connect with up to three fighters online and featuring an exclusive 3DS mode.

Pokémon Omega Ruby and *Pokémon Alpha Sapphire* are Game Boy Advance remakes due in 2014, allowing customizable areas to be shared via StreetPass.

Nintendo also looked ahead to 2015, with amiibo figurines promised for the 3DS. For more on Nintendo's physical characters, check out our Toys-to-Life feature on pp.144–45.

IOS & ANDROID

The new graphics software, Metal, in iOS 8 (due late 2014) allows developers to tap in to previously unused power within the A7 processor chip.

Monument Valley – also on Android – was a critically acclaimed app in 2014 with a beautiful visual style, while *Hearthstone: Heroes of Warcraft* was acclaimed on iPad, Windows and Mac. The *World of Warcraft*-based card game allowed players to duel online.

Elsewhere, mobile gamers could plug their iPhones into a console-style controller such as the MOGA Ace Power (below).

NVIDIA SHIELD

Running an NVIDIA Tegra 4 processor, the NVIDIA Shield Portable is able to multitask. It plays games, apps and movies from the Google Play store and can stream PC games at 1080p over wi-fi. NVIDIA GameStream opens up MOBA titles such as *League of Legends* and *World of Warcraft*, while the Shield's display can run on a TV.

Camera and cabling

Speakers and cabling

3D top screen

Nintendo 3DS
Released in 2011, the handheld was the successor to the DS and had sold more than 44 million units by the end of June 2014.

128 MB Fujitsu RAM

ABXY buttons

1,252,777
apps available in the Apple App Store as of 10 July 2014.

PlayStation Portable: the first Sony handheld was introduced in 2004.

MOGA Ace Power: slotting an iPhone into the Ace Power allows access to console controls as well as a battery boost.

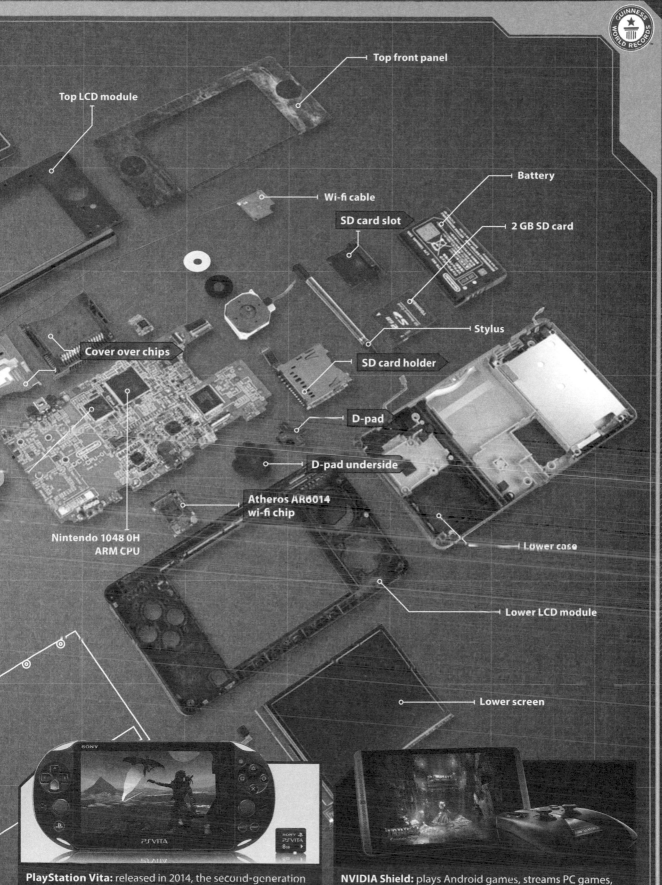

Top front panel

Top LCD module

Wi-fi cable

Battery

SD card slot

2 GB SD card

Stylus

Cover over chips

SD card holder

D-pad

D-pad underside

Atheros AR6014 wi-fi chip

Nintendo 1048 0H ARM CPU

Lower case

Lower LCD module

Lower screen

PlayStation Vita: released in 2014, the second-generation Vita had lost weight and quickly became known as the Slim.

NVIDIA Shield: plays Android games, streams PC games, and can be used to watch movies as well.

HARDWARE ROUND-UP

Although it's generally software that steals the limelight, 2014 was a groundbreaking year for gaming hardware. While the PS4 and Xbox One battled it out for eighth-gen supremacy, microconsoles were sneaking under our TVs, PC gaming grew ever stronger, and the Wii U was under scrutiny once again as developers tried to work out its future. Our virtual-reality dreams were dashed when Oculus Rift went another year without a release, but with Project Morpheus hot on its heels, it can't be long before VR goes mainstream.

INSIDE THE AMD R9 295X2

Radiator

1,018 MHz graphics chip (one of two)

Dual-link DVI

GDDR5 card (total memory of 8 GB)

AMD

AMAZON'S ON FIRE
Among the slew of microconsoles fighting to get under your big screen, the $99 (£TBA) Amazon Fire TV allows you not only to stream movies and TV shows through the box, but also to play games on its Android OS. Amazon has big gaming ambitions having set up its own in-house games team and is also working with Mojang and Telltale Games to create bespoke titles.

WII U ON THE UP?
Things haven't been easy for the Wii U, but perhaps the tide is turning. The release of *Mario Kart 8* increased UK Wii U sales in June 2014 by 666%! In the longer term, utilizing the built-in NFC capabilities of the GamePad, interactive amiibo figures for *Super Smash Bros.* (below) have proved a hit (see pp.144–45) and are set to appear with more Nintendo titles.

GRAPHICS REVOLUTION
PCs that leave consoles trailing graphically are more affordable than ever, and advancements in graphics mean that 4K gaming is well and truly here. The AMD R9 295X2 (see main image above), launched in April 2014, is one of the most powerful graphics cards for gaming ever. With a liquid cooling system and 8 GB of memory, the R9 295X2 can really do justice to games such as *Assassin's Creed: Unity* (pictured).

Connecting tube

Cold plate

8-pin power connector

Machined aluminium chassis

AMD
RADEON
GRAPHICS

asetek

Voltage regulator fan

Water-cooling unit

$2,437,429
pledged to the Oculus Rift
project on Kickstarter by
9,522 backers.

Oculus

DIY GAMING
Handhelds don't come
much more hands-on than
the DIY Gamer Kit (below),
which you have to build
before you can play. Made
by Technology Will Save
Us, the device comes in
40 components that have
to be soldered together.
Once the hardware's
finished, the creativity
doesn't stop: you can also
design games with it.

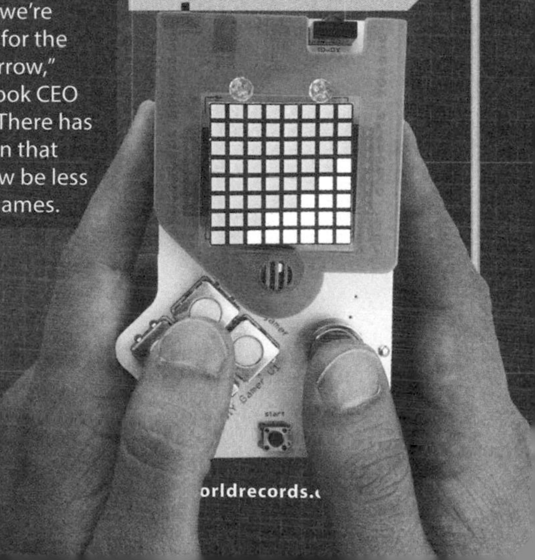

RISE OF THE STEAM MACHINES
The 13 Steam Machines officially announced by Valve at CES
in 2014 include CyberPowerPC's offering, shown below. With
AMD or Intel components available at $499 (£299) and $699
(£420) respectively, this particular Steam Machine comes
with the Valve-made Steam Controller (below right) and
runs the Linux-based Steam OS. Valve still has its eyes on the
living-room technology sector, but the question is, can it
really bridge the gap between PC and console gaming?

FACEBOOK GOES VIRTUAL
One of the biggest tech
news stories of 2014 was
Facebook acquiring Oculus
VR for $2 bn (£1.2 bn).
"Mobile is the platform
of today, and now we're
also getting ready for the
platforms of tomorrow,"
announced Facebook CEO
Mark Zuckerberg. There has
been some concern that
the device may now be less
focused on videogames.

HANDHELD HEAVEN

From the earliest days of the videogame it became apparent that gamers wanted to spend every available moment honing their skills. Enter the handheld game machine, putting gaming on the go at any time and any place. Following on from the history of home consoles in *Gamer's Edition 2014*, here's a lowdown on the history of the handhelds…

1979 MICROVISION

The Microvision, the **first handheld to have interchangeable game cartridges**, marked a big step on from Auto Race. The console itself was little more than the LCD screen and battery, while each of the game cartridges contained a mini microprocessor and control buttons that clipped on to the rest of the unit. By today's standards the games look incredibly basic, but they did allow gamers to play arcade-style games on the go, such as *Star Trek: Phaser Strike* and *Sea Duel*.

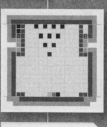

KEY TITLES

BlockBuster ▲
Bowling ▲

1976 MATTEL AUTO RACE

A big round of applause for Mattel's *Auto Race*, the **first handheld electronic game**. It launched in 1976, just four years after the **first videogame console**, the Magnavox Odyssey. The aim of the game was to steer a car (represented by a red rectangle) along a course while avoiding other cars (more red rectangles). The entire game was coded on to just 512 bytes of memory. Mattel followed up their pioneering title with *Football*, *Hockey* and *Missile Attack*.

APRIL 1989 GAME BOY

Like some kind of gigantic, friendly monster, the Game Boy still looms large over the handheld gaming landscape. It's fair to say that, while not the first handheld device, the Game Boy popularized portable gaming in the same way Sony's Walkman made portable audio a massive industry. Its popularity eclipsed all rivals, selling 118 million units worldwide to become the third best-selling console ever. The original version of the Game Boy was pretty chunky, with an LCD screen, two action buttons, start and select buttons and an eight-directional d-pad – just the same as a NES gamepad.

The Game Boy's success was largely down to two simple factors: impressive battery life (10 to 30 hours on four AA batteries) and a great line-up of games, such as the seminal puzzler *Tetris*: the **best-selling puzzle game** ever, with sales of 30.26 million across all platforms as of 23 June 2014.

KEY TITLES

Tetris ▶
Pokémon Red and Blue

GUNPEI YOKOI

The precursor to the Game Boy was Nintendo's Game & Watch LCD game series of simple, single-game handhelds (1980–91). These were designed by the late Gunpei Yokoi, who went on to design the Game Boy. Yokoi's philosophy was based around using older, cheaper technology in new ways. He believed that tech did not need to be cutting-edge to be fun. This led to the low price-point of the Game Boy and ultimately influenced the creation of the Nintendo Wii.

KEY TITLES

Shadow of the Beast ▲
Toki ◄

OCTOBER 1989 LYNX

Released to compete with the Game Boy, the Atari Lynx had superior graphics, a unique console design that meant two players could use the same machine to compete with each other at the same time, and the ability to link up with other players via a wired connection. But most significantly, the 16-bit handheld was also the **first handheld console to have a colour LCD screen**. In 2008, the Lynx won an Emmy Award for "Handheld Game Device Display Screen Innovation".

1990 GAME GEAR

The early 1990s saw Sega and Nintendo fight it out in both the home console and handheld markets. While the Mega Drive (Sega Genesis in the USA) went toe-to-toe with the SNES (Super Famicom in Japan) – outselling it in some territories – the Game Gear came a distant second to the Game Boy, with total sales of 10.62 million. On paper it appears that the Game Gear should have had the upper hand: full-colour graphics and a faster processor made it much more powerful than the Game Boy, but all that power came at the cost of battery life. Added to that, the Game Gear never had quite as strong a line-up of games, partly due to Sega focusing heavily on its home consoles.

KEY TITLES

Earthworm Jim ▲
Sonic the Hedgehog ◄

2001 GAME BOY ADVANCE

The Game Boy had bossed the 1990s handheld market, so Nintendo had a tough act to follow at the turn of the millennium. When their Advance came out, it was clear that Nintendo had decided to stick with what it knew while pumping up the power and bright colours. The Advance could play games with a graphical sophistication that matched the SNES. The machine was backwards-compatible with Game Boy and Game Boy Color games, too. It proved popular – sales totalled 81.5 million – while 2003's Advance SP included a brighter backlit screen, plus a clamshell design that would hint at what was to come next for Nintendo…

KEY TITLES

Advance Wars ▲
Metroid: Zero Mission ◄

HANDHELD HEAVEN

HANDHELL

Gizmondo (2005)
Released by Tiger Telematics, the Gizmondo was packed with then-fancy features such as GPS, Bluetooth, a digital camera and SMS messaging. But it was scuppered by having very few games, supply problems and Tiger Telematics declaring bankruptcy following some rather dubious goings-on by the company's executives.

Nokia N-Gage (2003)
The N-Gage combined gaming, phone functions and a music and video player, but the lofty launch price of $299 (£179) and its rather gaudy design didn't appeal to gamers.

game.com (1997)
The **first touchscreen console** also allowed gamers access to the internet via an external modem, but game.com's problems were all down to a lack of quality software: only 20 games were released in total.

KEY TITLES

*Metal Gear Solid:
Peace Walker* ▸
Patapon ▾

DECEMBER 2004
PLAYSTATION PORTABLE (PSP)

Compared with the phenomenal DS, Sony's PSP has been a "failure" with its sales of 80.79 million. The PSP is a power-packed handheld with amazing graphics and a massive 4.3-in (10.9-cm), bright LCD screen. As well as games, a range of films have been released on the PSP's UMD disc format. What's more, the PSP can be connected to the PS2 and PS3 as well as to other PSP units wirelessly. The problem is its shortage of fun, easy-to-play titles. It has largely relied on games that are very close to their home console versions without taking into account the different way gamers use handhelds.

NOVEMBER 2004 DS

Just like the Wii, the Nintendo DS placed innovation above raw power. And just like the Wii, it triumphed, becoming the **best-selling handheld console**, with sales of 154.88 million as of 23 June 2014. The DS has two screens in a clamshell, with the bottom screen being touch-sensitive. The restrained styling of the handheld – plus the inclusion of a stylus – gives the DS more adult appeal, with a host of titles such as the massively successful *Dr Kawashima's Brain Training: How Old Is Your Brain?* designed to tap into the emerging adult gamer market. In tandem with the Wii, the DS has attracted new generations of gamers from kids through to senior citizens. No other handheld has had so significant an impact before or after.

PERIPHERALS

Game Gear TV Tuner
Sega decided that playing games wasn't enough for its super-powered handheld – they wanted gamers to be able to watch TV on the go, too. Enter the battery-guzzling TV Tuner. It could receive an analogue signal for terrestrial channels. Most of the time.

KEY TITLES

Brain Training ◂
Professor Layton

KEY TITLES

Super Mario 3D Land ◄
Fire Emblem Awakening ▲ ►

FEBRUARY 2011 3DS

Sticking closely to the design of the DS, the unique selling point of the 3DS is the fact that it is the **first handheld to support glasses-free 3D**. The 3D effect, which can be switched off, only works if you look at the screen at exactly the correct angle, but it is quite astonishing. That said, very few games have made good use of it, and Nintendo say that "the use of the 3D feature by children aged six and under may cause vision damage". This explains, in part, why Nintendo released the 2DS in 2013, which is effectively a 3DS without the 3D and clamshell design. Despite the confusion, the 3DS has sold a relatively healthy 41.58 million units.

PERIPHERALS
Game Boy Camera and Printer
This nifty addition to the Game Boy allowed users to take and then print their very own black-and-white photos. However, the low-resolution spec of the Game Boy Camera meant that its pictures looked basic to say the least.

DECEMBER 2011 PLAYSTATION VITA

The sequel to the PSP has seriously upped the processing power. It plays host to some of the best-looking handheld games of all time, including *Uncharted: Golden Abyss*, the **most graphically advanced handheld platform game**, which displays 260,000 on-screen polygons. Adding a touchscreen plus a touchpad on the reverse of the machine indicates that Sony was using some of the same ideas that made the DS so successful. The Vita boasts a 5-in (12.7-cm) widescreen display, the **largest screen on a handheld**, but battery life has been a problem, often lasting only around five hours before needing a charge.

KEY TITLES

Tearaway ▲
Uncharted: Golden Abyss ▼

KEY TITLES

Candy Crush Saga ►
Clash of Clans ▼

2009-PRESENT MOBILE

The iPhone and its Android rivals, such as the Samsung Galaxy series, have changed the way many of us consume games. More than any other platform, mobiles have opened up games to users who would never have bought a dedicated gaming machine. People of all ages who perhaps wouldn't consider themselves gamers are playing the likes of *Flappy Bird*, *Candy Crush Saga* or *Clash of Clans* on their way to work or during moments of downtime. In some cases, these games are just as sophisticated as anything on the 3DS or Vita, but only time will tell whether mobile gaming can render dedicated handheld devices completely obsolete.

CONTRIBUTORS

These are the experts who contributed to *Gamer's Edition 2015*, sourcing and writing the records, facts, figures and trivia that go into the book. This year's *Gamer's Edition* includes writers who ply their trade at *Edge*, *Official PlayStation Magazine*, *Eurogamer.net* and *GamesRadar*.

LOUISE BLAIN

Previously a staff writer at *Official PlayStation Magazine*, Louise is now a freelance games and technology journalist as well as a member of the BAFTA Scotland games jury. She currently writes for *GamesMaster*, GamesRadar and TechRadar.

Which game did you play most in 2014? *Velocity 2X*.

What was the most exciting gaming event of 2014? E3 finally having a chance to show off what the new generation of hardware can do in terms of games.

MATT BRADFORD

Matt is a Canadian freelancer whose words have been spotted at GamesRadar, Twin Galaxies, WHAM! Gaming and past *Gamer's Editions*. His ramblings on gaming and pop culture can be heard on the weekly *Video Game Outsiders* and *Zombie Cast* podcasts.

Which game did you play most in 2014? *Dark Souls II*. Not always because I wanted to, but because I couldn't let it beat me.

What was the most exciting gaming event of 2014? E3 2014. Sure it's grown into a crowded, corporate monster, but it never fails to get me pumped up about what's around the corner.

ROB CAVE

Rob started gaming life in the 1980s with a second-hand Binatone TV Master IV, a first-generation British games console. He has been playing games on various PCs and consoles ever since. A passionate lover of comics and videogames, he has written about both subjects and has been a part of *Gamer's Edition* since it launched in 2008.

Which game did you play most in 2014? I'd say *The Last of Us* is probably the game I've enjoyed and returned to the most over the past year.

What was the most exciting gaming event of 2014? The most exciting thing about gaming in 2014 is how more and more people are making playing games part of their daily lives, playing a little, but often. I was also excited by Sony's announcement at Gamescom 2014 of "Share Play" as part of a firmware update on the PlayStation 4.

DAVID CROOKES

David started his gaming life with an Amstrad CPC. This led him to write for *Amstrad Action* in 1993, kickstarting his journalistic career. For the past 10 years he has written for *Retro Gamer*. He also pens many articles for *gamesTM* magazine and *The Independent* newspaper. He was the former news editor of Nintendo magazine *N*Revolution* and he curated the mammoth Videogame Nation exhibition.

Which game did you play most in 2014? *The Last of Us*.

What was the most exciting gaming event of 2014? The emergence of Project Morpheus.

ANDREW DAVIDSON

Andy is the editor of *Angry Birds Magazine*. Previously, he was editor of *Moshi Monsters Magazine* and *Toxic* (for whom he also reviewed videogames). A collector of retro gaming machines, Andy wrote about the history of consoles for *Gamer's Edition 2014*.

Which game did you play most in 2014? *Shovel Knight* (3DS).

What was the most exciting gaming event of 2014? For me, it has to be Evo 2014.

MATTHEW EDWARDS

Writing for the likes of Eurogamer.net, *Edge*, *gamesTM*, *Retro Gamer*, *Official Nintendo Magazine* and *Play*, it's fair to say that Matthew gets around.

Which game did you play most in 2014? *Ultra Street Fighter IV*.

What was the most exciting gaming event of 2014? Seeing a European Rose player win Evolution 2014 on a PlayStation pad.

RACHAEL FINN

Rachael is from London, UK, and helps fund her passion for soccer and videogaming by working for sports television broadcaster *Eurosport*.

Which game did you play most in 2014? Supercell's *Clash of Clans* has become something of an obsession. I'm in a clan with some friends and a group of players in Brazil and I've learned how to say phrases like "Please send archers" in Portuguese!

What was the most exciting gaming event of 2014? Facebook's acquisition of Oculus Rift.

ELLIE GIBSON

Ellie's career in videogames began the same week the PS2 launched, so she is an industry veteran! She started out writing manuals for PlayStation games and went on to work for Eurogamer.net. Ellie has written for the *Gamer's Edition* since its launch in 2008.

Which game did you play most in 2014? I really liked exploring Lara Croft's new island home in *Tomb Raider*.

What was the most exciting gaming event of 2014? EGX London at Earls Court. It's the UK's biggest and best games show.

STACE HARMAN

Stace is a freelance writer, editor and videogame consultant. He has been playing games since he was old enough to sit upright and is reasonably sure that zombies will one day roam the Earth.

Which game did you play most in 2014? Blizzard's *Hearthstone: Heroes of Warcraft*.

What was the most exciting gaming event of 2014? *The Last of Us* Live – seeing scenes from a videogame performed live on stage speaks volumes for how far writing and performance in the medium have progressed.

TYLER HICKS

Tyler is a freelance game reviewer and eSports pundit, expressing his opinions through blogging, livetweeting and articles. He's spent thousands of hours across the *Halo* and *Diablo* franchises, including coaching MLG *Halo* teams, but now sticks to *League of Legends*.

Which game did you play most in 2014? *League of Legends*. Rising through the ladder to prove I'm as good as I think keeps me coming back for more.

What was the most exciting gaming event of 2014? Evo 2014. When it comes to gaming event hype, there's no comparison to that brought by the fighting game community.

PHIL IWANIUK

Phil is staff writer at *Official PlayStation Magazine* and a racing games obsessive. His love for high-octane games started with *F1 Race* on the Game Boy, and led him to play *Gran Turismo 5* for 24 hours straight.

Which game did you play most in 2014? *NBA 2K14*.

What was the most exciting gaming event of 2014? Hideo Kojima announcing a new *Silent Hill* game in collaboration with Guillermo Del Toro at Gamescom 2014 via a playable teaser.

JOHN ROBERTSON

John has been involved with the videogame industry since 2007, working for publishers and media outlets. This experience of working on games as well as commenting on them as a journalist has given him a well-rounded view of the industry – from how it operates to how it achieves success.

Which game did you play most in 2014? *Hearthstone: Heroes of Warcraft*.

What was the most exciting gaming event of 2014? The growth of virtual-reality technology.

DAN WHITEHEAD

Dan has been playing games since 1982 and writing about them since 1991. He has written for *Official Xbox Magazine*, *Planet PlayStation* and Eurogamer.net, and his favourite game ever is Julian Gollop's 8-bit strategy classic, *Chaos*.

Which game did you play most in 2014? *Earth Defense Force 2025*.

What was the most exciting gaming event of 2014? The long overdue arrival of actual, affordable virtual-reality games. Now let's get to work on the whole "personal jetpack" thing.

BEN WILSON

Ben is a former editor of *Official PlayStation Magazine* who now writes about games for the *Daily Mirror*, *Stuff*, *OXM*, *GamesMaster* and more. His previous jobs include roles at *Zoo*, *More!*, *Bliss* and Nickelodeon.

Which game did you play most in 2014? *FIFA 14* on the PS4.

What was the most exciting gaming event of 2014? The *WWE* series coming to next-gen. Those wrestler faces look unreal.

ALEX WILTSHIRE

Alex is a former editor of *Edge* magazine, and currently works as communications manager for Hello Games and as a co-curator on a forthcoming exhibition about videogames for the Victoria and Albert Museum. He lives in Bath, UK, with his wife and two children.

Which game did you play most in 2014? *Mario Kart 8* has consumed my household and shows no sign of letting go. It's been a joy to watch my children become so skilled at a game I've been playing for 20 years. I'm convinced I've still just about got the edge on them.

What was the most exciting gaming event of 2014? For me, it was seeing *No Man's Sky* on stage at Sony's E3 press conference. Being involved in a project that moved so many people was incredible, especially one that inspired so much wonder.

GAMES AND DEVELOPERS

24: The Game SCE Studio Cambridge, 2006

2014 FIFA World Cup Brazil EA, 2014

ABBA: You Can Dance Ubisoft, 2011

Advance Wars Intelligent Systems, 2001

Advanced Dungeons & Dragons: Treasure of Tarmin APh Technological Consulting, 1983

Adventure Atari, 1979

Adventure Time: Explore the Dungeon Because I Don't Know! WayForward Technologies, 2013

ALF Sega, 1983

Alien Atari 2600, 1982

Alien 3 Probe Entertainment/Eden Entertainment, 1992

Alien Trilogy Probe Entertainment, 1996

Alien: Isolation The Creative Assembly, 2014 TBC

Alien: Resurrection Argonaut Games, 2000

Alienation Housemarque, TBC

Aliens: A Comic Book Adventure Mindscape, 1995

Aliens: Colonial Marines Gearbox, 2013

Aliens: The Computer Game Activision/Mr Micro, 1986

Aliens Versus Predator Rebellion, 1999

AlienX YoYo Games, 2014

Anarchy Online Funcom, 2001

Angry Birds Rovio, 2009

Angry Birds: Friends Rovio, 2012

Angry Birds: Go! Rovio/Exient Entertainment, 2013

Angry Birds: Rio Rovio/Fox Digital/Blue Sky Studios, 2011

Angry Birds: Star Wars Rovio/Exient Entertainment, 2012

Angry Birds: Star Wars II Rovio, 2013

Animal Crossing Nintendo, 2001

Apotheon Alientrap, 2014 TBC

Assassin's Creed Ubisoft, 2007

Assassin's Creed III: Liberation Ubisoft, 2012

Assassin's Creed IV: Black Flag Ubisoft, 2013

Assassin's Creed: Brotherhood Ubisoft, 2010

Assassin's Creed: Revelations Ubisoft, 2011

Assassin's Creed: Unity Ubisoft, 2014 TBC

Asteroids Atari, 1979

Baby PAC-Man Bally Midway, 1982

Bad Piggies Rovio, 2012

Baseball Nintendo, 1983

Bastion Supergiant Games, 2011

Batman Ocean, 1986

Batman: Arkham Asylum Rocksteady, 2009

Batman: Arkham City Rocksteady, 2011

Batman: Arkham Knight Rocksteady, 2015 TBC

Batman: Arkham Origins Warner Bros. Games, 2013

Batman: The Brave and the Bold WayForward Technologies, 2010

Batman Forever Probe Entertainment, 1995

Batman: Rise of Sin Tzu Ubisoft, 2003

Battlefield series: EA Digital Illusions CE/Visceral Games, 2002–13

Battlefield 2 DICE, 2005

Battlefield 3 DICE, 2011

Battlefield 4 DICE, 2013

Battlefield: Bad Company DICE, 2008

Battlefield: Hardline Visceral Games, 2015 TBC

Bayonetta Platinum Games, 2009

The Beatles: Rock Band Harmonix, 2009

Bionicle series, various, 2001–06

BioShock 2K Games, 2007

BioShock 2 2K Games, 2010

BioShock: Infinite Irrational Games, 2013

The Black Eyed Peas Experience Ubisoft/iNiS, 2011

Boom Beach Supercell, 2013

Borderlands Gearbox, 2009

Borderlands 2 Gearbox, 2012

Borderlands: The Pre-Sequel! 2K/Gearbox, 2014 TBC

Boyfriend Maker 36 You Games

Braid Number None, Inc/Hothead Games, 2008

Brain Age: Train Your Brain in Minutes a Day!, aka *Dr Kawashima's Brain Training* Nintendo, 2005

Brothers: A Tale of Two Sons Starbreeze Studios, 2013

Burnout Paradise Criterion Games, 2008

Caesar Impressions Games, 1992

Call of Duty Infinity Ward, 2003

Call of Duty 2 Infinity Ward, 2005

Call of Duty: Advanced Warfare Sledgehammer, 2014 TBC

Call of Duty: Black Ops Treyarch, 2010

Call of Duty: Black Ops II Treyarch, 2012

Call of Duty: Ghosts Infinity Ward, 2013

Call of Duty: Modern Warfare 3 Infinity Ward/Sledgehammer, 2011

Call of Duty: World at War Treyarch, 2008

Candy Crush Saga King, 2012

Castlevania Konami, 1986

Castlevania: Rondo of Blood Konami, 1993

Catwoman EA Games/various, 2004

Centipede Atari, 1981

Championship Soccer, aka *Pelé's Soccer* Atari, 1980

Clash of Clans Supercell, 2012

Computer Baseball Strategic Simulations, Inc, 1981

Contra Konami, 1987

Coolson's Artisanal Chocolate Alphabet Things Made Out Of Other Things Ltd, 2013

Cosmo Police Galivan Nihon Bussan, 1985

Counter-Strike Valve, 1999

Counter-Strike: Condition Zero Valve/Gearbox/various, 2004

Counter-Strike: Global Offensive Valve/Hidden Path Entertainment, 2012

Counter-Strike: Source Valve/various, 2004

The Counting Kingdom Little Worlds Interactive, 2014

Crash Bandicoot Naughty Dog, 1996

Crash Bandicoot 2: Cortex Strikes Back Naughty Dog, 1997

Crash Bandicoot 3: Warped Naughty Dog, 1998

Crash Team Racing Naughty Dog, 1999

Creatures Creature Labs, 1996

The Crew Ivory Tower/Ubisoft, 2014 TBC

CrossFire SmileGate, 2007

Crysis Crytek, 2007

Crysis 3 Crytek, 2013

Crysis Warhead Crytek, 2008

Cuphead Studio MDHR, 2015 TBC

Curiosity – What's Inside the Cube? 22Cans, 2012

Dance Central Harmonix, 2010

Dance Dance Revolution Konami, 1998

Dance Dance Revolution Hottest Party Konami, 2007

Dance Dance Revolution Pocket Edition Konami, 2013

Dark Souls II From Software, 2014

Daylight Zombie Studios, 2014

DayZ Bohemia Interactive, 2013

DC Universe Online Sony Online Entertainment, 2011

Dead or Alive Team Ninja, 1997

Dead or Alive 5 Team Ninja, 2012

Dead Rising 3 Capcom, 2014

Dead Space 2 Visceral Games, 2011

Dear Esther The Chinese Room, 2012

Defense of the Ancients (DotA) Valve, 2005

Defender Williams, 1980

Defiance Trion Worlds/Human Head Studios, 2013

Destiny Bungie, 2014 TBC

DEVICE 6 Simogo, 2013

Devil May Cry Capcom, 2001

Diablo III Blizzard, 2012

Diddy Kong Racing Rare, 1997

Disney Infinity Avalanche Software, 2013

DJ Hero 2 FreeStyleGames, 2010

Donkey Kong Nintendo, 1981

Donkey Kong Jr. Nintendo, 1982

Doom id, 1993

Doom 3 id, 2004

DotA 2 Valve, 2013

Double Dribble Konami, 1986

Dr Kawashima's Brain Training, aka *Brain Age: Train Your Brain in Minutes a Day!*, Nintendo, 2005

Dragon Age II BioWare, 2011

Dragon Age: Inquisition BioWare, 2014 TBC

Dragon Nest Eyedentity Games, 2010

Dragon Quest series: Square Enix/various, 1986–2014

Driveclub Evolution Studios, 2014 TBC

Duet Kumobius, 2013

The Dukes of Hazzard: Racing for Home SouthPeak Games, 1999

Dungeon Siege III Obsidian Entertainment, 2011

Dying Light Techland, 2015

Earth Defense Force 2025 Sandlot, 2013

Earthworm Jim Shiny Entertainment/Playmates Interactive Entertainment, 1994

An Elder Scrolls Legend: Battlespire Bethesda, 1997

The Elder Scrolls Online ZeniMax Online Studios, 2014

The Elder Scrolls Travels: Stormhold Bethesda, 2003

The Elder Scrolls III: Morrowind Bethesda, 2002

The Elder Scrolls IV: Oblivion Bethesda, 2006

The Elder Scrolls V: Skyrim Bethesda, 2011

Electrocop Epyx, 1989

Elite David Braben and Ian Bell, 1984

Epic Mickey Junction Point Studios, 2010

ESPN NBA Basketball Visual Concepts, 2003

E.T.: The Extra-Terrestrial Atari, 1982

EVE Online CCP Games, 2003

Everybody's Gone to the Rapture The Chinese Room/SCE, 2015 TBC

The Evil Within Tango Gameworks, 2014 TBC
Evolve Turtle Rock Studios, 2015
F1 Race Stars Codemasters, 2012
Fable Simbiosis Interactive, 1996
Fable Big Blue Box/various, 2004
Fallout Interplay, 1997
Fallout 3 Bethesda, 2008
Fallout: New Vegas Obsidian Entertainment, 2010
Family Guy: The Quest for Stuff TinyCo, 2014
Far Cry Crytek, 2004
Far Cry 2 Ubisoft, 2008
Far Cry 3 Ubisoft, 2012
Far Cry 3: Blood Dragon Ubisoft, 2013
Far Cry 4 Ubisoft, 2014 TBC
Far Cry: Vengeance Ubisoft, 2006
Farm Heroes Saga King, 2013
FarmVille Zynga, 2009
FarmVille 2 Zynga, 2012
Fester's Quest Sunsoft, 1989
2014 FIFA World Cup Brazil EA, 2014
FIFA 06: Road to FIFA World Cup EA, 2006
FIFA 09 EA, 2008
FIFA 12 EA, 2011
FIFA 13 EA, 2012
FIFA 14 EA, 2013
FIFA 15 EA, 2014 TBC
FIFA International Soccer Extended Play Productions, 1993
FIFA Soccer World Championship EA, 2000
FIFA Street EA, 2005
FIFA Street EA, 2012
FIFA Street 2 EA, 2006
FIFA World Cup 2006 EA/various, 2006
FIFA: Road to World Cup 98 EA, 1997
Final Fantasy Square, 1987
Final Fantasy V Square, 1992
Final Fantasy VII Square, 1997
Final Fantasy VIII Square, 1998
Final Fantasy X Square, 2001
Final Fantasy XIII Square Enix, 2009
Final Fantasy XIV Square Enix, 2010
Final Fantasy XIV: A Realm Reborn Square Enix, 2014
Fire Emblem Awakening Intelligent Systems/Nintendo, 2012
Flappy Bird Dong Nguyen, 2013
Flick NBA Basketball Freeverse, 2009
Flick Soccer! HD Full Fat, 2011
Flickers DigiPen, 2013
Fonz Sega, 1976
Football Mattel, 1979
Football Manager 2014 Sega, 2013
Forza Horizon 2 Turn 10/various, 2014 TBC
Forza Motorsport 4 Turn 10, 2011
Forza Motorsport 5 Turn 10, 2014 TBC
FRAMED Loveshack, TBC
Frogger Konami, 1981
Game of Thrones Telltale Games, 2014 TBC

Gears of War Epic Games, 2006
Gears of War 2 Epic Games, 2008
Gears of War 3 Epic Games, 2011
Gears of War: Judgment Epic Games/People Can Fly, 2013
Girl's Garden Sega, 1984
Goal Storm Konami, 1996
Goat Simulator Coffee Stain Studios, 2014
God of War SCE, 2005
God of War II SCE, 2007
God of War III SCE, 2010
God of War: Ascension SCE, 2013
God of War: Chains of Olympus Ready at Dawn/SCE, 2008
God of War: Ghost of Sparta Ready at Dawn/SCE, 2010
Gone Home The Fullbright Company, 2013
Gorogoa Jason Roberts, 2014 TBC
Gotcha Atari, 1973
Gothic Piranha Bytes, 2001
Gran Turismo SCE/Cyberhead, 1997
Gran Turismo 3: A-spec Polyphony Digital, 2001
Gran Turismo 4 Polyphony Digital, 2004
Gran Turismo 5 Polyphony Digital, 2010
Gran Turismo 6 Polyphony Digital, 2013
Gran Turismo PSP Polyphony Digital, 2009
Grand Theft Auto DMA, 1997
Grand Theft Auto III DMA, 2001
Grand Theft Auto IV Rockstar, 2008
Grand Theft Auto V Rockstar, 2013
Grand Theft Auto: London, 1969 DMA, 1999
Grand Theft Auto Online Rockstar, 2013
Grand Theft Auto: San Andreas Rockstar, 2004
Grand Theft Auto: Vice City Rockstar, 2002
Green Day: Rock Band Harmonix, 2010
Guacamelee! Super Turbo Championship Edition Drinkbox Studios, 2013
Guitar Hero: Aerosmith Neversoft, 2008
Guitar Hero III: Legends of Rock Neversoft, 2007
Guitar Hero World Tour Neversoft, 2008
Gun Neversoft, 2005
Half-Life Valve/Gearbox, 1987
Half-Life 2 Valve, 2004
Half-Life 2: Episode Two Valve, 2007
Halo Bungie, 2001
Halo 2 Bungie, 2004
Halo 3 Bungie, 2007
Halo 4 343 Industries, 2012
Halo 5: Guardians 343 Industries, TBC
Halo: Combat Evolved Anniversary Bungie/343 Industries/various, 2011
Halo Wars Ensemble Studios, 2009
Happy Trails Activision, 1983

Hard Time MDickie, 2007
Hard Truck: 18 Wheels of Steel SCS Software, 2002
Hattrick Hattrick, 1997
Haunted House Atari, 1982
Hay Day Supercell, 2012
Hearthstone: Heroes of Warcraft Blizzard, 2014
Heavenly Sword Ninja Theory, 2007
Heroes of Newerth S2 Games, 2010
Home Improvement: Power Tool Pursuit! Imagineering Inc, 1994
Hyper Light Drifter Heart Machine, 2014 TBC
Ice Hockey Nintendo, 1988
Imagine: Babysitters Visual Impact, 2008
inFAMOUS Sucker Punch Productions, 2009
inFAMOUS: Festival of Blood Sucker Punch Productions, 2011
inFAMOUS: Second Son Sucker Punch Productions, 2014
Injustice: Gods Among Us NetherRealm Studios, 2013
Inside Playdead Studios, 2015 TBC
International Superstar Soccer Konami, 1994
International Superstar Soccer Pro Evolution 2 Konami, 2001
Jak and Daxter: The Precursor Legacy Naughty Dog, 2001
Joe Danger Hello Games, 2010
Joust Williams Electronics, 1982
Jr. PAC-Man Bally Midway/Atari, 1983
Jurassic Park: Trespasser DreamWorks Interactive, 1990
Just Dance Ubisoft, 2009
Just Dance 3 Ubisoft, 2011
Just Dance 4 Ubisoft, 2012
Just Dance 2014 Ubisoft, 2013
Just Dance 2015 Ubisoft, 2014
Just Dance Now Ubisoft, 2014
Karaoke Studio TOSE, 1987
Katamari Damacy Namco, 2004
Kerbal Space Program Squad, 2011
Kick Off Dino Dini, 1989
Killzone: Shadow Fall Guerrilla Games, 2013
Kim Kardashian: Hollywood Glu Mobile, 2014
Kinect Sports Rare, 2010
Kingdom Hearts Square, 2002
Kingdom Hearts II Square Enix
Kingdom Hearts 358/2 Days Square Enix, 2009
Kingdom Hearts: Birth by Sleep Square Enix, 2010
Kingdom Hearts: Chain of Memories Jupiter, 2004
Kingdom Hearts: Dream Drop Distance Square Enix, 2012
Kingdom Hearts: Final Mix Square, 2002
Knack SCE, 2013
Knight Rider Pack-in-Video, 1988
The Last of Us Naughty Dog, 2013
The Last of Us Remastered Naughty Dog, 2014

League of Legends Riot Games, 2009
Left 4 Dead Turtle Rock Studios/Valve, 2008
The Legend of Zelda Nintendo, 1986
The Legend of Zelda: A Link Between Worlds Nintendo, 2013
The Legend of Zelda: A Link to the Past Nintendo, 1991
The Legend of Zelda: Link's Awakening Nintendo, 1993
The Legend of Zelda: Ocarina of Time Nintendo, 1998
The Legend of Zelda: Skyward Sword Nintendo, 2011
The Legend of Zelda: Twilight Princess Nintendo, 2006
The Legend of Zelda: The Wind Waker Nintendo, 2002
LEGO Batman: The Video Game Traveller's Tales/TT Fusion/ Robosoft Technologies, 2008
LEGO Batman 2: DC Super Heroes Traveller's Tales, 2012
LEGO City Undercover: The Chase Begins TT Fusion, 2013
LEGO Harry Potter: Years 1–4 Traveller's Tales/Feral Interactive, 2010
LEGO Harry Potter: Years 5–7 Traveller's Tales, 2011
LEGO The Hobbit Traveller's Tales, 2014
LEGO Island Mindscape, 1997
LEGO The Lord of the Rings TT Games, 2012
LEGO Marvel Super Heroes TT Games, 2013
LEGO Star Wars: The Video Game Traveller's Tales/Griptonite Games/Aspyr Media/Giant Interactive Entertainment, 2005
LEGO Star Wars: The Complete Saga Traveller's Tales, 2007
LEGO Star Wars II: The Original Trilogy Traveller's Tales, 2006
Life Goes On Infinite Monkeys Entertainment, 2013
Life is Strange DONTNOD, 2014 TBC
Limbo Playdead, 2010
LittleBigPlanet Media Molecule, 2008
LittleBigPlanet 3 Sumo Digital/ XDev, 2014
LittleBigPlanet Karting United Front Games/Media Molecule, 2012
LittleBigPlanet PS Vita Double Eleven/Tarsier Studios/XDev, 2012
Little Computer People Activision, 1985
Loading Human Untold Games, TBC
LovePlus Konami, 2009
Luxuria Superbia Tale of Tales, 2013
Mad Dog McCree American Laser Games, 1990
Madden NFL 15 EA Tiburon, 2014
Madden NFL 25 EA Tiburon, 2013

Magic: The Gathering MicroProse, 1997

Mankind O2 Online Entertainment, 1998

Mario & Sonic at the Olympic Games Sega, 2007

Mario & Sonic at the Olympic Winter Games Sega, 2009

Mario Kart 7 Nintendo, 2011

Mario Kart 8 Nintendo, 2014

Mario Kart 64 Nintendo, 1996

Mario Kart Arcade GP Namco, 2005

Mario Kart Wii Nintendo, 2008

Mario Maker Nintendo, 2015 TBC

Mark of the Ninja Klei Entertainment, 2012

Marvel vs. Capcom series, Capcom/Rutubo Games/ Probe Entertainment, 1994– present

Mass Effect BioWare, 2007

Mass Effect 2 BioWare, 2010

Mass Effect 3 BioWare, 2012

Max Payne 3 Rockstar, 2012

Mega Man Capcom, 1987

Metal Gear Konami, 1987

Metal Gear Online Kojima, 2008

Metal Gear Solid Konami, 1998

Metal Gear Solid 2: Sons of Liberty Konami, 2001

Metal Gear Solid 4: Guns of the Patriots Kojima, 2008

Metal Gear Solid V: Ground Zeroes Kojima, 2014

Metal Gear Solid V: The Phantom Pain Kojima, TBC

Metal Gear Solid HD Collection Various, 2011

Metal Gear Solid: Peace Walker Kojima, 2010

Metal Gear Solid: Snake Eater 3D Kojima, 2012

Metal Gear Solid: The Twin Snakes Silicon Knights, 2004

Metal Slug SNK Playmore, 1996

Metroid Nintendo, 1986

Metroid Prime Retro Studios, 2002

Metroid: Zero Mission Nintendo, 2004

Michael Jackson: The Experience Ubisoft, 2010

Microsoft Flight Simulator series, various, 1980–2012

Millipede Atari, 1982

Minecraft Mojang, 2011

Minecraft: Xbox 360 Edition 4J Studios, 2012

Minesweeper Curt Johnson, 1992

ModNation Racers United Front Games, 2010

Monument Valley Ustwo, 2014

Mortal Kombat NetherRealm Studios, 1992

Mortal Kombat: Armageddon Midway Games, 2006

Mortal Kombat: Deception Midway Games, 2004

Mortal Kombat vs. DS Universe Midway Games, 2008

Mortal Kombat X NetherRealm Studios, 2015 TBC

Moshi Monsters Mind Candy, 2007

Moto-Cross Sega, 1976

Motor Toon Grand Prix SCEI, 1994

Ms. PAC-Man Bally Midway, 1982

Mushroom 11 Untame, 2015 TBC

NaissanceE Limasse Five, 2014

NASL Soccer Mattel, 1979

NBA 2K1 Visual Concepts, 2000

NBA 2K2 Visual Concepts, 2001

NBA 2K3 Visual Concepts, 2002

NBA 2K9 Visual Concepts, 2008

NBA 2K11 Visual Concepts, 2010

NBA 2K13 Visual Concepts, 2012

NBA 2K14 Visual Concepts, 2013

NBA Jam Midway, 1993

NBA Live series, EA, 1995– present

NBA Live 14 EA Tiburon, 2013

NBA Live 15 EA Tiburon, 2014 TBC

NBA Live 95 Hitmen Productions, 1995

NBA Live 2003 EA Canada, 2002

NCAA Basketball Sculptured Software, 1992

Need for Speed series, various, 1994–present

Need for Speed: Hot Pursuit EA, 1998

Need for Speed: Most Wanted EA, 2005

Need for Speed: Motor City Online EA, 2001

Need for Speed: Rivals Ghost Games, 2013

Need for Speed: Underground 2 EA, 2004

Need for Speed: World EA, 2010

Need for Speed: World Online EA, 2010

Neverwinter Nights BioWare, 2002

Neverwinter Nights 2 Obsidian Entertainment, 2006

New Super Mario Bros. Nintendo, 2006

New Super Mario Bros. 2 Nintendo, 2012

New Super Mario Bros.: Wii Nintendo, 2009

NHL EA, 1991–present

NHL 2K2 2K Sports, 2001

NHL 09 EA/HB Studios, 2008

NHL 12 EA, 2011

NHL 14 EA, 2013

NHL 15 EA, 2014 TBC

NIM Ferranti, 1951

Ninja Gaiden Black Team Ninja, 2005

Nintendo Land Nintendo, 2012

Nintendogs Nintendo, 2005

No Man's Sky Hello Games, 2015 TBC

No Time to Explain tinyBuildGames, 2011

Nova-111 Funktronic Labs, 2014 TBC

The Office Reveille, 2007

Olympic Gold U.S. Gold, 1992

One Piece: Romance Dawn Three Rings, 2012

The Orange Box Valve, 2007

The Order: 1886 Ready at Dawn/ SCE, 2015 TBC

The Oregon Trail MECC, 1971–2012

Ori and the Blind Forest Moon Studios, 2014 TBC

Overlord Triumph Studios/4J Studios, 2007

OXO A S Douglas, 1952

PAC-Man Namco, 1980

PAC-Man Championship Edition DX Mine Loader Software Co, 2010

Papers, Please Lucas Pope, 2013

Payday 2 Overkill Software/ Starbreeze Studios, 2013

Petz Various, 1995–2011

Phantasy Star Online Sonic Team, 2000

Pikmin Nintendo, 2001

Pikmin 2 Nintendo, 2004

Pinball Construction Set BudgeCo, 1983

Pitfall Activision, 1982

Plants vs. Zombies PopCap Games, 2009

Plants vs. Zombies 2 PopCap Games, 2013

Pokémon series, Game Freak/ Creatures Inc, 1996–present

Pokémon Alpha Sapphire Game Freak, 2014 TBC

Pokémon Blue Game Freak, 1996

Pokémon Emerald Game Freak, 2004

Pokémon Gold Game Freak, 1999

Pokémon Green Game Freak, 1996

Pokémon Omega Ruby Game Freak, 2014 TBC

Pokémon Red Game Freak, 1996

Pokémon Silver Game Freak, 1999

Pokémon Stadium Nintendo, 1999

Pokémon X Game Freak, 2013

Pokémon Y Game Freak, 2013

Pong Atari, 1972

Poöf vs the Cursed Kitty Arkedo, 2013

Popeye Nintendo, 1982

Portal Valve, 2007

Portal 2 Valve, 2011

Predator Pack-in-Video, 1987

Pro Evolution Soccer BG Entertainment, 2001

PES 2009 Konami, 2008

PES 2010 Konami, 2009

PES 2011 Konami, 2010

PES 2012 Konami, 2011

PES 2014 PES Productions, 2013

PES 2015 PES Productions, 2014 TBC

Professor Layton Level-5, 2007– present

Professor PAC-Man Bally Midway, 1983

Project Cars Slightly Mad Studios, 2014 TBC

Project Spark Team Dakota/ SkyBox Labs, 2014 TBC

Punch-Out!! Nintendo, 1987

Puzzle & Dragons GungHo, 2012

Quantum Break Remedy Entertainment, 2015 TBC

Ratchet & Clank Various, 2002– present

Ratchet & Clank: Quest for Booty Insomniac Games, 2008

Ratchet & Clank: Up Your Arsenal Insomniac Games, 2004

Ratchet & Clank Future: Tools of Destruction Insomniac Games, 2007

Rayman Legends Ubisoft, 2013

Rayman Origins Ubisoft, 2011

R.B.I. Baseball Namco, 1986

Red Dead Redemption Rockstar San Diego, 2010

Red Dead Redemption: Undead Nightmare Rockstar San Diego, 2010

Red Dead Revolver Rockstar San Diego, 2004

Resident Evil Capcom, 1996

Resident Evil 2 Capcom, 1998

Resident Evil 4 Capcom, 2005

Resident Evil 5 Capcom, 2009

Resident Evil 6 Capcom, 2012

Resident Evil Code: Veronica Capcom, 2000

Resident Evil: Revelations Capcom, 2012

Ridiculous Fishing Vlambeer, 2013

Rise of the Tomb Raider Crystal Dynamics, 2015 TBC

Risen 3: Titan Lords Piranha Bites, 2014

Risk of Rain Hopoo Games, 2013

River Raid Activision, 1982

Road Construction Simulator rondomedia, 2011

Rock Band Harmonix, 2007

Rocksmith Ubisoft, 2011

RuneScape Jagex Games Studio, 2001

Ryse: Son of Rome Crytek Frankfurt, 2013

Saints Row Volition, Inc, 2006

Saints Row IV Volition, 2013

Saints Row: The Third Volition, 2011

Samba de Amigo Sonic Team, 1999

Sangokushi Taisen Sega, 2005

Scalebound Platinum Games, TBC

ScreamRide Frontier Developments, 2015 TBC

Sensible Soccer Sensible Software, 1992–2007

Shadow of the Beast Reflections/ The Creative Assembly, 1989

Ship Simulator 2006 Lighthouse Interactive, 2006

Ship Simulator Professional VSTEP, 2009

Sid Meier's Alpha Centauri Firaxis Games, 1999

Sid Meier's Civilization: Beyond Earth Firaxis Games, 2014 TBC
Silent Hill Konami, 1999
SimCity Maxis, 1989
SimCity 2000 Maxis, 1994
The Simpsons: Tapped Out EA, 2012
The Sims Maxis, 2000
SingStar London Studio, 2004
SingStar ABBA SCE London Studio, 2008
SingStar Bollywood SCE London Studio, 2007
SingStar Singalong with Disney SCE London Studio, 2008
SingStar Dance SCE London Studio, 2010
Sir, You Are Being Hunted Big Robot, 2013
Size DOES Matter DOS Studios, 2013
Skullduggery! ClutchPlay Games, 2014
Skylanders: Giants Toys for Bob, 2012
Skylanders: Spyro's Adventure Toys for Bob, 2011
Skylanders: Swap Force Vicarious Visions, 2013
Smash T.V. Williams, 1990
SMITE Hi-Rez Studios, 2014
Snake's Revenge Konami, 1990
Sniper: Ghost Warrior 2 City Interactive, 2013
SNK vs. Capcom: Card Fighters DS SNK Playmore, 2007
Sonic Adventure 2 Sonic Team USA, 2001
Sonic & All-Stars Racing Transformed Sumo Digital, 2012
Sonic Battle Sonic Team, 2003
Sonic Boom: Rise of Lyric Big Red Button Entertainment/Sanzaru Games, 2014 TBC
Sonic Boom: Shattered Crystal Big Red Button Entertainment/Sanzaru Games, 2014 TBC
Sonic the Hedgehog Sonic Team, 1991
Sonic the Hedgehog 2 Sonic Team, 1992
Sonic: Lost World Sonic Team, 2013
The Sopranos: Road to Respect 7 Studios, 2006
South Park: The Stick of Truth Obsidian Entertainment/ South Park Digital Studios, 2014
Space Invaders Taito, 1978
Spelunky Derek Yu/Andy Hull/ Blitworks, 2009
Splashy Fish redBit Games, 2014
Splatoon Nintendo, 2015 TBC
Spore Maxis, 2008
Sportsfriends Die Gute Fabrik, 2013
Spyro the Dragon Insomniac Games, 1998
Spyro: Year of the Dragon Insomniac Games, 2000
The Stanley Parable Davey Wreden, 2011

Star Citizen Cloud Imperium Games/Behaviour Interactive/ CGBot/voidALPHA, 2015 TBC
StarCraft Blizzard, 1998
Star Trek: Phaser Strike Milton Bradley, 1979
Star Wars: Battlefront Pandemic Studios, 2004
Star Wars: The Clone Wars Pandemic Studios, 2002
Star Wars: Knights of the Old Republic II – The Sith Lords Obsidian Entertainment, 2004
Star Wars: The Old Republic BioWare, 2011
Stikbold! Reign Bros, 2014
Street Cleaning Simulator Astragon, 2011
Street Fighter Capcom, 1987
Street Fighter II: The World Warrior Capcom, 1991
Street Fighter X Tekken Dimps/ Capcom, 2012
Ultra Street Fighter IV Dimps/ Capcom, 2014
Sunset Overdrive Insomniac Games, 2014 TBC
Super Mario 3D Land Nintendo, 2011
Super Mario 3D World Nintendo, 2013
Super Mario 64 Nintendo, 1996
Super Mario Bros. Nintendo, 1985
Super Mario Bros. 2 Nintendo, 1988
Super Mario Bros. Special Nintendo, 1986
Super Mario Galaxy Nintendo, 2007
Super Mario Galaxy 2 Nintendo, 2010
Super Mario Kart Nintendo, 1992
Super Mario Land 2: 6 Golden Coins Nintendo, 1992
Super Mario Sunshine Nintendo, 2002
Super Mario World Nintendo, 1990
Super Meat Boy Team Meat, 2010
Super Metroid Nintendo, 1994
Super PAC-Man Namco, 1982
Super Princess Peach TOSE, 2005
Super Smash Bros. HAL Laboratory, 1999
Super Smash Bros. Brawl Nintendo, 2008
Super Smash Bros. for Nintendo 3DS Sora Ltd/Bandai Namco, 2014 TBC
Super Smash Bros. for Wii U Sora Ltd/Bandai Namco, 2014 TBC
Super Smash Bros. Melee HAL Laboratory, 2001
System Shock 2 Irrational Games/ Looking Glass Studios, 1999
Team Fortress 2 Valve, 2007
Tearaway Media Molecule, 2013
Tekken Namco, 1994
Tekken 3 Namco, 1997
Tenchu: Stealth Assassins Acquire, 1998
Tennis for Two William Higinbotham, 1958
Tetris Alexey Pajitnov, 1984

Theatrhythm Final Fantasy: Curtain Call Square Enix 1st Production Department, 2014
Thief: The Dark Project Looking Glass Studios, 1998
Thief: Deadly Shadows Ion Storm, 2004
Thief II: The Metal Age Looking Glass Studios, 2000
The Three Stooges Incredible Technologies, 1987
Tiger Woods PGA Tour 14 EA Tiburon, 2013
Tiger Woods PGA Tour 99 EA, 1998
Titanfall Respawn Entertainment, 2014
Toki TAD Corporation, 1989
Tom Clancy's Rainbow Six: Siege Ubisoft, 2015 TBC
Tom Clancy's Splinter Cell Ubisoft, 2002
Tomatos Role Willow Flame Productions, 2013
Tomb Raider Core Design, 1996
Tomb Raider Crystal Dynamics, 2013
Tomb Raider II Core Design, 1997
Tomb Raider: Definitive Edition Crystal Dynamics, 2014
Tomb Raider: Rise of the Tomb Raider Crystal Dynamics, 2015
Tomodachi Life Nintendo, 2013
The Tomorrow Children Q-Games, 2015 TBC
Tony Hawk's Pro Skater Neversoft, 1999
Trainz N3V Games, 2001
Tropico PopTop Software, 2001
Tropico 5 Haemimont Games, 2014
True Love Software House Parsley, 1995
UFC Undisputed 3 Yuke's, 2012
Ultima 1: The First Age of Darkness Richard Garriott, 1981
Ultima Online Origin Systems, 1997
The Ultimate 11: SNK Football Championship SNK, 1996
Uncharted 2: Among Thieves Naughty Dog, 2009
Uncharted 3: Drake's Deception Naughty Dog, 2011
Uncharted 4: A Thief's End Naughty Dog, 2015 TBC
Uncharted: Drake's Fortune Naughty Dog, 2007
Uncharted: Golden Abyss SCE Bend Studio, 2011
Utopia Don Daglow, 1981
Vancouver 2010 Eurocom, 2010
Velocity 2X Futurlab, 2014 TBC
VVVVVV Terry Cavanagh, 2010
The Walking Dead: The Game Telltale Games, 2012
Wasteland Interplay Productions, 1998
Watch_Dogs Ubisoft, 2014
We Love Katamari Namco/NOW Production, 2005
Wii Fit Nintendo, 2007
Wii Party Nd Cube/Nintendo, 2010
Wii Party U Nd Cube/Nintendo, 2013

Wii Play Nintendo, 2006
Wii Sports Nintendo, 2006
Wii Sports Resort Nintendo, 2009
Wild Gunman Nintendo, 1984
Wing Commander Origin Systems, 1990
Winter Olympics: Lillehammer '94 Abstract Images/ID Software/Tiertex Design Studios U.S. Gold/1993
The Witcher CD Projekt RED, 2007
The Witcher 2: Assassins of Kings CD Projekt RED, 2011
The Witcher 2: Assassins of Kings Enhanced Edition CD Projekt RED, 2012
The Witcher 3: Wild Hunt CD Projekt RED, 2015 TBC
Wolfenstein: The New Order MachineGames, 2014
World Basketball Manager series, Icehole, 2003–present
World of Tanks Wargaming, 2010
World of Tanks: Xbox 360 Edition Wargaming West, 2014
World of Warcraft Blizzard, 2004
World of Warcraft: The Burning Crusade Blizzard, 2007
World of Warcraft: Cataclysm Blizzard, 2010
World of Warcraft: Mists of Pandaria Blizzard, 2012
World of Warcraft: Warlords of Draenor Blizzard, 2014 TBC
World of Warcraft: Wrath of the Lich King Blizzard, 2008
World of Warplanes Wargaming, 2013
World of Warships Lesta Studio/ Wargaming, 2014 TBC
WWE 2K14 Yuke's/Visual Concepts, 2013
WWE 2K15 Yuke's/Visual Concepts, 2014 TBC
WWE All Stars THQ San Diego, 2011
WWE SmackDown vs RAW 2008 Yuke's/Amaze Entertainment, 2007
WWF SmackDown! Yuke's, 2000
WWF SmackDown! 2: Know Your Role Yuke's, 2000
The X-Files Game HyperBole Studios, 1998
Xbox Fitness Microsoft Studios, 2013
XCOM: Enemy Unknown Firaxis Games, 2012
XCOM: Enemy Within Firaxis Games, 2013
Yaiba: Ninja Gaiden Z Team Ninja/ Spark Unlimited/Comcept, 2014
Yoshi's Woolly World Good-Feel/Nintendo, 2015 TBC
YouKai Watch 2: Ganso and Honke Level-5, 2014
Zaxxon Sega, 1982
Zombies Ate My Neighbors LucasArts, 1993

INDEX

INDEX

PICTURE CREDITS

6 Paul Michael Hughes/GWR
7 Richard Bradbury/GWR, Paul Michael Hughes/GWR
10 Mike Blake/Reuters, Alamy, Carlos Barria/Reuters
12 Reuters
13 Rex Features, Jonathan Alcorn/Reuters
14 Yoshikazu Tsuno/Getty Images
17 Stephen Butler/BAFTA
18 Paul Michael Hughes/GWR
20 Alamy, Kevork Djansezian/Reuters, Kevork Djansezian/Reuters
21 Mario Anzuoni/Reuters, David McNew/Reuters
22 Arcade Flyer Archive
26 Moby Games, Alamy, Alamy, Kobal
27 Moby Games, Kobal, Alamy, Alamy, Buena Vista/Alamy, Moby Games, Jean-Paul Pelissier/Reuters
28 NBC/Getty Images, Alamy, Alamy, Fox Broadcasting
29 Cartoon Network, Noam Galai/

Getty Images, Alamy, Alamy
32 Armando Arorizo/Alamy
34 Alamy
35 Alamy
36 Benoit Tessier/Reuters
38 Nigel Raymond
40 Alamy
41 Patrick Gosling, Patrick Gosling, Richard Bradbury/GWR
62 Gus Ruelas/Reuters, Alamy
71 Jochen Tack/Alamy, Jason Morgan
83 Jesse Grant/Getty Images
86 Media Molecule, Nathan King/Alamy
87 Paul Michael Hughes/GWR
91 Alamy
94 Alamy, Alamy
98 Rex Features
106 Torsten Silz/Getty Images
115 Ranald Mackechnie/GWR
116 David Parker/Alamy, Alamy, Sean Pavone/iStock, Sangokushi Taisen
120 Hampus Andersson
121 Helena Kristiansson

122 Shannon Stapleton/Reuters
128 Carlton Beener
130 Zhang Jingna
131 Bryan Bedder/Getty Images
133 Gus Ruelas/Reuters
134 DreamWorks Pictures
136 Alamy
137 Paul Michael Hughes/GWR
138 Halkin Mason Photography, Chris Payne
155 Moby Games
156 Alamy
168 Jamie Simonds/BAFTA
170 Paul Michael Hughes/GWR
172 Robert Matton/Alamy
173 Alamy
180 Alamy
186 Evan Amos, Alamy
189 ifixit.com
190 ifixit.com
191 ifixit.com
192 ifixit.com
214 Paul Michael Hughes/GWR

DID YOU GUESS THE HEADGEAR?

How did you get on with our headgear quiz on p.49?
Will you be wearing a mortarboard or a dunce cap?

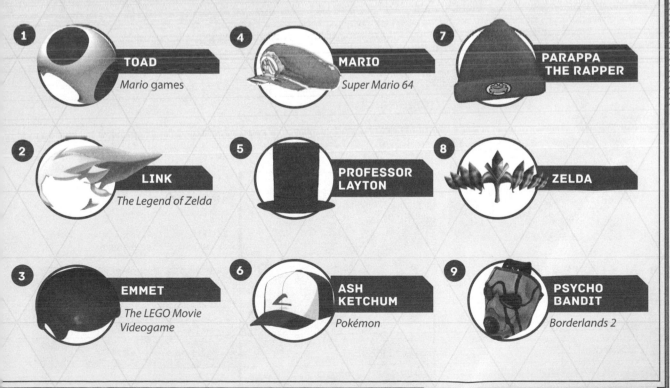

1 **TOAD**
Mario games

2 **LINK**
The Legend of Zelda

3 **EMMET**
The LEGO Movie Videogame

4 **MARIO**
Super Mario 64

5 **PROFESSOR LAYTON**

6 **ASH KETCHUM**
Pokémon

7 **PARAPPA THE RAPPER**

8 **ZELDA**

9 **PSYCHO BANDIT**
Borderlands 2

GLOSSARY

100-PERCENT COMPLETION Completing all tasks and missions in a game, often associated with speed-runs

AAA "Triple A" refers to a videogame that benefits from a large budget and development team, and one expected to be hugely successful, particularly if supported by a generous marketing campaign; the videogaming equivalent of a blockbuster movie

AI Artificial Intelligence: computer-generated opponents that adapt and react realistically to humans

ALPHA The first phase of software testing, usually conducted exclusively by the developers; *see also BETA*

BAFTA British Academy of Film and Television Arts; established the annual British Academy Games Awards in 2004 (hived off from the BAFTA Interactive Entertainment Awards)

BETA Phase of software testing that comes after alpha (see *ALPHA*) – usually open for public use

CHIPSET A crucial part of a computer's integrated circuitry that relays data between the processor and other components on the motherboard, such as the memory disks and the external ports

CLAN A team, guild or faction of gamers, usually at the same skill level, playing as an organized group; typically, a clan's members work together in multiplayer games, such as MMORPGs and strategies

CUTSCENE Non-playable sequence in a game used to advance the plot

DAU Daily average users; often used to measure the popularity of Facebook games

DEV Short for "developer"

DLC Downloadable content

EASTER EGG A joke, mini-game, bonus or hidden message implanted inside a game by the coders as a reward for those with the patience – or luck – to uncover it

FPS First-person shooter, with action from the player's point of view

FRAGFEST A multiplayer deathmatch

FREE2PLAY Games that are free for the most part, with extras generally available at a cost

GLITCH A bug in the programming. Some can be exploited in speed-runs

HDD Hard-disk drive

HIT POINTS/HP A number in RPGs that determines how much damage a character can take before expiring

COMBO
A series of actions performed in sequence, typically in fighting games, to produce a more powerful, accumulative effect; pictured is street fighter Abel pulling off a Focus Attack combo in *Ultra Street Fighter IV*

ANY-PERCENTAGE COMPLETION Completing a game without finishing all tasks and missions, often associated with speed-runs

AUTOATTACK The default means by which a unit deals damage in *League of Legends*

HACK AND SLASH
Sub-genre of action-adventure, RPGs and MMOs that involves heavy combat and plenty of sword action. Pictured above is the deadly Bayonetta from the hack-and-slash game of the same name, wielding her trusty katana *Shuraba*, which sucks the very soul from those unlucky enough to feel the sting of its bloodthirsty blade

JRPG Japanese role-playing game

KILL-TO-DEATH RATIO The number of enemies you eliminate divided by the number of lives you lose; also known as kill:death ratio

MACHINIMA An animated film created by manipulating videogame graphics to establish a story-telling narrative, often unrelated to the original game

MAU Monthly average users; often used to measure the popularity of Facebook games

MELEE KILL A kill achieved without the use of a gun, typically with a knife, machete, sword or blunt instrument

MMO Any kind of massively multiplayer online game – includes (and is often used interchangeably with) MMORPG (see definition). These "massive" games feature persistent "worlds"

MMORPG A type of MMO game that is specifically a role-playing game (RPG)

MOBA Multiplayer online battle arena, aka action real-time strategy

ISOMETRIC
A form of rendering objects in games so that they are viewed from a perspective – typically with 120° between the x, y and z axes – that makes them seem 3D; pictured is the isometric view in *Commandos 3: Destination Berlin*, showing its isometric projection

MOD Modification made to a game by a fan or a developer, from the smallest in-game tweak to a complete new version of a game (such as *Counter-Strike*, a take on *Half-Life*)

NES Nintendo Entertainment System, known as the Famicom in Japan; its successor was the SNES (Super Nintendo Entertainment System), known as the Super Famicom in Japan

NPC Non-playable character, controlled by the computer

NTSC National Television System Committee; the TV system used in North America

OS Operating system, such as Windows, Mac OS, iOS, Android or Linux – the software that runs the basic functions of a computer or device

OTAKU Japanese term for a fanatic; most similar to the English words "geek" or "nerd", it refers typically to those people obsessed with manga, anime or videogames

PAL Phase Alternating Line; the TV system used in Europe – consoles are produced for both NTSC (see definition) and PAL territories

TWIN-STICK CONTROL
Using two joysticks, one to control character movement and the other to control aim; pictured here is Japanese peripheral maker Hori's Xbox 360 dual joysticks designed for Sega's Xbox Live Arcade game *Virtual On: Oratorio Tangram*

POLYGON A two-dimensional computer graphic that, when combined with vast numbers of other polygons, can be used to build up 3D-looking graphics; the higher the polygon count, the more smooth and realistic the final graphic will appear to be

PORT The transfer of a game from one platform to another

PS PlayStation; can include: PS2, PS3, PS4, PSP (PlayStation Portable), PSN (PlayStation Network) and PS Vita

RPG Role-playing game

RTS Real-time strategy

SANDBOX Aka open-world, a game with an environment that can be explored and manipulated by the gamer, often with no objective in mind; in a more general sense, also refers to a game or level that has no artificial barriers

SCROLLER A game in which the playing area is limited to a window through which the gamer moves, either horizontally (a "side-scroller", usually left to right) or vertically (a top-down view)

SPEED-RUN A play-through of a whole game or a part of it, completed as quickly as possible

STEALTH A genre of gaming in which the object is to achieve goals without being detected by the enemy

STORY MODE Used in fighting games to describe the single-player fighting battles as a narrative unfolds, perhaps through linking cutscenes (see definition)

SKILL-SHOT Projectile-based, direction-targeted abilities in *League of Legends*; above, champion telepath Sona – Maven of the Strings – tackles her enemies by firing off a devastating surge of sound

TROPHY In general terms, an award earned beyond an individual game (e.g., in a central, platform-wide network such as the Xbox 360's Gamerscore System) for completing a level, reaching a given score, securing a number of kills, and so on

TURN-BASED A game (such as chess) in which the players are not active simultaneously but take turns to move

UI User interface; the means by which a gamer interacts with a game, such as on-screen icons, buttons and messaging

UX User experience; a key concern for videogame developers

XP Experience points – usually gained through battles and achieving goals; they help to raise the level of a character, often in an RPG

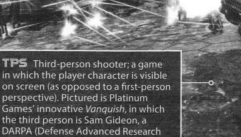

TPS Third-person shooter; a game in which the player character is visible on screen (as opposed to a first-person perspective). Pictured is Platinum Games' innovative *Vanquish*, in which the third person is Sam Gideon, a DARPA (Defense Advanced Research Projects Agency) agent clad in an Augmented Reaction Suit

STOP PRESS!

LONGEST-RUNNING COMBAT GAME SERIES

One-on-one physical contact gaming records include the **longest-running annual combat game series** (see p.57) and the **longest-running fighting game series** (p.47). But in absolute terms, the granddaddy of all fighting games is *Street Fighter*. The multiple record holder made its debut in 1987 and in 2014, some 27 years later, *Ultra Street Fighter IV* – apparently the final version of *SF IV* – found its way from the Japanese arcades to consoles and PC to critical acclaim.

MOST CRITICALLY ACCLAIMED PS3-EXCLUSIVE GAME

Uncharted 2: Among Thieves has a GameRankings rating of 96.38%, with only a pair of non-exclusive *Grand Theft Autos* – *IV* and *V* – sitting above the hit Nathan Drake outing at No.1 and No.2 respectively. For more on the PlayStation-exclusive *Uncharted* series, turn to pp.90–91.

HIGHEST-RATED PLAYER ON *WORLD OF TANKS*

Gamer "Der_Weïsse_Mongol" had a tank-destroying score of 11,804, as of 21 August 2014. The personal rating is a reflection of overall performance, including elements such as victories, damage, average experience per battle and player-survival ratio.

The **highest hit ratio on *World of Tanks*** is 97.93%. The sharp-shooting record was set by gamer "diligentia".

The **most vehicles destroyed in *World of Tanks*** is 110,166, trashed over 53,642 battles by "Marxist".

MOST KILLS ON *RESIDENT EVIL: REVELATIONS* ON WII U

As of 24 June 2014, gamer "checko" had racked up a score of 614,418 on the 2013 release *RE: Revelations*. The achievement took 729 hr 28 min 45 sec of game time.

Over on the desktop, the **most kills on *RE: Revelations* on PC** stands at a total of 1,021,262, achieved by "wangyong".

MOST CONSECUTIVE BASKETBALL FREE THROWS ACHIEVED ON *NBA 2K9*

Tristen Geren (USA) achieved 114 free throws in a row on 1 July 2014 while playing *NBA 2K9*. Keen record-breaker Tristen currently holds 15 videogaming world records, including **most three-pointers made in one minute on *NBA 2K14***, with a total of six on 25 June 2014.

BEST-SELLING THIRD-PARTY WII PLATFORM GAME

Epic Mickey, developed by Warren Spector, Junction Point Studios and Disney Interactive, has sold 2.94 million units. The game features the famous Mr Mouse combating enemies with a magic paintbrush and holds the No.6 sales spot on the Wii, behind *Mario* and *Donkey Kong* games.

FASTEST TIME TRIAL FOR "ANCIENT LAKE" ON *DIDDY KONG RACING*

Jean-Baptiste Barois (France, left) set a time of 47.36 sec on the "Ancient Lake" track of the N64's *Diddy Kong Racing* on 6 February 2014. Playing another kart classic, Bandon David Byrd (USA) set the **fastest lap of "D.K.'s Jungle Parkway"** in *Mario Kart 64*, with a time of 4.65 sec on 28 May 2014.

FASTEST LAP OF "LAGUNA SECA" IN *GRAN TURISMO 5*

Lewis Appiagyei (UK) reached the chequered flag in 44 sec exactly on 25 July 2014. He recorded his time on GWR's Challengers website at **www.guinnessworldrecords.com/challengers**.

MOST CRITICALLY ACCLAIMED SURVIVAL HORROR VIDEOGAME

Resident Evil 4 on the PS2 had an average rating of 95.85% on gamerankings.com as of 10 July 2014. The series is responsible for all top 5 placings with, in order, *RE 4* on the GameCube, *RE Code: Veronica* on the Dreamcast, *RE 2* on the PlayStation, and *RE 4* on the Wii at No.5.

MOST CRITICALLY ACCLAIMED STEALTH GAME

Metal Gear Solid 2: Sons of Liberty has an average score of 95.09% on GameRankings. For more sneaky *Metal Gear* records, see below and turn to pp.124–25.

LONGEST GAME END SEQUENCE

Have the popcorn and your most comfortable chair at the ready when you complete *Metal Gear Solid 4*. The ending lasts for an epic 1 hr 9 min 4 sec.

MOST VIDEOGAME CONCERTS PERFORMED

On 17 August 2014, Video Games Live (VGL) staged its 286th concert celebrating the best in gaming music. Drawing on the resources of full-size symphony orchestras, choirs and world-class soloists, VGL recreates epic gaming soundtracks alongside video projections of the games – often played live by audience members – and this latest gig featured the Xi'an Symphony Orchestra at the Jiaotong Siyuan Stadium in Xi'an, China. VGL is the brainchild of American audio pioneer Tommy Tallarico (the **most prolific videogame composer**, with over 300 titles to his name).

FASTEST COMBINED COMPLETION TIME OF *MINESWEEPER*

As of 21 August 2014, Kamil Murański (Poland) had completed classic puzzler *Minesweeper* on all three difficulties in a total of just 38.65 sec.

MOST DOWNLOADED MOD FOR *FALLOUT: NEW VEGAS*

As of 21 August 2014, a total of 2,027,756 users of the popular Nexus mods website had downloaded the *Weapons Mod Expanded – WMX*. Uploaded on 16 January 2011, the mod was coded by Joseph "Antistar" Lollback and brings further enhancements to *Fallout: New Vegas*'s weapons-modding system.

LARGEST COLLECTION OF *MOSHI MONSTERS* MEMORABILIA

Lucy Neath (UK) is 12 and, as of 20 May 2014, was sharing her home in Milton Keynes, Buckinghamshire, with 1,914 individual *Moshi Monsters* items. Lucy has been collecting over four years and her YouTube channel, themoshimonsterkitty, has had almost 15,000 subscribers and 10 million views. Her favourite piece among the toys, cushions, T-shirts, magazines, perfumes and mugs is Furnando the Mystic Moggie, an extremely rare Moshling.